Confessions of a Puppetmaster

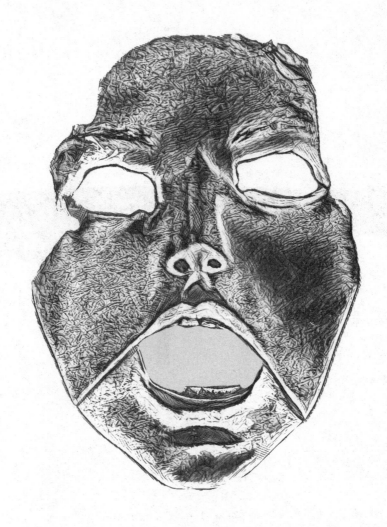

Charles Band
with Adam Felber

WM

WILLIAM MORROW
An Imprint of HarperCollins*Publishers*

CONFESSIONS *of a* PUPPETMASTER

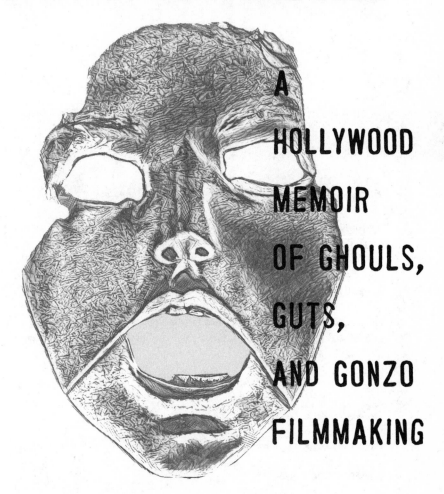

A
HOLLYWOOD
MEMOIR
OF GHOULS,
GUTS,
AND GONZO
FILMMAKING

Title page illustration and insert photographs courtesy of the author

HarperCollins books may be purchased for educational, business, or sales promotional use. For information, please email the Special Markets Department at SPsales@harpercollins.com.

FIRST EDITION

Designed by Bonni Leon-Berman

Library of Congress Cataloging-in-Publication Data has been applied for.

ISBN 978-0-06-308734-7

21 22 23 24 25   LSC   10 9 8 7 6 5 4 3 2 1

CONTENTS

Confessions of a Puppetmaster

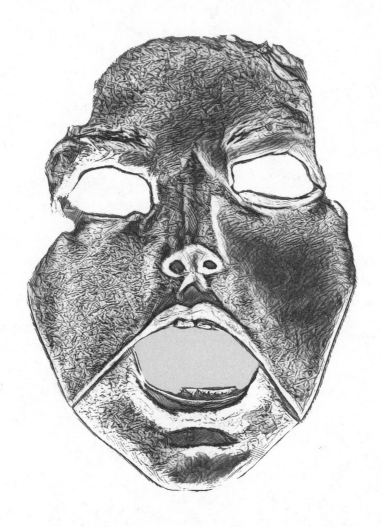

Introduction

CONTAGION

Unaware of just how insane things had gotten outside her door, Barbie took a shower. In her clothes.

She let the water run down her fit, toned body, cleansing it of the contagion. She sang to herself, "Happy birthday to me . . . happy birthday to m—"

—the door flew open, revealing the filth-covered zombie, inches from her face, growling and lunging toward her! Oddly, she noticed, it was wearing a surgical mask.

She screamed.

It was gone.

Ten minutes later, she was on the phone. "Hey girl, are you, like, *sure* it was just a hallucination?" Kendra asked.

"I mean, I think so," said Barbie, now in a crop top and short shorts, looking and sounding every bit the stereotypical Valley Girl. "I mean, I'm not in the belly of some 'corona zombie,' so . . . I *guess*." She sank down on the couch, iPhone pressed up against her face as she commiserated with her friend.

It was back to reality, but right now reality was *the worst*.

On the TV, President Trump was saying that he hoped he could reopen the country by Easter. But from what Kendra was saying, it sounded like the shutdown could last a lot longer than that.

"This lockdown sucks," Barbie pouted. "It's only been like two hours and I'm already *bored.*"

"I know, right?" Kendra sympathized. "And it's Taco Tuesday!" Which was a huge bummer for Barbie. I mean, *tacos* . . .

But then Barbie brightened. Out of nowhere, she remembered her old boyfriend, and she squealed in sudden happiness. "Wait! Remember Jim Bob? He was like some kind of survivalist. And he left some of his survival shit in my garage."

"And . . . ?" Kendra was dubious.

"And . . . there's toilet paper!"

"Girrrl! You lucky bitch! Go Barbie!"

"Mm-hmm!" Barbie chanted. "I'm a rich bitch! I'm a rich bitch!" Hands in the air, grinding her hips party-girl style, she celebrated on the couch as Kendra whooped into the phone. Moments later, she went to check out her stash. "Come on, toilet paper," Barbie called. "I know you're in here."

It was only the first day of lockdown in California, but toilet paper had been scarce for weeks, ever since it became obvious that the pandemic was going to be, like, a *thing.* Barbie tiptoed into the garage, the afternoon sun streaming in behind her. She peered under the blue tarps that Jim Bob had covered the shelves with. A mannequin, ammunition, some dried food rations (like, *eww*!). But then, toward the back . . .

"Yes! I hit the motherfucking mother lode!"

Charmin. A twenty-four-pack of the BIG rolls. Costco-tastic! She was *set.* She turned to leave the garage when she heard a noise behind her. When she swung around . . .

. . . she found herself face-to-face with a zombie. A real one this time.

Bigger and grosser than the one she'd imagined, parts of his throat ripped out, his face a blighted, bloody mess, his torn surgical mask revealing a mangled nose, a missing upper lip, bloodstained teeth, and what might have been part of a jawbone showing beneath . . . It laughed, burbled, and spoke one guttural word . . .

"*Co-ro-na . . .*"

It moved toward her.

Barbie screamed. And screamed.

"Cut! And that's a wrap!"

Confession: I love yelling, "That's a wrap!" I've done it more than 340 times in my insane career, and it never gets old.

But this one was special. It was Friday, March 20, 2020. The first day of California's coronavirus lockdown order. And in that one day, I had begun *and* wrapped principal photography on my new feature film, *Corona Zombies*.

Look, by the time you read this, there will be a *lot* of entertainment that uses our worldwide pandemic nightmare as a backdrop. There will be "very special episodes" of popular sitcoms that take place during lockdown. There will be Important Documentaries.

There will be feature films that use COVID-19 as a device. Romantic comedies where the couple getting a divorce have to shelter together and rediscover why they loved each other in the first place. Brad Pitt or Meryl Streep or—I don't know, maybe Kristen Stewart in unconvincing "scientist glasses"—may have already collected an Oscar for their brilliant portrayal of the heroic researcher who battled the odds and the damn bureaucrats and found the cure.

And that's fine. All I know is that long before that, on April 10, 2020, just as people were adjusting to the quarantine and looking for something to stream, Full Moon Features released *Corona Zombies*.

That, my friends, is the very definition of an "exploitation film." It takes whatever you're thinking about right now, the thing that's in the wind, and recontextualizes it as a piece of entertainment. Quick, silly, down-and-dirty. It gives you a thrill, a scare, and hopefully a few good laughs. Long before the corporate behemoths can get something approved, and written, and rewritten, and negotiated, and shot and edited and slotted into their schedules, we true independents have already gone ahead and made something, released it, and moved on to whatever the next thing is. I guarantee that by the time Ms. Streep accepts her award, I will have made a dozen more movies.

[An aside: The term "exploitation movies" makes it sound like someone is being exploited. In case you're new to this stuff . . . no. What's being exploited is an opportunity, a cultural or historical moment. No actors or actresses are harmed in the making of these motion pictures. In fact, if they're on my sets, they're generally having a blast.]

"Baht . . . baht . . ." he stammered in his thick Eastern European accent as he interviewed me for Germany's edition of *Rolling Stone*. "Baht why does she take za shower in her clothes?"

A fair question. Showering while fully clothed would look weird in any movie. And *Corona Zombies* was a Full Moon feature, so there's kind of an expectation of a little tasteful nudity.

"That's a really good question, Horst," I said. Though I have no memory as to whether his name was actually Horst. Just go with it.

I went on: "The truth is that we figured that Barbie's character was so ditzy that she misinterpreted the rules about how you were supposed to deal with washing after you went out."

"Ah, I see. Zat makes sense."

But it didn't, really. The explanation was a lie. Or at least it wasn't the whole truth. I was doing like five Zoom interviews a day to promote *Corona Zombies,* and I didn't have time to get into the full story of the Surprisingly Chaste Shower Scene.

That full story requires knowledge of the insane timeline of how *Corona Zombies* came to be. Madness. Utter madness.

Thursday, March 12, 2020

Billy Butler and I were having dinner at BOA on Sunset, right where West Hollywood becomes Beverly Hills. Billy's a friend and one of my top collaborators: actor, writer, director. I first used him in 1987, on *Ghoulies II.* He came up with the story for the first *Gingerdead Man* (starring Gary Busey. Jesus, there are some stories *there*!).

The place was empty, because people were already freaking out about the coming pandemic. Bright side: *great* service!

We were desperately trying to figure out something we could do during the impending Shutdown of Life as We Know It. I'd been watching what was happening with COVID-19 in Italy. More than most Americans, because I grew up in Italy, on the sets of epics and spaghetti westerns made by guys like John Huston and my dad, Albert Band. I will supply a metric ton of crazy stories about that later, but for now all you need to know is that

I'm deeply connected to Italy. They had just gotten absolutely gobsmacked by the coronavirus. And I knew it would be as bad or worse here, because if we're ever called upon, we Americans can and will rise to the occasion and be stupider than absolutely anybody.

So I wanted to figure out a way to keep working. For more than forty-five years I've been making movies in Hollywood and Rome and Romania. That's what animates me. I'm not going to let a little thing like a deadly plague stop me!

Or am I? Billy and I were at a loss, or at least I was. Billy pitched me an idea about repurposing my old movies: dubbing in new, funny dialogue, like in *What's Up, Tiger Lily?* That sounded fun, but not nearly fresh enough for my fans. They'd already seen my movies.

Lockdown was looming, and we had nothing. We ordered another couple of vodka martinis.

That night, at like eleven o'clock, I suddenly had the idea. I jotted it down.

Friday, March 13, 2020

You know when you wake up and read the note you wrote right before you fell asleep and it's either completely unintelligible or completely stupid?

This wasn't one of those times. It was all there: Make a movie about some ditzy girl who doesn't quite get what's going on with the coronavirus. She's learning about it on TV while sheltering in place at her apartment.

But . . . it turns out the coronavirus isn't just a virus. It's a contagion that turns people into flesh-eating zombies, which totally works because zombification in movies is *always* about a virus. I figured we'd intercut real news footage with fake stuff and segue between the girl, the TV, and a real, recut zombie movie with completely new dialogue dubbed in—the *What's Up, Tiger Lily?* treatment.

I call Billy and tell him what we're doing. He loves it. Then I call Roudebush.

First thing you need to know about Kent Roudebush is that his name is not Kent Roudebush. He's a successful Hollywood writer, and like a lot of my people he's a union guy and can't use his real name. He wrote all of my *Evil Bong* movies (the first of which starred Tommy Chong). He *gets* horror comedy. And he's fast.

Kent says, "Okay, when do you need it?"

"Forty-eight hours."

Pause.

"You're shittin' me."

"No."

"Okay, Charlie . . ."

"Look, I swear to god, we are heading for a national lockdown. If we don't shoot this thing next week, it's all over. We're done. It's only a couple of—"

"I *said* okay, Charlie."

Roudebush is the best.

Saturday & Sunday, March 14 & 15

My movies are usually short. I don't want to bore you. Hell, I don't want to bore *me*. So I won't go into the gory details of the next couple of days, even though they're important. It's what my Jewish ancestors called "schlepping"—the necessary stuff that you have to slog through to get from one place to another.

Only in this case, I had to do it at warp speed. I had to turbo-schlep.

I call my people. I need a location or two, an AD, art director, cinematographer, sound, etc. Hours of phone calls. The only thing that makes it easier is that I know everybody's about to be out of work. So . . . yay, virus?

[I'll let you in on one of my best tricks for making good-looking movies on a tiny budget: spend what money you have on hiring great department heads. That's it. The rest is easy. The kids who work in their departments will work for next to nothing, and they'll be glad to do it because they're learning from someone who really knows their stuff. The department heads get some cash, their kids get experience and make connections, and I get a movie that looks better than it has any right to look.]

Sunday afternoon, like clockwork, Roudebush's script comes in. It's good. The whole ridiculous venture is taking shape. Now all I have to do is select a couple of my old zombie movies to slice 'n' dice.

There's just one problem: I realize that I do not in fact make zombie movies.

Monday, March 16

Okay, I made *one* zombie movie. In my delirious feast-or-famine career, 2012 was definitely one of the famine years. But I managed to make a movie called *Zombies vs. Strippers*.

Wait—it's not what you think! Unless you think it's about a bunch of half-naked strippers fighting off a zombie horde in a frenzy of spurting blood. In which case it's *exactly* what you think. It takes place in a rough neighborhood, at a down-and-out strip joint called the Tough Titty. (Come on, what else would it be called?)

But although it has a couple of scenes we might be able to repurpose, it's really not the right vibe. I need something a little older, a classic. And because we're replacing the dialogue, it doesn't have to be in English.

I call Bill Lustig, who licenses old genre movies. A lot of Italian stuff, too, which is close to my heart. As I said, I grew up there. Also, I bought Dino De Laurentiis's old movie studio there and ran it for several years. Also also, for a couple of decades I owned a castle there. An actual medieval castle. Don't worry, I'll get to that.

Anyway, Bill has exactly what I need: *Hell of the Living Dead*, a gloriously bad 1980 flick directed by Bruno Mattei. It's got it all—scientists, native tribesmen, jungles, factories, and lots of shambling zombies busily disemboweling anyone they can catch up with, in the most repulsive and gory ways. It's perfect.

We set our shoot day for Friday. Yes, a one-day shoot. But hey, it's only like four or five scenes, probably less than ten minutes on the screen. Three locations, all in the same house. A couple of actors. No problem.

Thursday, March 19

Los Angeles mayor Eric Garcetti announces a shelter-in-place order, effective the next day at midnight.

Hours later, California governor Gavin Newsom announces an identical, statewide order, effective immediately.

Now we have a problem. I need to think. We are literally

shooting in a few hours. After some careful strategizing, I come up with a clever plan that can be summed up in nine words:

Hell with it. We're going to do it anyway.

Friday, March 20

The shoot goes amazingly smoothly, considering.

As Barbie, Cody Renee Cameron is a total pro, delivering the lines with hilarious airhead gusto. Lots of jokes about hand sanitizer and face touching and toilet paper and all the obsessions of that moment in history. 2020, kids. It was a weird time.

Barbie's best friend Kendra, only heard on the phone, works as a perfect foil. Not surprising. She's *my* actual best friend, my girlfriend, Robin Sydney.

Greg, our makeup guy, spends six hours getting our zombie ready for his one-and-only moment, that thrilling toilet paper/garage scene. One shot, but we need it. And Greg nails it.

By the time we get to the shower scene, I've already thought it through: We've got three weeks until we release this thing (god help us!). Which means we need to get all the publicity out there ASAP. Like, *yesterday.*

So I'm not just thinking about the movie. I'm thinking about the PR. We'll need to use pretty much everything from today in the trailer. Including, *especially,* the helpless chick in the shower, a horror film staple ever since Norman Bates first yanked back that curtain and got all stabby on Janet Leigh.

But one thing I knew for sure was that although I'd be able to show a mutilated, bloody zombie on YouTube, no problem . . . a human breast would be an instant dealbreaker. American corporate media is weird that way.

And without a YouTube trailer, this project was going nowhere.

So that's that. For the sake of the trailer, I tell Cody to shower with her top on. It works just fine.

We moved fast. By Monday we had a teaser. A real trailer soon followed, and it quickly picked up a quarter million views on YouTube. It got press, of course, even though a lot of it wasn't positive. People get *touchy* about deadly worldwide pandemics! COVID-19 was just beginning to ravage the American population, and a lighthearted horror parody like mine . . . well, it's not for everybody. One media outlet called it "the worst possible taste." Which was unfair: I can do, and have done, *much* worse!

Anyway, we slammed our way through dubbing and scoring and editing and mixing, and on April 10, *Corona Zombies* dropped on FullMoonFeatures.com and all the Full Moon apps.

Ironic bonus for zombie fans: How long was the premiere from the moment I had the idea? My friends, it was . . . twenty-eight days later.

It got us a couple thousand new subscribers, thousands of downloads. By these strange modern standards, it was a hit.

The reviews were mixed. *Film Threat* called it "a hilarious satire," and likened it to *What's Up, Tiger Lily?* and *MST3K.* Horronews.net called it "awesome" and "the film we need right now."

Meanwhile, others called it "pathetic," "perfunctory and sad," and "bottom of the barrel opportunism. Do everything possible to socially distance yourself from it."

I used *all* of the above reviews and more in a new promotional poster.

The downloads kept coming.

Well, now I had invented a fun, quick-and-dirty type of movie that I could continue to make while everyone else was shut down—my editors and voice actors could do all their work while safely at home. We immediately started work on another dubbed-and-recut satire, *Barbie and Kendra Save the Tiger King,* a satire of *Tiger King,* which was a worldwide phenomenon at that moment.

I was psyched. This wasn't the first time I'd helped create mini-industries within the movie business, and it wouldn't be the first time I'd profited off it. But hopefully I've already experienced the *last* time that I completely lose my shirt. I really miss that castle!

In my forty-five years in the industry I've worked with an amazing menagerie of geniuses and clowns. I came up the ladder with guys like Stan Winston and John Carpenter. I helped discover up-and-comers like Viggo Mortensen, Demi Moore, Helen Hunt, and Bill Maher. I even had a brief fling with one of them, and because these are my confessions, I'll tell you about it (here's a hint: it wasn't Maher). I've dined and partied with just about everybody, often in Hollywood, but always as an outsider.

I'm going to tell you all of that, but I'm going to tell it my way: quick and dirty, and loaded with blood and guts and jump scares and boobs and madness.

Our story starts in Europe. And like any grindhouse classic, it involves Nazis and gunplay and death and dismemberment. Oh, and the most famous blond bombshell in history. Let's start with her.

The Italian Job

(1951–1970)
Studio City, CA, 1952

From my window, I saw her get out of the car. She was twenty-five years old, impossibly blond; the evening sun filtered through the loose folds of her simple but stylish dress. She was aware of my neighbors' eyes on her, and couldn't resist vamping it up a little, her shoulders back, her hips feinting left and right, a human calliope of Sex. Even though she was not yet rich—not by a long shot—*The Asphalt Jungle* had made her somewhat famous, and her name would've been on the lips of many an onlooker: "Marilyn. It's Marilyn Monroe!"

And she was coming to see me.

I sat there, preoccupied, but I could hear her heels clacking up the stone path, the knock on the door, the approaching voices . . . and all at once she burst through my open door and she was with me. No longer performing, just arriving. Open, honest, moving more simply now, but no less a goddess. Distracted though I was, I looked up at her as she drew near. I could smell her—light perfume, soap, and something else. She put her hands on her knees and bent forward, her red lips parting, her fulsome cleavage now exposed, dangling, almost in my face.

"Hello, Charlie. I'm Norma Jeane. I've heard a lot about you," she cooed.

At least that's how I imagine it happening. One of the tragedies of my life is that I can't remember it. Even though part of me believes that this is where it all started with me and women. That weird cocktail of worship and lust that made me want to capture them on film—moving, always moving—whether fleeing from a zombie horde or indulging in a sorority pillow-fight . . .

But I don't remember. I'm just bullshitting here. It was 1952. I was a few months old, and Marilyn Monroe was my babysitter.

No, I don't have any pictures, dammit. But Dad told me about it. He was friends with Marilyn. He was John Huston's assistant director on *The Asphalt Jungle,* he was there at her audition, and they remained close for years. They even hung out in Rome together—Dad, my mom, Marilyn, and her husband Joe DiMaggio.

To understand all that, we have to flash back again. Back to those Nazis that I promised you.

My grandfather was getting a little tired of the White House.

I mean, he liked the place. He especially liked his new friend, Franklin Delano Roosevelt. But he was homesick.

Do I have your attention?

Max Band was a well-known artist, living in Paris with his wife and his young son, Albert Band, my future father. Along with his friend Marc Chagall, Max was one of the founders of the famed "School of Paris" artistic movement. He was famous enough that in 1940 he was given the opportunity to come to America and sculpt a bust of the president of the United States.

No, really. The sculpture still sits in the White House.

Anyway, sitting together like that, he and FDR really hit it off. Which turned out to be a good thing, because a few weeks after Max arrived in the U.S., he got an urgent call from a friend back home.

The Nazis had taken Paris. They'd raided and ransacked hundreds of homes, made arrests. Of course they'd hit the home and studio of the well-known Jewish artist Max Band. They trashed his place. My grandfather had nothing to go home to.

Fortunately, unlike so many sudden refugees, when Max got the call, he happened to be hangin' with the president of the United States.

FDR intervened and saved my family—he greased the wheels and made them citizens, and he graciously offered to help resettle Max wherever he wanted within the States. Max didn't know a ton about the U.S., but his sixteen-year-old son had been paying a *lot* of attention to a certain American export and knew exactly where *he* wanted to go.

Grandpa indulged him. They moved to Hollywood.

Toward the end of his life, my dad finally got around to writing his memoir. It's pretty great. I'll get it published someday.

It's entitled "John Huston and My Breakfast Money," and it's an amazing tale of an amazing life. The opening sentence is, "We were there at the beginning, John Huston, the bimbo, and me."

Don't judge. It was a different time. They were trying to *cast* a bimbo, but they struck . . . gold. Marilyn.

Dad goes on: "In the history of film, only Huston was of any importance in 1949. He was the Academy Award–winning writer and director whose work would become legend. 'The Huston Touch,' they would call those special moments in such films as *The Maltese Falcon*. . . ."

My dad had talked his way into Huston's orbit and made himself useful enough to become his AD. He ended up adapting Huston's next film, *The Red Badge of Courage*, for the screen.

See, after getting resettled thanks to FDR, Dad's adolescence had been sprinkled with glittering cameos—my grandpa's studio became a gathering place for Orson Welles, Edward G. Robinson, Zero Mostel, and my dad's personal hero, Charlie Chaplin.

In fact, when my dad was a teenager, he directed Chaplin's son in a Molière play. Chaplin really enjoyed it, visited my dad backstage, gave him some notes . . . and in no time they became friends. Before he knew it, he was at Charlie Chaplin's house, having dinner with his hero and Chaplin's very pregnant wife, Oona. Postwar Hollywood was a strange, giddy place, and an enterprising, competent kid like my dad could really go places.

But that's my dad's story. My story began in 1951, a year after *The Asphalt Jungle*, and by the time I can remember anything, my family, along with a certain segment of the movie industry, had moved to Europe. We lived in Paris for a while, where I finished first grade. All I remember of France is hating my school and its stupid uniform—my brother Richard and I, miserable, stuffed into knee pants and a starched shirt and tie and even, so help me, a goddamned beret. And I remember my dad, one evening, making a speech to the family: Things weren't going well. There was no work and no money. We had to leave.

We caught a night train to Rome. It was scary. I vividly remember my mother sewing our remaining money into my dad's pants, just in case we got robbed. But we didn't get robbed—instead there was just seven-year-old me and my little brother and my parents on a dark train at night, heading for a country I'd never been to, where they spoke a language I didn't know. The hope was that Dad could drum up some film work in Italy, maybe produce or even direct a couple of movies, and then head home to our grandparents in L.A.

We stayed for twelve years.

I loved Rome. I love it still, but it's different now. My brother and I had fantastic childhoods, really. We thrived there, attending the Overseas School of Rome.

Not that I liked school. I never liked to be told anything, never liked having to submit to anybody's authority, which is why I've been my own boss basically my whole life. But the scene was *cool:* my friends were kids from all over the world, all kinds of races and nationalities. To this day I feel deeply uncomfortable when I'm in a group of people who are all the same, even when it's all white people. *Especially* if it's all white people. We're uniquely fucked up.

When we weren't in school, we roamed Rome, getting in and out of trouble. And every Friday night was movie night at the American embassy, where someone would bring first-run features, often prerelease. See, the foreign market was becoming huge for Hollywood, so new movies had to be sent around the world to be dubbed—meaning that we ended up with the 35mm prints for movie night.

Also there were the sets. I spent huge chunks of my childhood on movie sets with my dad, watching people create epics, historical dramas, and spaghetti westerns. Big, splashy films with giant casts (and usually a couple of imported American stars). I hung out, asked questions, learned from everyone—the cameramen, the sound guys, the ADs, and the actors and the extras. I loved movies, and being on set was magical. Still is. I still can't believe I get to do this!

But what shaped me most about Rome was Rome itself. The Italian attitude. See, in Italy, anything is possible. "No" doesn't mean "no." "No" is an opening move in a negotiation that will eventually lead to "yes" if you're smart enough and persistent enough and charismatic enough. And I had all of that. I was a happy, gregarious, handsome American in Europe (if I do say so myself!)—I could get away with absolutely anything, talk my way out of any trouble. By the time I was fifteen I was also having actual, real-life sex—my first serious girlfriend, Meda, and I, caught in the thrall of exploding hormones, would grab any and every opportunity to sneak off and hump like bunnies. It seemed like the fun would never stop.

Right up until the time Meda's dad walked in on us.

He went straight to my dad and demanded I stay away from his daughter. Which didn't work, of course. So then he left Rome and yanked his family back to Pittsburgh, taking the first love of my life away from me. Not cool, Mr. Robertson. Not cool.

But I got my revenge five years later, when I asked Meda to leave college and come out to Los Angeles and marry me. And she said yes.

But that comes later.

So maybe you're wondering . . . what made a perfectly happy kid like me develop a lifelong obsession with horror and grotesquerie? I don't know. Maybe it's a natural tendency. Maybe it involved my deep fascination with and love of Marvel Comics, which were a constant presence throughout my childhood.

And maybe it had to do with a couple of near-death experiences in nightmarish third-world-style hospitals. That'll do it.

I was nine years old, and the family had decamped to Yugoslavia. We were living in a hotel in Belgrade while my dad was producing *The Avenger,* an epic starring Steve Reeves and based on Virgil's *Aeneid.* Someone—probably my dad—had cut a deal with the Yugoslavian dictator Tito. And get this: Tito didn't just allow us to shoot in his country, no, he provided literally thousands of extras by ordering his troops to be in the film. Some directors can seem like tyrants, but our de facto AD was the genuine article!

Oh, there was another notable player in *The Avenger.* As Aeneas's curly-haired young son, the cinematic debut of Charlie Band!

To be honest, I didn't really enjoy acting. It seemed to me that all the action was happening on the *other* side of the camera. But I liked Steve, and I can attest that, as a former Mr. America, he was the most qualified guy on earth to play an ancient Greek demigod. He was a kind, gigantically muscled action figure of a man—the early model for all our modern steroidal, ripped movie heroes.

Anyway, one day I woke up with a really bad stomachache and couldn't join my dad on the set, which was a bummer. I lived for those sets, so you *know* I was hurting. It got steadily worse, agonizing really, and my mother called a doctor.

He looked me over. Prodded around. His brow wrinkled and he became worried in a super obvious way, which is never comforting. He said he had to press my abdomen to see if it was appendicitis. Okay . . .

He pressed.

In a flash that was literally blinding I felt the worst pain of my entire life. And passed out. I was rushed to the hospital, where they had to operate. My appendix had exploded. It didn't look good for me, that was the word they gave my mom.

Someone was dispatched to the set to let my father know that his oldest son's appendix had burst, and that they were cutting me open, and that I probably wasn't going to make it. Dad had to travel two hours back to Belgrade, and it was two of the worst hours of his life, *willing* the car to move faster, hoping to get a last look at his son before he died. Years later, Dad still couldn't tell the story without getting all teary-eyed.

SPOILER ALERT:

I lived.

But it wasn't easy. This was my first of several stays at third-world hospitals, and it was painful and gruesome. I was there for weeks on end, stuck on a dark, dank ward with maybe a dozen other patients, all of them in some kind of agony, struggling, bleeding, dying. Limbs were amputated, lives were lost. It sucked.

It wasn't the gore. For some reason, I've always been okay with blood and guts. But the *feel* of the place, the endless, dreary misery as I lay there, in pain, unable to eat, pricked with needles and fed through tubes, unable to escape, feeling my body wither away to nothing . . .

Yeah, maybe that's what drew me to horror.

I also learned from those weeks in Yugoslavia that I could live through absolutely anything. Through every giant success and horrific bust, through every lousy break that life has thrown at me, I've always reminded myself: Yeah, it's bad. But it's not as bad as Yugoslavia.

My dad was my rock during all that. My mom was a sweet but somewhat distant woman, like a lot of parents at that time. Dad was a Jewish mother and a Jewish father all rolled into one. When he left the hospital at night, he'd leave a handkerchief, smelling of his signature Jean Naté cologne, to get me through the night, so that I could smell something other than suffering and disinfectant and death. A reminder that outside the four hellish walls where I was penned up in misery, there was a larger, better world. A world with family and friends and sunlight.

I recovered. I began to eat. I was released from hell and headed out into the daylight, vowing I would never go back to such a place.

And then it happened again.

I don't want to dwell on this, but when I was fourteen I suddenly felt that same pain in my abdomen again, was rushed to a hospital in Rome, and had to undergo emergency surgery *again*. It turned out that my operation had created intestinal adhesions. In fact, they told me, this awfulness might recur periodically for the rest of my life.

Again I was holed up in a hospital that was not up to American standards. Again I was stuck with needles and fed through tubes while I wasted away to what looked like a human skeleton. After a few weeks I was cleared to eat again, and I remember my mom feeding me a tiny spoonful of broth . . . and for the first time in what seemed like forever, flavor exploded in my mouth. It was the most amazing thing I ever tasted. It's easy to take life's gifts, like the taste of food, for granted. Because of those terrible times, I try not to.

A year or two later it happened *again*. I was getting used to it, but that didn't make it suck any less. Once again, I became a human pincushion, lost almost half my body weight, suffered horribly. I remember exactly when this happened, though. It was July 1967, the Summer of Love. I remember because Dad showed up with a portable record player and a brand-new album he knew I wanted: *Sgt. Pepper's Lonely Hearts Club Band.*

My dad. So much cooler than other dads. I listened to it endlessly as I made it my job to Not Die. And by this point, I knew I would fight my way out. Look, I was a hyperactive, endlessly industrious kid. I had friends and plans and schemes, and by the third time this nonsense happened, I also had Meda in my life. I could've been seeing movies (by that point I was into some of the great Italian directors, like Fellini and Antonioni), and romancing Meda and making my little art films. I was always running some scheme or another, but I kept hitting this damned medical roadblock. I learned a lot from those months, but NOT patience. Every time I was released, it was like being shot out of a cannon, and I emerged eager to hit the ground running, faster and harder than I had before.

Which is probably why I started the illegal underground night-club in the subterranean ruins of ancient Rome.

Okay, you're a fifteen-, sixteen-year-old foreign kid in Rome, and you're too young to hit the really cool clubs. But you need a joint—a cool place to gather all your friends together, students from your school and other schools, a place to party and dance and laugh and be free. Where do you find that?

Well, there was "Teen Club," but that was in a *church basement.* No. I had to make it myself.

Understand, I wasn't constructing some kind of Roman orgy or drug den. Italy in the sixties, for all its worldliness, was an oddly innocent place. Sure, there was an endless supply of food and drink and music and the ever-present hint of sex . . . Sure. But in a way that was almost cute.

Me, I gathered some friends and hatched a plan. I'd create a social club, let a hundred or so of my closest pals buy memberships to get in on the ground floor, as it were, and use that money to help pay for it all. What could possibly go wrong?

Meda and I walked around our target neighborhood, the area around the Fountain of Trevi. It's a beautiful, old, old neighborhood, full of narrow cobblestone streets and ancient buildings. Absolutely lovely and very expensive, but there were ramshackle old places on the back streets that you could rent for a song. Almost immediately we found a small cantina, sunk below street level. It was cramped and dank and unlovable, but I didn't care. I wanted what was underneath.

See, Rome is built on . . . Rome. Like, layers and layers of previous Romes. It's Rome all the way down. So underneath the cantina we rented was a cavernous, scary room from truly ancient times. The guy who rented it to me had let me know that although it was bricked up, we were free to open it up if we wanted. And we did. It was ideal.

Okay, if you want to quibble, I'll admit the place didn't have a lot of . . . hmm, what's the word I'm looking for? Oh yeah: *air*. But that was just a detail. We could blast our music and party all night long!

We found some lights, ran some extension cords. Meda was a terrific artist, and she painted the walls with murals that would glow under black light (remember, it was the sixties!). We brought in a record player. I sent word around that on an upcoming Friday night, in a subterranean Roman ruin, the Ultimate ChaBa Club would open. ("ChaBa"? That's for Charles Band, naturally). I printed up lifetime membership cards and sold them to kids from my school and other nearby American schools. Ten thousand lire apiece, which was about eight bucks. And I sold over a hundred of 'em!

Opening night was fantastic. My parents came, all dressed up for the occasion, because as I said, they were much, much cooler than normal parents. They knew it wasn't legal, but they also knew they couldn't stop me, so they went with it. Despite the lack of air, the night was a huge success, and I was a fifteen-year-old nightclub impresario!

Until the joint got shut down in a police raid a week later.

We'd had some, um, operational challenges along the way. For instance, as a club manager, I should have known not to put my stoner friend Stefano in charge of the bar. He brought in lots of beer for us to sell, yes, but then got so high that he started giving it all away, handing a bottle to anyone who asked with a bleary-eyed, benevolent smile. Lesson learned. But it wasn't giving free alcohol to teenagers that sank us.

The problem was those goddamn scooters. *Motorini,* we called them. Vespas and such, with foul-smelling little two-stroke engines. We kids used 'em to get everywhere, because for some reason the legal age to drive a scooter in Rome was fourteen. And no, we didn't wear helmets, because sixties. Naturally, all the Ultimate ChaBa Club patrons showed up on their scooters, parked them on the sidewalks, and came down to the ruins to party.

And when we closed the club for the night, probably around 1:00 A.M., everybody got on their scooters and went home. Except that we're talking about these incredibly loud little two-stroke engines, all gunning it at once, on the tiny, echoey stone streets of a family neighborhood. The neighbors were not pleased.

So a week after opening came the inevitable police raid.

It was a bust, but it was a bust done Italian style. Casual. I'd already told my guys at the door that if something like this happened, they should bring the police to me. I may have been a delinquent and technically a criminal, but I wasn't *dishonest*! Plus, I was no coward.

In perfect Italian, I explained to the cops that I was a student and told them my name. To prove this was all on the up-and-up, I even showed them the Ultimate ChaBa membership card, so help me, I did. The cop in charge examined it. He was my height, with a rubbery, expressive Roman face, casually projecting authority. I think he was partially stunned by the fact that this weird American kid was actually trying to talk his way out of this.

He returned my card. "Very industrious. But look, we are going to have to shut you down. You can't do this."

"Really?" I asked, radiating surprised innocence. "Why?"

"Well, first of all, you're fifteen years old."

"That's a problem?"

"Yes. And secondly . . . there's no air down here. You could all die."

I gasped in concern. Complimented his keen powers of perception. Sent everyone home. In no time, I had talked my way out of any serious trouble—out of any trouble at all, in fact. But the Ultimate ChaBa Club was dead.

I said goodnight to the cops and thanked them for protecting us ignorant Americans and the city at large. I vowed to never do it again.

About a month later, I did it again.

See, everyone had been on me about it. They wanted the club back, plus there was the little matter of those lifetime memberships. I didn't want to give all that money back! There was only one solution: we needed another space. It took some time, but I assured everyone that the new club was in the works.

This time we chose a more discreet location. My friend Tamara told me about a street near the Pantheon. We walked the neighborhood and found the perfect place—another cantina! Bigger, cooler, and removed from the street. You had to walk through a door, across a courtyard, and through another door. Plus it had all the modern amenities, and by that I mean "air." We grabbed it, and I gave the place a typically understated nightclub name: GODSIN.

This time my friends had to park far away, in the piazza. They had to knock on the door. But my adolescent brain somehow missed the fact that if you pack 150 American teens into the basement of a residential building, it might get loud.

The police weren't as friendly this time.

I didn't run and hide, though. They struggled to ask in English, "Is-a this place you have . . . You have-a the permits?"

I answered that I didn't have-a the permits. But I answered in fluent Italian. That makes a huge difference. Now they could *talk* to me. And in Rome, if you can talk, you can negotiate.

I got off again. But my nightclub career was over.

A fun side note: Forty years later, after decades of movies and madness, I was in Rome with my girlfriend, Robin, when my old friend Tamara got in touch with me. She was living in Rome again!

"Charlie, you won't believe this," she said, "but you guys have to come visit us in our new apartment."

We went to the address. The neighborhood, not far from the Pantheon, was now super-expensive. The street Tamara lived on was now famous, lined with beloved antique shops.

We knocked on the door and Tamara came and greeted us. I couldn't contain myself as she walked us across the courtyard.

"Tamara—this is the neighborhood! This is the place where—"

"No," she said. "This isn't the neighborhood."

"It's not?"

"No," she said, with an uncontainable smile as she led us. "This is the *exact building*. You see this door?"

I did. It was the door to GODSIN. Swear to god. She now lives upstairs from our old club.

I was suddenly gobsmacked by memory. I looked at the ol' door. "And if some enterprising young kids with ambition and gumption open a nightclub down here?" I asked.

"Yeah. I'm totally calling the cops."

And then, around the time I graduated high school, it was time, at long last, to go home. The sixties had ended and my childhood had, too. The film industry was changing. Plus, my grandparents were getting old, and Dad wanted to get back to them.

I'd been back to America a couple of times. I was excited to see what life would be like in Hollywood. I wasn't sentimental. I knew I'd come back to Italy (though I didn't know that I still had a studio to run and a castle to buy there!). I headed home with a sense of optimism and adventure and endless possibilities.

Within a couple of months I weighed eighty-five pounds and was wasting away, half-dead, in a roach-infested Mexican hospital.

Head of the Family and THAT TONGUE

Dark, hopeless medical wards from which there is no escape. Weird surgeries. Mayhem and despair. If you're a fan of my stuff, you've probably seen one of my favorite versions of all this, *Head of the Family*.

It's pure southern Gothic. A young diner owner stumbles upon the Stackpool family, a terrifying quartet of inbred siblings: a hulking enforcer, an oversexed bombshell, a geek with super-sharp senses, and a disgusting giant-brained head on a tiny shrunken micro-body. Essentially, the Head (Myron) wants to be a real boy with a full-sized body, and he's willing to experiment upon an unlimited supply of kidnapped drifters until he figures it out. Meanwhile, he's suddenly being blackmailed by this young businessman and his girlfriend . . .

So . . . as the movie approaches its horrifying conclusion, the blackmailer's girlfriend, Loretta, captured, makes a desperate play: she strips off her dress and tells Myron that she *loves* him, like, she's totally horny for the Head. A pretty transparent ruse when you're hopelessly cornered by a grotesque madman, maybe, but you gotta admire the girl's spirit! Also, a giant malformed head like Myron hasn't had a lot of girls come on to him, so . . . he goes for it. Wants to show her what he can offer.

That's when he extends his tongue. And does unspeakable things with it.

Okay, I'll speak of it. SPOILER ALERT: His unbelievably gross, bumpy, slimy tongue extends from his mouth . . . farther and farther . . .

impossibly long . . . until it gently and horrifyingly and sensually licks Loretta's right breast. Jiggles it. Teases the nipple a little. Leaves a trail of slime.

It is *foul*. All the more so because Jacqueline Lovell really nails that state of being utterly repulsed while knowing her life depends on *not* being repulsed.

I'm proud of the fact that almost all the effects in *Head of the Family* are done using forced perspective, a technique dating back to the silent era. We'd place Myron's head close to the camera to make it look huge, and place other actors in the background to shrink them. Then you make it work with trick lighting and training the actors to look at empty air so it looks like their eyelines are right. Nowadays you mostly do that stuff with CG, but I do like that Peter Jackson famously revived the good old-fashioned forced perspective technique throughout the Lord of the Rings trilogy. Elijah Wood ain't *that* short!

Anyway, the tongue was different. It was a real, physical, practical effect. And that tongue scene is totally the money shot of the whole movie, that wished-for moment when the audience screams and laughs and can't believe what they're seeing. Anyone who tells anyone about *Head of the Family* absolutely mentions the Tongue.

The Tongue was three feet long, a monstrous latex thing slathered in K-Y Jelly to make it slimy and shiny. It lived on a platform that supported an elaborate rig. Cables came out of the back of the Tongue and fed into a system of pulleys and levers. It took three people working those pulleys and levers to bring it to life, and those guys literally had to practice for hours just to get it to perform a realistic licking motion for five seconds or so.

Then came the day of the shoot. Jackie, on her knees, half-naked in the flickering torchlight of the Stackwell dungeon. In front of her was the Tongue, and behind it were three guys operating the Tongue. We coated it with goo and moved the rig toward Jackie . . .

There was a lot of laughing. My sets are fun places to begin with, but this was just so clearly sick and wrong, and in the best possible way. The camera rolled, the guys began their choreographed robotongue dance, extending and undulating the monstrous appendage forward as Jackie held still . . . and . . . *Shluuuuuuuurrrrrp!*

It only took a couple of takes. I yelled "cut," everybody cheered, and Jackie recoiled hilariously and said, "Oh god. I feel like my *soul* needs a shower." We all agreed.

That night I had my editor Steve Nielson cut the scene together. Michael Citriniti, who played Myron the Head, was also a fucking riot in the scene, speaking so civilly, so genteelly . . . and then slowly, painfully, beginning to extend his (real) tongue out of his mouth . . . then cut to that horrifying shot, that awful licking moment . . . then back on Jackie's face, trying not to look disgusted . . .

Standing there behind Steve in the edit bay, chuckling at what we'd done, I said, "Love it or hate it, nobody's going to forget this."

I dare you to try!

2

Coming to America

(1971–1976)

Making my first horror movie was a trip. *The Eyes of Dr. Chaney*, I called it, but if you want to see it you'll have to find it by its later title, *Mansion of the Doomed*. It's about a deranged surgeon, played by the wonderful Richard Basehart (whom you might remember from *Knight Rider* or *Voyage to the Bottom of the Sea*. Then again, you might not!). Anyway, Dr. Chaney's daughter loses her eyes in a car accident that was *his fault*! To make amends, her father decides to start harvesting people's eyeballs in the hopes of restoring her sight.

So . . . you know, like a typical Charles Band joint.

But wait. In order to make the first real Charlie Band movie, I needed to meet people, get to know Hollywood, rub elbows with Chicago mobsters, invent a business, and nearly die in Mexico.

We'll start with that last one.

Steve was an Italian prince of some sort, my pal from Rome who happened to be living in America around the time I arrived. His real name was Stefano Cacace, and he was the son of the Baron Amadeo Cacace. A tall, blond, perennially stoned goofball (you may remember him as my nightclub's overly generous bartender!), Steve was easily as crazy as I was. So it was perfectly logical, in the spring of 1971, for Steve to suggest we drive from Los Angeles all the way to the bottom-most tip of South America. And it made just as much sense that I said yes.

I remember he called me from San Francisco not long after I arrived in L.A., and gave me his insane sales pitch: "Charlie, before you get too busy, let's do it. You and me. We'll buy a giant American muscle car and drive to the tip of South America." Like it was the most obvious thing in the world that two friends could do; either go get a burger or drive seven thousand miles to the ass-end of the world. Take your pick.

I agreed. What could possibly go wrong?

First there was a need for a suitable vehicle, and man, we found it. An Oldsmobile 442, one of the goofiest, burliest hot rods to emerge from the sixties. It was essentially the automotive version of Arnold Schwarzenegger. We loved it.

Steve started to get nervous, though. We were going to be driving through some pretty rough neighborhoods. And by "rough neighborhoods" I mean "desperately impoverished Latin American dictatorships." What if we went to sleep in a hotel and some bad guys tried to break into our trunk or steal our engine? To this day it amuses me that we were more worried for the Oldsmobile than for ourselves.

At the last minute I hit upon a solution. We took the car to a shop that was willing to weld cartoonishly gigantic locks on the hood and the trunk. The Olds was a beast beforehand; now it was straight outta *Mad Max*.

Then there was the problem of my compromised digestive system. I wasn't too far removed from my second stay in that Roman hospital. And between us and the healthier cuisines of Central and South America lay the gastric minefield known as Mexico.

But Steve had a plan for getting his pal Charlie to the other side. In the back of our Olds he placed a five-gallon drum of nuts—a kind of trail mix, I guess, but mostly peanuts—which was to be my diet until we passed through the danger zone. Perfect.

We set off, two skinny longhairs in frilly Italian hippie clothes, roaring down the highway in a spectacular automotive desert beast, happily munching nuts and blasting the radio, heading south . . .

The adventure lasted all of three days before I nearly died.

If you know anything about nutrition, you probably saw this coming. But I knew nothing about nutrition, so I was pretty surprised when that intestinal agony came over me again. Steve dragged me into a hospital in the Mexican city of Guaymas, where a doctor told me that I had catastrophic intestinal blockage and that he'd have to operate.

The culprit? Nuts. The doctor looked at me with an expression of pity laced with condescension. "To eat only nuts for three days . . . You realize that it's like putting glue in your intestines, don't you?"

Well, *now* I did.

Weeks in the hospital ensued. It wasn't as bad as Yugoslavia—nothing would ever be as bad as Yugoslavia—but it wasn't fun. There were giant cockroaches, weird shit happening, people in agony everywhere. One of those people was me. I had a roommate, but I don't remember anything about him. I do remember Stefano visiting, lounging around the room, obliviously slurping down a giant, juicy, sliced avocado topped with spices. Have

I mentioned how heightened and fragile your senses are when you're in that kind of gastric agony? Steve's nasty avocado was a form of torture.

Steve left. My dad arrived, because *of course* he did. He brought Meda with him, and she even donated blood for me (more about our reunion in a moment!). Together we got me back on my feet, and soon I was well enough to get on a plane and get back to my new life in Los Angeles.

Before I left, the doctor served up the bad news, which I'd heard before: my condition was chronic. "One day," he said, "this will come back and strangle your intestines again." Thanks, Doc!

But here's the cool thing: More than forty years later, it hasn't come back. Not once. As soon as I hit Los Angeles, I read everything I could get my hands on about diet and health. A lot of hippie shit, yes—it was, after all, 1971. But also a lot of good, science-based information. I learned to find balance, avoid excess, and listen to my body. Thanks to that, my medical nightmares were behind me—and I could buckle down to the important business of creating nightmares for other people!

So now we're back in Los Angeles, and it's the seventies, and my real career is about to begin. I want to tell you all about that, but first I have to set the stage and establish our cast of characters. You've already met Charlie Band and his remarkable dad, Albert. And my brother, Richard, who was becoming quite the musician.

Then there was Meda, the first love of my life.

I'd never lost touch with Meda. Even after her straitlaced, conservative dad caught us in flagrante and dragged her back to Pittsburgh, we wrote to each other constantly. Love letters crossed the Atlantic, back and forth, every week. I even saved up money and visited her one Christmas in Pittsburgh. Imagine—

it's December at the height of the Vietnam War, in a by-the-book buzz-cut Nixon-loving "America: Love It or Leave It" household. And here comes this long-haired, half-Jewish Italian despoiler-of-women in gay-looking fringed Continental hippie clothes.

We actually had a great time. The strict rule that Meda and I were not to engage in Naughtiness was violated within the first few hours, when she snuck into my bedroom, and our Christmas magic began.

A few years later, I called her from my new Los Angeles home. I said, "Meda, what are you doing wasting your time in Pittsburgh? I've got a life [*I didn't*] and a business [*not really*] and I'm gonna make movies [*I hoped*]. You should be part of this." Meda knew me well enough to know that a lot of my Big Hollywood Success was what those in the software industry now call "vaporware." But we were in love. She came to Los Angeles, and within a few months we were married.

So that's my family during the weird, grimy start of the 1970s. Oh, and there was one more important addition: the amazing Frank Ray Perilli, the comedian–manager–screenwriter–crazy man who personally introduced me to Shecky Greene and sushi and Chicago mob bosses and hard-core pornography and Barbra Streisand.

You're gonna love this guy. I did, too.

Lou Garfinkle was a dear old friend and collaborator of my dad's. He wrote *The Young Guns* (1956) and *I Bury the Living* (1958), both of which Dad directed. He eventually wrote the story to *The Deer Hunter*. But when we Bands arrived in Hollywood, Lou was writing a movie with a big, crazy, funny Italian guy with enormous, bushy eyebrows named Frank Perilli. Frank started out as both a comedian and a businessman—he'd worked with *and* managed his friends Lenny Bruce and Shecky Greene, for instance. He and my dad became fast friends, and he became my cultural Sherpa, helping me navigate the weird landscape of early-seventies L.A. Frank seemed to be comfortable absolutely everywhere, and he was happy to show me around.

"Kid, you ever have sushi? Ever in your life?" he asked me one afternoon. I hadn't. Within an hour we were at the tiny sushi counter at the legendary Imperial Gardens restaurant on the Sunset Strip (a site that would eventually become the just-as-legendary nightclub the Roxbury). In those days there were maybe two sushi places in all of Los Angeles, and that cozy little six-seat counter became a mecca for me—I absolutely fell in love with the stuff. And just about every time I went to Imperial Gardens with Frank, I found myself crammed in there with Barbra Streisand.

She was in her late twenties at the time, stylish and hip and with this fantastic energy about her. She was also quiet and unfailingly nice, and although we became friendly, we never really became friends. We weren't there to make friends; we were there for the fish. Besides, Frank and I had somewhere to be.

See, for Frank, sushi at the Imperial Gardens was just an appetizer (though he would tuck down literal pounds of that appetizer!). The real meal was across Sunset, at the equally legendary Italian joint, the Martoni Marquis.

Now that was a weird transition. Stepping into Martoni's was like stepping into a Scorsese or Coppola movie. Dark and red and full of smoke and wise guys and laughter. The crowd was older and well-to-do, either genuine or honorary Italians. And everybody knew Frank. He'd wave at film people and mob bosses and occasionally head to their tables to pay his respects. I have no idea what all those Chicago dons made of me—I probably came across as Frank's young gay boyfriend. Or his youthful ward—Robin to his improbable Batman. I didn't care, though. Frank was a true friend, and always a good time.

It was at Martoni's that Frank introduced me to legendary comedian Shecky Greene. Which quickly became important in one of young Charlie Band's earliest business ventures, the one that was going to fund *The Eyes of Dr. Chaney.*

Frank also took me to my first porno, at the famous Pussycat Theatre on the Strip. "Come on kid, you gotta do it at least once," Frank said. Well, if I gotta, I gotta . . . I shrugged and went along to a screening of the cultural milestone known as *Deep Throat.*

I didn't like it one bit.

I tell ya, you kids today with your iPads and laptops with a dazzling world of absolute filth just a click away: you have no idea what it was like at the dawn of the modern age of porn.

Not that I was all that innocent, but even though those were the days when porn was going "mainstream," when open-minded suburban couples were going out to see *Deep Throat* and *The Devil in Miss Jones,* even though I considered myself worldly . . . I couldn't get into it. Sitting in a theater with all these men, watching close-ups of brightly lit humping and sucking on a giant screen, sitting next to a fifty-five-year-old who looked like a Mafia guy. No. Just no.

"Frank," I said after fifteen minutes, "I can't do this. This is really gross and weird."

Frank wasn't hurt. "Okay, kid. But I'm gonna stay and watch this . . ." Which was fine by me.

A few minutes later, out on the Strip, I realized I'd lost my wallet. Oh, god.

Frank loved telling the story: "So I get back to watching the movie, which was okay—only okay—and suddenly I hear this rustling sound from the floor. I look down and it's Charlie! Kid had snuck back into the theater with some story about 'losing his wallet'!"

He never let me live it down. But for the record, I totally *had* lost my wallet. And despite all the sexy movies I've made, I never once made a hard-core porno. I don't even look at the stuff. Except for once a while, on the Internet. For research purposes, of course.

Okay, so you've met The Cast. Now, as in any good caper movie, you need to know The Plan.

Well, I didn't have a Plan. What I *did* have, suddenly, was forty years' worth of the *New York Times*. Somehow, that was going to have to turn into something.

It did.

I was in New York for some reason, and picked up a copy of the *Village Voice*. I loved the *Voice,* and I also loved thumbing through their classified ads, particularly the "Miscellaneous" section, where you could find odd people trying to sell some of the weirdest shit imaginable. It was the eBay of its day, but even more random.

Anyway, I came across an ad that fascinated me. Some dude in Texas was selling forty years' worth of the *New York Times*. Like, every single day of the *Times,* in perfect condition, for the low, low price of twenty-five hundred dollars! I knew I had to have it.

Please note: I had no idea what I was going to do with it. Nor did I have twenty-five hundred dollars.

In point of fact, I had basically no money. I was living hand to mouth. But I always had a scheme or two on the burner, and I just *knew* I could make this happen. I called the guy and told him I wanted the papers. He wanted five hundred bucks up front before he loaded it on a truck and had his son drive all those papers out to me in Los Angeles.

Somehow I scraped together the money, and all of a sudden I had a ticking clock: some big kid from Texas was on his way with a truckload of old newspapers and the expectation of two thousand dollars *that I didn't have*!

By the time he got to L.A., I had his money and a few places to store the papers—mostly in the garages and spare rooms of friends and family members who were used to bizarre requests from Charlie. I have no idea how I managed it. But manage it I did, and soon I found myself staring at my new possessions—gigantic ceiling-high stacks of the *New York Times*.

Okay . . . I thought. Now what?

I had an idea.

It probably seems obvious now, but absolutely nobody was doing anything like this at the time. Imagine this:

You are beloved comedian and Las Vegas legend Shecky Greene, enjoying a midmeal smoke at the Martoni Marquis on Hollywood's Sunset Strip. It's your birthday. Suddenly, your buddy Frank's weird young hippie friend wishes you a happy birthday and hands you a present. You unwrap it.

It's a book of some sort. It's huge. Beautiful, leather-bound, and on the front in tasteful gold lettering is the title:

SHECKY GREENE
April 8, 1926

You open it up, and inside you find the *New York Times* from April 8, 1926! The Gray Lady. The Paper of Record. From the very day you were born. Somehow, this nutty long-haired nobody has given you a truly fascinating and touching birthday keepsake.

In truth, I gave away several of those, not just to Shecky. I'd found an insane Eastern European bookbinder and had these birthday books made up for everybody I knew who I considered Important. It was the seventies equivalent of reaching out to influencers. So now I was spending money I didn't have to give presents to rich people! But I had that crazy entrepreneurial energy and my Italianate conviction that poverty was a temporary condition to be cured by a concoction made of inspiration and stubbornness and sheer *balls*. I had no intention of stopping— who *wouldn't* want these things? Maybe I could whip up one for Streisand and slide it down the sushi counter to her at the Imperial Gardens. Of course, first I had to somehow find a way to pay the bookbinder . . .

A couple of weeks later, Shecky Greene places an order. Days later, he walks across the stage of *The Tonight Show,* and on live national television he presents the host with a gift. A book:

JOHNNY CARSON
October 23, 1925

Johnny loved it. Just like that, I was in *business*.

I don't know why Meda put up with it. She ended up handling most of our rapidly exploding business as I threw myself into turning all that money into movies (and cars and great meals and stuff!). Plus, I'd named the company after another woman.

Wait, I can explain. Which is probably what I told Meda at the time.

This isn't easy . . . but okay: Remember I told you how after her dad shipped her back to the States, Meda and I exchanged love letters and kept the flame alive? That is entirely true. What is also true is that I was a seventeen-year-old kid. A thousand pounds of raging, romantic hormones packed into a 150-pound body. I met a girl. A cool, incredibly blond, incredibly adorable chick from Marymount, one of the other American schools in Rome. Joyful, hip, creative, and really into Charlie Band. She loved hanging out with me, loved that I made my crazy little student art films, even happily carrying the film canisters for me. Her name, improbably enough, was Jan Miracle.

We had fun. Even while Meda and I were exchanging letters, I was, regrettably, two-timing her with Jan Miracle. At some point Jan was shipped off to school in Switzerland, but we vowed to stay in touch. It was insane. And the insanity lasted until one day, shortly after my Christmas in Pittsburgh, Jan dropped by my place in Rome and discovered my letters from Meda.

And that was that.

Except that *wasn't* that. I was never a one-night-stand guy. I've only had like five meaningful relationships with women in my life. And Jan was one of them. So although it was totally over, and I haven't seen her since, Jan mattered to me. Which is why, when the book business started, I went to Meda and told her my idea for a company name.

"I want to call it . . . Miracle Vintage Papers."

Meda looked at me. "You're kidding."

But she understood, bless her, despite what she knew about me and Jan. Sadly the Jan/Meda two-step wasn't the only time women I truly loved were angry at me like that and—truth to tell—with good cause.

But that story will have to wait. Miracle Vintage Papers took off, money started rolling in. It's hard to explain how huge and sudden it was. Within a few weeks of Shecky's *Tonight Show* appearance, we had two hundred thousand dollars in orders! And my costs? Well, ten bucks for the bookbinding, about a dime per newspaper, and I sold each one for fifty dollars. The math isn't complicated—by my standards at the time, we were *rich*. And it was time for Charlie Band to take that hard-earned money and recklessly plunge it into the most unsafe business on the planet: independent film.

I always tell people that my first movie was *Mansion of the Doomed.* This is a lie.

There's a lot of truth to that lie. I mean, as soon as Miracle Vintage Papers started taking off, I started thinking about poor Dr. Chaney, the brilliant, crazed eye surgeon determined to restore his daughter's sight. I knew I wanted to make a horror movie, and I knew that I could use my newfound income to fund it.

And then Frank Perilli talked me into making something completely different.

All I'll tell you about the movie itself is that it was a parody of the recently released, super-controversial Marlon Brando erotic film *Last Tango in Paris.* Frankie wrote a funny script, I directed it, and it was called *Last Foxtrot in Burbank.*

To my knowledge there are no copies of it out there, not anywhere, and this is a good thing.

Honest to god, I have no idea how Frank got me to do this. Maybe he just had . . . a gift. Or maybe I was an idiot. Probably both. But although the movie itself was terrible, it did lead to a couple of good stories. And in my defense, I was a completely insane twenty-two-year-old. Why *anyone* thought I should be producing and directing a feature film is beyond me. Then again, I was pretty persuasive, and making a movie at twenty-two wasn't

all that different from creating a Roman nightclub at fifteen—
you just *do it* until somebody stops you.

The movie starred Michael Pataki, a beloved character actor
and hilarious coked-up wild man who (1) did a great Brando
impression and (2) was buddies with Frank. As far as I can tell,
those two facts were the entire artistic justification for *Last
Foxtrot in Burbank.* But I liked Michael. Everybody liked Michael, so when it finally came time to make *Mansion of the Doomed,*
I had Michael direct it.

Michael wasn't the only guy who worked on *Last Foxtrot* who
became part of my "crew." There was this amazingly energetic,
scrawny film nut named John Carpenter who I'd been hanging
out with. We were an odd couple when we went out to dinner. I
had evolved healthy, moderate habits as a result of my intestinal
sagas. John would sit down and have a pre-dinner cup of coffee
while smoking a cigarette, and then proceed to order mountains
of fried food that would somehow disappear into his lanky, man-
tislike body. But on the subject of movies, which we were both
obsessed with, we were totally simpatico. John became my editor
on *Foxtrot,* credited as "John T. Casino."

That was the crew I found myself running with, my brothers
in arms. And another thing that unites us is that to my knowledge, after 1973, none of us ever, ever again spoke of *Last Foxtrot
in Burbank.*

As soon as John finished editing, I launched the thing. I knew
way too little, and I spent money like I was feeding pigeons on
the piazza, recklessly tossing out cash, because I *had* cash and we
had a Real Movie, and it was bound to at least earn its money
back, right?

Of course not.

I four-walled two theaters, one in Westwood and one on Hollywood Boulevard. For the uninitiated, "four-walling" a theater

means you essentially rent the joint for an exorbitant price, and you own everything except the concession stand. The two theaters I rented cost me eight thousand and six thousand dollars for the opening weekend, which was a ton of money at the time. I'd have to earn it all back on ticket sales—which, by the way, didn't count the giant premiere, because those seats were free.

And I really did up the premiere in true Hollywood style, spending everything that was left of my money (and probably a good amount of other people's). Red carpets, klieg lights, booze everywhere. Something like five hundred people showed up. Dustin Hoffman was there, a friend of somebody's. The atmosphere was electric, the assembled partiers were beautiful, and my Hollywood career was off to a glittering, dazzling, triumphant start. I was on my way!

The second showing had about fourteen paying customers in Hollywood. Maybe six in Westwood. I was doomed.

Like Max and Leo from *The Producers,* I suddenly realized that I'd made a terrible mistake, and I retreated to my home to monitor the receipts and plot my inevitable desperate flight from Los Angeles and show business. Maybe I could get my mom to sew my last few dollars into my pants.

I'd made literally zero good decisions. I felt like a guy who wins the lottery, puts the money in a sack, walks into a Vegas casino, saunters up to a roulette table, and puts it all on 7.

For example, I'd been told that the theaters might cheat me out of all those lucrative ticket receipts, and it'd be wise to station a guy at both theaters with a hand counter to keep tabs. So what did I do? I flew my crazed Italian buddy Stefano down from Carmel to monitor the Westwood crowd. Which means that American Airlines earned more money on *Last Foxtrot* than I did.

One vivid memory: It was just after the third or fourth screening had started, and I was at home stewing in my despair, when

I got a call from Stefano. He was breathless. "Charlie! Charlie! Dude, I have amazing news," he sang into the phone excitedly. My heart jumped. Maybe the disastrous second screening had been a fluke, a natural hangover from the premiere! Maybe we had a hit on our hands, or at least a chance to break even!

"What, Steve?" I asked. "Is there a real crowd?"

"No, man. There are only like four people in the audience. But two of them are John Lennon and Yoko Ono!"

You know what? That *was* cool. I was still utterly ruined, but that was cool.

You can still rent my *real* first movie, *Mansion of the Doomed*. I make sure it's always available on my Full Moon channels, too. It's got a solid cast and offers some good, shocking, gross moments. Like so many of my movies, a lot of the people involved went on to Hollywood glory. It starred Richard Basehart and Oscar-winner Gloria Grahame, and featured Vic Tayback (the beloved Mel, of Mel's Diner, from the sitcom *Alice*) and Lance Henriksen (who would soon become famous in the role of Bishop in the film *Alien*).

Behind the scenes, I had my guys. My dad supervised the production, and my brother pitched in as well. Frank wrote the script, and our frenetic friend Michael Pataki directed. Michael was a constant whirlwind of manic energy, up to his neck in drugs and girls, enjoying orgies by night and telling stories *about* those orgies the next day, a walking party of a man. It was hilarious being around Michael, but also completely exhausting.

All the vital, necessary gross-out stuff—the eyes being pulled out of living patients, the horrifying scar tissue, the mauled, empty eye sockets of Dr. Chaney's pathetic prisoners . . . all of that was supplied by my new friend Stan Winston.

Stan (or "Stanley Winston," as he was billed at the time) was a true sweetheart of a man. He'd come to Hollywood to act, I think, but by the time I met him he was a makeup guy. By the mid-eighties he was winning Oscars for special effects, and he became a full-fledged Hollywood legend for movies like *Aliens* and the Terminator, Predator, and Jurassic Park franchises. You know, intimate little art-house flicks!

It was impossible to dislike Stan. He had an easy manner and he was a really deep thinker about his craft. "Things have to feel organic, Charlie. Like from nature. Humans are great at spotting things that are phony, but if what you're showing them feels like something from the natural world, they believe it." That was how he approached things, whether he was making an eyeball for me or a T. rex for Spielberg, and he loved walking us through his process. Sometimes we called him "The Rabbi."

He was also a great friend, and our families were very close, especially throughout the eighties. Stan always made time to help on my projects, too—when I needed a disgusting title creature for my 3-D movie *Parasite* (starring Demi Moore), Stan built it for me. Even though he'd become super successful and was hard at work helping create the effects for big movies (including our friend John Carpenter's *The Thing*), Stan not only created the Parasite, he was there on my set to make sure it moved right.

In a lot of ways, *Mansion of the Doomed,* for all its gore and horror, wasn't just my first real movie; it was also the beginning of me really doing the thing I loved. I created a set filled with smart, funny, talented people who all had a great time making something together. It was like the sets I grew up on, but now I was in charge, making sure it all came together, making sure everybody was happy and had what they needed.

The Mansion was an actual mansion, a beautiful house I rented in the posh Fremont Place neighborhood, where 90 percent of the film takes place. Most of the mayhem happened there, and although I'd like to think I had permission to do all the stuff we did . . . Well, if you lived in that neighborhood and looked out one morning to see some filth-covered woman with gory, empty eye sockets emerging from a basement window, staggering across a lawn, screaming in terror and agony, and then being dragged back into a house by an evil doctor and his assistant . . . um, sorry.

Oh, and also—somehow, *Mansion of the Doomed* made money. I was now a moviemaker with a track record! A Young Turk with boundless energy. The sky was the limit.

I still had no idea what I was doing.

The Hollywood Kid

(1977–1979)

This chapter of my life begins with a deadly car crash and ends with a firebombing. Only one of those is fictional.

Along the way I'll destroy fifty more cars, blow up a gas station, make a naughty fairy tale musical loaded with naked people, then another, and help invent the home video industry. I can't help it—I'm a showman. I'll say anything to get you into the tent. But in this case it's all true, I swear.

Now come on in!

"You gotta do a car crash movie," Frank said.

It wasn't a dumb idea. At that moment, they were hot in B-movie circles. Roger Corman, the patron saint of exploitation, was making them, including *Death Race 2000* and *Eat My Dust,* starring Ron Howard.

[Sidebar: Roger semi-bribed Ron to do that one, promising to fund Ron's directorial debut in exchange for Ron spending ten days acting on *Eat My Dust.* To me, you have to admire both guys for cutting that deal!]

Anyway, it wasn't a dumb idea. But I'd already let Frank talk me out of doing a horror movie once, and if I was going to make a car crash movie, it was going to have to be *my* kind of car crash movie.

That's what led me to come up with the plot for *Crash!* A young woman finds a weird one-eyed figurine at a flea market and uses it as a key chain. Next thing you know, her much older wheelchair-bound husband tries to kill her by loosing a vicious dog into her moving convertible. While she's still unconscious in the hospital, the key chain possesses her, enabling her in turn to possess her car from afar, wreaking horrible mayhem on the California highways. You know, *that* old story.

To my everlasting delight, years later Stephen King, one of my heroes, had some very nice things to say about *Crash!* He of course would write his own possessed car story, *Christine.* But let's be clear: *Christine* bears almost no relationship to my movie. I've had much less worthy people than Stephen steal things from me, so I know what that looks like, and this ain't it. To be honest, I would've loved it if he *had* borrowed from me—it would've been an honor.

Crash! starred Sue Lyon (the original Lolita) as the young wife and José Ferrer (who had won an Oscar for *Cyrano de Bergerac*) as the crippled old husband, and featured a cameo from the great John Carradine.

Let me say this: Stocking my movies with well-known but kind of, um, past-their-prime stars was never my intention. But we independent moviemakers were always under pressure from our distributers to "get a few Names in there." For me, that directive came from Brandon Chase of Group 1 International Pictures, a friend of Frank's who advanced some of the cash to make my first three movies. You'll note that in this book I haven't said a bad word about hardly anybody. I have always had a habit of seeing the best in people. Keep that in mind when I tell you that Brandon was . . . not completely honest with me. He always spoke of all the money "we" were going to make on my movies, but it turned out to be the imperial "we." I never saw any of that cash.

All that said, I absolutely loved working with those "Name" actors. For one, I was a huge film buff, and getting to work with my idols, no matter their age, was an honor and a privilege. Also, they were almost always fantastic, gracious presences on set. They knew they were "past it" by Hollywood standards, they knew they were in B movies and that that's how they were going to spend the twilight of their careers . . . and they were fine with that. They were glad to be on a set, doing their job, and they showed up eager, happy, and prepared. They had style, class, great stories, and—in the case of Roddy McDowall—a firm connection to black market goods. More on that in a minute!

Anyway, now that I had a cast and a script and some funds, I needed those other vital elements that a car crash movie required: cars. And someone to crash them.

I bought the cars myself. Dozens of them. Old cars, derelicts, junkers, anything I could find that could hold a coat of paint long enough to be pushed into a ravine and blown sky high. It was a simple formula: Buy 'em for minuscule amounts of cash, blow 'em up, and move on to the next one. Why not?

I would soon find out that there were some really good legal reasons Why Not. But not right away.

To mash up, bash up, and blow up all these cars I found a Hollywood legend, a crazy man named Harry Woolman. Just now I actually had to look him up on the Internet to find out his last name, because he was never called "Harry Woolman." Everybody knew him as "Three Finger Harry." Or "Dynamite Harry." And yes, that second nickname was the cause of the first.

We were a dangerous combo. Harry, a sixtysomething former stuntman and daredevil, happy to create a pyrotechnic nightmare to order. And me, twenty-six years old, with tons of energy and absolutely no sense. I remember discussing how we were going to blow up a gas station for one important scene in *Crash!* I told Harry I wanted it big. He surveyed the small vacant lot we'd rented.

"How big?" Harry asked, stone-faced.

"Just . . . the biggest fucking thing," I said, waving my arms. "Like, atom bomb level."

Harry nodded.

We built a gas station, mostly out of papier-mâché, on that tiny lot. We were supposed to blow up the station and then have a car roll out through the flames and onto the road, peeling away from the destruction.

That was what was *supposed* to happen. Remember, this was done without CGI and on a very limited budget. We'd only get one shot per stunt, hopefully with multiple cameras. One thing I learned quickly is that you can't un-explode a car!

So anyway, we get the cameras rolling and Harry blows up our gas station and it's cataclysmic—a giant orange ball of fire rising menacingly over the landscape, great fountains of flame all around it. But in the chaos our driver gets disoriented and doesn't make the turn. Instead the car veers way off course and piles into a brick wall belonging to the house next door to the lot . . . and utterly destroys it.

It's a pretty great shot. But another thing I learned quickly is that Hallmark doesn't make a "Sorry I Smashed Your Wall in an Apocalyptic Automotive Fireball" card. I sent my brother Richard to ring the neighbor's doorbell, but there was nobody home. So Richard wrote a nice note with our phone number and a promise to fix the wall, and left it in the guy's mailbox. Meanwhile, my crew backed the car out of the rubble and got the hell out of there.

We never heard from the owner. A few weeks later, Richard confessed that he just *might* have given the guy the wrong number.

Don't feel too bad for Richard, though. Sure, he had to do a lot of the nitty-gritty production work on the movie. But he also got to sleep with Lolita!

I'm not sure how it happened. I was busy. Sue Lyon was now thirty, fifteen years removed from her notorious screen debut. But she still *looked* like Lolita. I mean, boyfriends must have felt oddly naughty about having sex with her when she was *sixty*. Anyway, I slowly became aware that she and Richard were hooking up throughout the production.

Well, good for Richard. I wasn't jealous. I was happily married to Meda. In fact, it was while we were filming *Crash!* that Meda informed me that I would soon have to add another job to my burgeoning résumé: Dad.

Also, I was completely obsessed with my movie, which was absolute madness. My stunt coordinator, Von Deming, and his sons were not only the maniacs who were driving and crashing all my cars—Von also designed our "driverless" possessed car, and he and his sons took turns piloting it from a metal capsule tucked in the back seat. He could barely see from his hidden vantage point, and if something bad happened, I don't think he would've been able to exit quickly. If at all. But it looked *great*!

And then there was the day when we dropped two cop cars

into a ravine while we shot from below. That looked great, too—until one of the cars came tumbling down the slope toward us. Because, see, we were shooting *up* at it from the bottom of the ravine, and you know . . . gravity, man. It's a bitch.

I swear to god, it was the kind of slapstick, poor-grasp-of-physics choice that you usually see made by a certain famous cartoon coyote. But in this case it was real. And terrifying. Like true moviemakers, our first thought was for our gear. In one panicky moment, my crew and I grabbed all our impossibly heavy, expensive cameras and stuff and ran to safety. Idiocy. Glorious idiocy.

Speaking of idiocy, it was some time toward the end of *Crash!*, while we were editing, that I started getting notices from the DMV: I had to pay the registration on a car. Okay.

And then I got another DMV notice, for a different car. Yet another car was found, destroyed, in a junkyard. There were assessments and fines. And they just kept coming.

See, in my zeal to make the movie, I had bought all those cars—fifty cars—*in my own name.* I guess I just figured that once a car was dead, it was gone. Game over. But it turned out the law didn't work like the movies. Soon I owed something like eight grand, which I couldn't (and didn't) pay. Talk about possessed vehicles—those damn cars haunted me for years, and until I eventually took care of it I was a fixture on the DMV's Most Wanted List.

But so what if I was a fugitive from automotive justice? I'd done it. I'd brought in *Crash!* on time and more-or-less on budget—which in this case meant "in three months" and "about three hundred thousand dollars." It did really well (again, for Brandon Chase, not for me), and with a decent crash movie and a horror movie under my belt, Frank and Brandon were sure of the logical next step for their young friend:

An erotic fairy tale musical.

Wait, what?

"Wait, what?" I asked Frank.

Frank explained. Bill Osco, who was briefly a big name in exploitation films, had just scored a huge hit with a soft-core erotic musical version of *Alice in Wonderland*. I know: the seventies were weird. But it's true—starring Kristine DeBell (who would later appear opposite Bill Murray in *Meatballs*) as the horny young title character, *Alice in Wonderland* grossed an unbelievable ninety million dollars worldwide. Kristine's previous incarnation had been as the Ivory Soap girl, so there was added pervy delight in seeing this snow-white symbol of purity getting nasty with the Mad Hatter. And Humpty Dumpty. And the Queen of Hearts. Again, the seventies were weird.

Brandon wanted a piece of that action. Frank had an idea for a movie. I had . . . reservations. But in a matter of weeks, I was making *Cinderella*.

It was tough. Not the sex stuff. Look, like I said, although I was a hormone-fueled young straight guy, I wasn't a perv. I wasn't abusive. I didn't want to do any of that casting-couch crap. My feeling was that as long as I found people who were willing to do the stuff the part required, and I kept the mood on the set happy and friendly and open, I could shoot sexy stuff without it getting weird. And I was right—the sexy scenes in *Cinderella* were the easiest to shoot. It was when the actresses and actors had their clothes *on*—*that's* where all the challenges were.

Elaborate costumes. Horses. Carriages. Sets. Musical numbers with choreography and lip-syncing. *Cinderella* had a four-hundred-thousand-dollar budget, and I used all of it. It was made by the same ol' gang: Michael Pataki directed, Frank Perilli wrote it. Even Meda was in it (fully clothed), and so was Frank (also fully clothed, thank god!).

It did well. And with *Cinderella* and *Crash!*, I was discovering a new thrill: Going to see my movies in regular theaters. Watching people gasp and cheer during fiery explosions, scream with disgusted delight at the gore, laugh and whoop at sexy shenanigans. I was *making stuff* that people were digging!

They were definitely digging *Cinderella*. I watched it with packed audiences in six-hundred-, seven-hundred-seat theaters, filled with smiling, laughing, mildly scandalized moviegoers. It made a lot of money for Group 1 and Brandon Chase.

It didn't make me a dime.

I hadn't paid much attention to the business side of my business, because it was boring. But now I started to pay at least a little bit of attention. Maybe I was paranoid, but I suspected that Brandon was robbing me blind. I went and talked to a lawyer.

"Brandon is robbing you blind," the lawyer told me. Some of that robbery was completely legal, too, the lawyer said. "Mr. Band, the worst word in this whole rotten contract is 'perpetuity.' He owns your work, well, forever." Damn. Well, I could make more. But not with Brandon. And I realized that sooner or later I was going to have to learn about my business.

But not right away. John Carpenter heard my tale of woe with sympathy, after which he told me to call a guy he had just started working with—Irwin Yablans, the brother of the famed president of Paramount, Frank Yablans. Irwin had just formed Compass International Pictures with a father-son lawyer team, Joe and David Wolf. As a guy who'd just made a fairy tale movie, I should've known not to trust a couple of Wolfs. But Irwin was nice, and he handled U.S. distribution, while I threw in my lot on the foreign markets with the unfortunately named Manson International Pictures. I was still pretty ignorant, really. But at least this let me go back to making movies.

Just like Brandon, Irwin wanted Names in the movies. Me, I wanted crazy shit in the movies. More specifically, at that moment I wanted to blow up the entire planet.

End of the World delivered on both accounts. Although the movie wasn't much of anything, I got a tip just before the shoot began that Christopher Lee was available. For the low, low price of $50,000. Which would've been fine if my budget wasn't $150,000.

But I paid it. I mean, come on—Christopher Lee!

The movie was a weird mess. It was about some aliens who disguise themselves as priests and nuns to infiltrate humanity and destroy the planet. The one disaster shot I paid for was the actual planet blowing up. The rest was preexisting real disasters—dams bursting, buildings burning—my introduction to the wonderful world of stock footage.

A mess. But it was a *competent* mess, which is actually important in the movie world. I'd proven myself to Irwin and the Wolfs. I was *in*. I had a couple of great ideas for sci-fi and horror movies.

Frank, of course, had other ideas. "Kid," he said, "let's make another sexy musical and get some of that *Cinderella* money that Brandon fucked you out of."

I didn't point out that it was Frank himself who'd gotten me into bed with Brandon in the first place. That would be rude.

Fairy Tales was actually a lot more fun than its predecessor. It still looks pretty good, stuffed to the gills with lewd jokes, really fun songs (written by Andrew Belling), big sets, lavish costumes, and—of course—endless, riotously bouncing boobies.

Also, if any of you who were born after 1980 happen to watch *Fairy Tales,* you might notice something strange a few inches beneath most of the actresses' belly buttons. That's not a special effect. That, kids, is something that historians call "pubic hair," or more colloquially, "bush." Seems weird now, I know, but it was everywhere in the seventies.

Anyway, the best story from *Fairy Tales* concerns The Shoe.

A lot of the movie is set in the Old Woman's Shoe. You know, from the nursery rhyme. Except in my movie it was, naturally, a bordello. And I wanted a real, giant set piece—a women's boot large enough for characters to lean out the windows and talk to the doorman a story or two below. As a producer, this created . . . challenges.

I found a carpenter named Joe Chavez who was willing to construct the shoe. It was going to be forty-five feet high when assembled, and Joe was naturally worried. "I can get it on a flatbed truck for you," he said tentatively.

"Great!" I said.

"But then what?" Joe asked. "You can't take it on the highway. It won't fit under underpasses. It'll knock down phone lines. And where are you going to shoot it?"

"Relax, man," I said with conviction. "You just build the shoe. I've got the rest of it taken care of."

I didn't have anything taken care of, of course. But I worked out a plan.

Griffith Park is a Los Angeles institution, a sprawling green oasis tucked in the hills between Hollywood to the south, Glendale to the east, and Burbank in the San Fernando Valley to the north. It's so big we don't think of it as just one place. The Hollywood sign? That's in there. The Griffith Observatory, the L.A. Zoo, even the wonderful Greek Theatre (from *Get Him to the Greek*) are nestled in those hillsides. A great place to shoot exteriors, too. In fact, the original Batcave from TV's *Batman* is in there.

All that said, it's in the middle of Los Angeles. You can't just sneak in with a forty-five-foot-tall shoe and shoot a movie.

Except that I did.

I got a permit, but it was the cheapest, flimsiest permit available. It allowed me to shoot for a couple of hours. It didn't allow for carpentry, set pieces, or trailers, and certainly not giant shoes. Then again, it didn't explicitly forbid *footwear,* or stipulate the size thereof.

We staged the operation like a heist, coordinating every move, communicating with walkie-talkies and pay phones. After midnight, the night before the shoot, I told the crew to go for it.

At 4:00 A.M. I get a call: the crew has arrived at Joe Chavez's place, and they've got the shoe on the flatbed. I tell them to go, but to stick to the route we'd charted, one with gentle turns and—we hoped—no low-hanging wires or trees.

At 7:00 A.M. I arrive in the park and start getting everything ready. Miraculously, the shoe is there. A gigantic, three-story women's boot, complete with windows and a giant arched door (right at the shoe's arch). (No pun intended.) (But I'll take it.)

Because of the flimsy permit situation, I want to work fast. We don't want to attract attention. But we've got our full cast of crazily costumed fairy tale pervs. Spangled doublets and bedazzled codpieces, buxom wenches and painted ladies in elaborate gowns. Little Bo Peep with her shepherd's crook and bright yellow bustle and truly astounding cleavage. Seven dwarfs in matching pajamas.

It wasn't subtle.

Even though we were there early, even though we'd found a less-traveled corner of the park, we started attracting a small crowd. I handled them. I was in full Producer Mode, treating the onlookers (who could destroy us all with a phone call) like honored guests, giving them snacks, showing them where to stand. Eventually there were about forty of them, watching as we completed shot after shot: comedy business at the front door, characters popping out of windows, musical numbers, the giant finale when the entire cast assembles in front of the shoe to see the Prince and his Sleeping Beauty off into their horse-drawn carriage. Somehow we got all of it before the sun set.

Exhausted, elated, I found myself yelling, "That's a wrap!" I thanked the applauding crowd, and instructed my cast and crew to break everything down and get lost as quickly as possible. Somehow, we'd done it. I'd planned out something impossible, and for once—for once!—I'd thought of everything.

Just then, my brother Richard sidled up to me with a question.

"Hey, Charlie, what do we do with the shoe?"

I'd thought of *almost* everything.

I know, it sounds like a planned moment from a slapstick farce. But it's exactly what happened. Soberly, Richard and I turned and looked at that giant, ridiculous fucking shoe, majestically towering over the landscape. And we knew what we had to do.

We ran away.

Over the next week or two I occasionally dropped by to visit the shoe. It was a good place to hang. Have a snack, sit on the ground looking out at the majestic park, and gaze upon the whimsical wonder that still stood there, a testament to big dreams (and poor planning).

By the second weekend, word had gotten out all over Hollywood. It was now a fun local mystery/conversation piece. I'd be at dinner or a party when someone would say, "Hey, have you seen the shoe in Griffith Park, man?" I'd seen it, I told them. I had.

After another couple of weeks the shoe started breaking down. People took parts as souvenirs, there was normal wear and tear, etc. To my knowledge, nobody ever injured themselves on the thing, thank god. I stopped coming by. Like every great pair of shoes, eventually you just have to let it go.

Okay, so now it's 1977 and everything is changing. Vietnam is over, Nixon is gone, and hippie culture has become just another commodity. Middle-class white people have discovered disco and cocaine, and they've started the important process of ruining both for everybody. A movie named *Jaws* has earned $471 million, just two years after *The Exorcist* had earned a similar amount, launching the age of the big-time movie blockbuster, and with that, the major studios are returning to the world of horror, sci-fi, and outlandish effects.

That's both good and bad for me. Good because there's a renewed interest in the kind of stuff I love. Bad because it's becoming big business, and I don't want to be part of a big business. I never liked working for anyone. I didn't even like working for distributers like Irwin, and I would soon be taking that stuff into my own hands.

But I'm seeing opportunity everywhere. For instance, I've got one of the first big-screen TVs in my house, and I've figured out how to run videotapes of studio movie prints on it. Okay, I actually pirated those tapes, and I'm using professional equipment—this was before consumer videotape machines. But I'm seeing possibilities there—a completely new paradigm for how people entertain themselves at home. Also, the first video game consoles are appearing in American homes, and the field looks wide open to me. In fact, I'm about to get involved in all of that.

First, though, I made my 1978 sci-fi epic *Laserblast.*

The idea was simple. A bullied high school kid finds a super-powerful laser gun left behind by aliens, and he goes on a revenge spree.

One thing I knew I wanted was some stop-motion animation to depict the aliens. I have always loved stop-motion animation, from my earliest encounters with Ray Harryhausen's groundbreaking effects as a kid. To this day, if you put one single shot of stop-motion animation in your trailer, you have sold a movie ticket to Charlie Band.

I was introduced to a young animator named David Allen, who at that time was famous for creating the Pillsbury Doughboy for TV commercials. We hit it off—he instantly knew he was talking to a true fan. He gave me a break, agreeing to make a few shots of aliens for *Laserblast* for way less than his normal price. But it still wasn't cheap. Also, it wasn't fast, which was hard on a guy like me. I pushed Dave, and he gently pushed right back: "Charlie, there's no way to hurry it. In my business, if we get a few seconds of film in a day, we've had a good day." This was mind-boggling to me, a man who could shoot an entire feature film in two weeks. Just to get those shots into my movie, the release would be delayed for months. I decided to wait. It was worth it. Also, that began a working relationship with the great Dave Allen that lasted for decades.

Like a lot of my movies, *Laserblast* wasn't exactly a critical darling. Some people got it, and some people really, really didn't. That's okay—I've never made movies for the critics. And their more creative bad reviews look great on a movie poster. But everybody, in every review I've read of *Laserblast,* loved the aliens that Dave Allen created. He was a truly gifted man,

While I waited for Dave to finish those shots, though, something else happened, with a different Allen: my friend Gary Allen, a fantastic, funny, big lug of a man whose long hair couldn't conceal his old-school Brooklyn roots. "Charlie, you gotta come down and see this fucking thing. You won't believe this fucking thing." Gary was a gifted editor, and he was cutting the trailer for a new film, and he wanted me to see some of the footage.

I took a look.

It was mind-blowingly great. Maybe I was naïve and too in love with sci-fi, but to me, this was clearly going to be the biggest movie ever.

I was obsessed with getting a reference to this sure-fire hit into *Laserblast*. I grabbed the movie's logo from a piece of pre-marketing, had it enlarged, I mean *really* enlarged . . . Which is why, if you went to see *Laserblast* in early 1978, impossibly enough, there's a shot of our hero using his giant, alien-tech gun to blow up a giant billboard for *Star Wars*.

It wasn't meant as a dig at the movie. I was a true fan. But I wanted moviegoers to see my movie and think, "How the hell did he do that? *Star Wars* just left the theaters!"

Roddy McDowall was the biggest Name I got to appear in *Laserblast,* and he wasn't just a good guy; he became a friend and a partner in crime.

We started talking about home video early on. I told him I was finding ways to get films transferred to the three-quarter-inch videotape format so I could show them in my home. Roddy's face lit up. He had the exact same quasi-legal hobby! "Charlie, lad," he said, "I have someone you must meet. Absolutely must."

Wally Heider is one of the most legendary recording engineers in music history. I'll let you look him up on Wikipedia, but suffice to say the guy created the San Francisco sound, and he recorded everyone from Bowie to the Grateful Dead to Herbie

Hancock to Fleetwood Mac. He was friends with Roddy, and he had a studio on Cahuenga and a ton of equipment.

Here's how our scheme worked: Roddy would use his clout to get prints of movies from the studios. For "private screenings." "Research." We'd rush the prints over to Wally, and Roddy and I split the cost of having the movies transferred onto videotape. Wally would dupe a copy for each of us, Roddy would return the print, and bam! Roddy and I built a library of classic films for our home-viewing pleasure.

This was a big deal. Until then, if you wanted to see a movie, any movie in the world that was more than a month or two old, too bad. You were pretty much out of luck. You'd have to either (A) wait until it played in some revival house, or (B) catch it on TV, usually late at night, sliced up to ribbons and festooned with lousy commercial breaks.

This changed all that.

I'm not a recluse, but I am the furthest thing from a party animal. I'm kind of a private guy. But suddenly, I was immensely popular. Every single weekend, both Friday and Saturday nights, there always seemed to be people at my house with me and Meda, there to watch a movie. Sometimes it was *Snow White,* sometimes it was *2001.* It didn't matter. People wanted to be at my place, where they could watch movies.

The message wasn't lost on me. This stuff was *powerful.*

One more huge event happened on *Laserblast.* I was out in the desert, getting some shots of mayhem and destruction, when a call came in for me. Remember, this was the seventies, so that meant that someone called someone who called our office who called the pay phone where one of my guys was stationed, so he could get on the walkie-talkie and get somebody to get in a Jeep and ride out to where I was on set so I could be taken to a phone so that I could get the news . . .

. . . that Meda had given birth to a daughter, our daughter, Taryn. My first child.

I couldn't wait to get home to meet her, and she did not disappoint. She was, and remains, an incredible lady.

Taryn's birth also brought home a simple fact: although I was still only twenty-six years old, I was now, inescapably, a grown-up. That didn't mean I had to *act* like a grown-up. I still don't. But it meant that I had to Provide. I had to make some good-faith efforts to carve out some real businesses for myself and try not to get ripped off again.

I was about to carve out some real businesses for myself. And then get massively ripped off again. Such is life.

That same year, 1977, producer Andre Blay struck a multimillion-dollar deal with 20th Century Fox to license fifty of their films, making his Magnetic Video the first to sell prerecorded movies for home video.

I became the second.

I couldn't compete, cash-wise. But I was a film buff; I knew where the bodies were buried. There were oceans of material out there. B movies. Cult films. Rock concerts. Just sitting in canisters, doing nothing. The licensing fees were pretty much zilch. Their potential was unlimited. I licensed some stuff, set up a company, and started running off copies of tapes and stuffing 'em in boxes. It was a lot of work for a small number of sales; videocassette recorders were a brand-new thing, only for the early adopters. The customer pool was small, but they were willing to pay fifty bucks to own a movie!

Also, this time I got smarter about one thing: I named my company Meda Home Entertainment.

My offices on Santa Monica Boulevard were becoming a cottage full of cottage industries. In front was where I planned my movies and held meetings. But in the back was where the real money was being made. One small room was filling up with videotapes and boxes for Meda Home Entertainment. In the next room the real Meda was binding books for our still-thriving newspaper business. (We'd run through a surprising amount of our supply of the *New York Times,* but supplemented it by buying years' worth of the *San Francisco Chronicle* and the *Los Angeles Times*!). Plus, we were raising a child. And raising money to make another movie.

Tourist Trap is one of my most highly regarded films, a cult horror classic about a bunch of young friends on a trip being stalked and killed by a battalion of ambulatory mannequins. Lots of fun. But in addition to all the thrilling fake murders, getting *Tourist Trap* made very nearly got me *actually* murdered. Like, for realsies.

Funding my movies had become a real challenge. The up-front money from the producer-distributors was never enough, and I found myself horse-trading, borrowing and making promises, robbing Peter to pay Paul. I hate relying on other people to come through with money, because sometimes they just . . . don't. Nothing kills a set like people finding their checks bouncing. Even if you fix it right away, it's a terrible feeling that never really goes away. At some desperate financial juncture during the production of *Tourist Trap,* one of my actors told me he knew "a guy named Jim who has money and loves movies." Was he an investor? No. He was just "a guy who loves movies." Who was willing to lend me money. I took the loan.

I know. There's no way to tell this story that doesn't sound like an obvious and stupid mistake, right out of a million crime movies. But in real life, when it happens, it doesn't feel like that. We were all working on a movie together, all pulling our oars through the water in the same direction, and when one of your comrades-in-arms sends you to someone he trusts . . . well, it feels reasonable and safe. Right up until the moment when it doesn't feel reasonable and safe anymore.

Looking back, I should've seen all the signs. I don't remember all the terms of the loan, but they were truly Shylockian—very short term, with a very large vig to be paid on top of it. At the time, though, I somehow succeeded in not seeing the obvious risks. It's a talent I have.

But other than my impending doom, everything was great. We had Chuck Connors, the Rifleman himself, fresh from his Emmy-nominated performance in *Roots.* We had Tanya Roberts, an impossibly hot young actress who would soon be tapped to join *Charlie's Angels.* And we had a crew of energetic young Texans who'd just arrived in Hollywood, Tobe Hooper's guys from *The Texas Chain Saw Massacre,* and another hopeful from their Austin film scene, our director, David Schmoeller.

One fun story from *Tourist Trap.* To shoot the bulk of the movie I had rented a house in the Franklin Village neighborhood of Hollywood (right near the famed, enormous Château Élysée, which had recently become—and still remains—the Scientology Celebrity Centre). Right after we began production I learned that another film crew had taken up residence in a house just a couple of blocks away. It was my old buddy John Carpenter, shooting a feature! I had kind of soured on Irwin Yablans and his Wolf team, but I didn't hold that against John. We had a lunch, then a dinner (yes, he still led off with coffee and a cigarette before ordering plates full of deep-fried foods that would've put me in the hospital). It was a lot of fun—we both still dug the same kind of freaky, scary film aesthetic—and we promised to visit each other on our respective sets.

To be honest, after we visited each other, I felt kind of bad for John. I had Chuck Connors and other bankable stars, I had some truly scary mannequins and those nutty Texans from *Chain Saw.* What did John have? Just the unknown *daughter* of some Hollywood stars. Oh, and he had a truly badass new piece of gear that he showed me with glee, a recent, super-expensive invention. Somehow, he'd gotten ahold of a Steadicam. This allowed him to do incredibly cool, smooth camera movements that would've been impossible a couple years before.

So I had a really pleasant visit with John. Still, I left his set feeling more confident than ever about *Tourist Trap.* I thought to myself that no one was ever going to hear of John's movie, *The Babysitter Murders.*

I was right. Nobody ever heard of *The Babysitter Murders.* All the big studios rejected it, leaving Irwin to distribute it by himself. Which he did, although before it hit theaters, he insisted on a name change:

Halloween. A lot of people *have* heard of that one.

Meanwhile, *Tourist Trap* was beginning to feel like a real trap for me. Things went fine on set, but behind the scenes, as we wrapped and moved into postproduction, the actor who'd arranged my loan started to get weirdly insistent about me paying his friend Jim back. Like, *pronto.* It hadn't seemed so dire and time-sensitive when I took the loan a month or so before, but suddenly it started to worry me. Also—a small detail—when we talked about his friend Jim, somehow his name was now Jimmy.

Not long after that I got an unpleasant phone call from someone who represented Jimmy. I didn't realize Jimmy was the kind of "friend" who had representatives who made phone calls for him, certainly not the types who'd sound unfriendly, calling my house, telling me, "Jimmy's going to need his money back." Yikes. I made a mental note to get Jimmy his money, though at that precise moment I just plain didn't have it. Jimmy would have to wait.

Jimmy didn't wait.

Midnight. The baby is finally down, and Meda and I are enjoying a peaceful night, dozing in our new little house in Laurel Canyon, nestled in among the trees and coyotes, hipsters and rock stars. It was a sweet setup—my mom and dad had a place right down the road. The street, I'll always remember, was Amor Road, which to most people meant "love." To Meda and me, it also meant "Roma" spelled backward, a constant reminder of our wild, passionate teenage exploits in Italy, then already a decade behind us.

A sound woke me up. Kind of a crash, I guess. Or maybe a boom and a whoosh. There might've been a screech of tires. Who knows? I'd been asleep. But all of a sudden, Meda and I were awake. There was a sound coming from outside. And even more disconcertingly, a flickering light. And a smell.

I ran to the window. Out back, our carport, right up against the house, was on fire. Not like a simmering electrical fire, this thing was *en fuego*. Ablaze. Flames everywhere, licking up against the side of our house.

It hit me pretty quickly. Three Finger Harry couldn't have done it better himself.

I'd been firebombed.

The next few minutes were a blur. We grabbed the baby, called 911, went out on the lawn. The fire department came unbelievably fast—you do NOT mess with fires in those canyons! My parents came by, and I think we might've spent the night over at their place.

I had no doubt about who did it, and there was nothing I could do about it. But standing on my lawn, talking to the firemen, seeing Meda's face as she clutched Taryn to her, I knew things had to change, and fast. Was I scared? Not exactly. I don't really get scared. I guess I'm just built to *deal* with things. Within hours I would be in touch with a lawyer, arrange to get Jim his damn money somehow, start to plan for the future. But I was scared for Meda and Taryn, I felt awful about how scared they were, and I knew I could never let something like that happen again.

I knew I wasn't beaten, that I wasn't going to quit. But I also knew that after I made this right, things were going to be different. I was going to have to figure out a way to never again have to be dependent on anyone, *machers* or mobsters, gangsters or *gonifs,* producers, distributers, studios . . . *no one.* Suddenly being an independent filmmaker no longer seemed like just a good idea. It seemed like a matter of life and death.

Plus, I had a ton of stuff I still wanted to make.

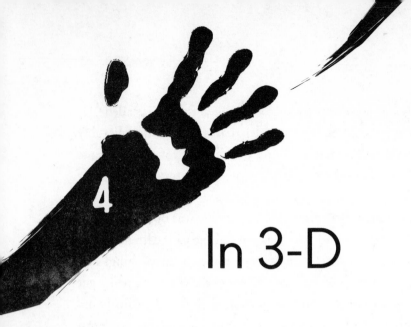

4

In 3-D

(1979–1982)

Tourist Trap ended up doing pretty well. Not with the critics, of course, though with one amazing exception. About two years after *Tourist Trap* hit the theaters, Stephen King wrote a book about horror, *Danse Macabre,* in which he called *Tourist Trap* a "sleeper" and a "gem" and said it "wields an eerie, spooky power, as wax figures begin to move and come to life in a ruined, out-of-the-way tourist resort."

Wow.

By the way, in that same book, King lists my dad's film *I Bury the Living* as one of the twenty scariest movies of all time. We thought it was awesome to find *both* of us name-checked there!

It's been more than forty years since I made *Tourist Trap,* and the movie now has a cult following. Which is cool, but I don't dwell on it. Nowadays, just like back then, my focus isn't on reconsidering the past. It's about figuring out my Next Thing.

As the seventies turned into the eighties, that Next Thing was getting my business and my career to a more secure place, so

I could avoid little inconveniences like cash flow problems and bounced checks. And firebombings.

And I largely succeeded in doing that over the next couple of years. Though in the process, I managed to blow up my life in a completely new and different way. What can I say? I have a gift.

Look, I absolutely *knew* that the home video business was the future. That's why I founded Meda Home Entertainment, licensed all those old movies. And that business was picking up. But then I took a chance on my first- and last-ever brick-and-mortar business.

I called my chain of video stores The Wizard of Vid. I'm not sure why, but it was probably a play on the popular comic strip *The Wizard of Id,* whose name was itself a play on *The Wizard of Oz.* Okay. And when I say "chain of video stores," I actually mean two stores, both in L.A., one on each side of my beloved Hollywood Hills. One on Robertson in Beverly Hills, the other on Ventura Boulevard in the Valley.

It wasn't a bad idea. But it was early. After all, this was even before the advent of the video rental. No, really—that business was still a few years in the future. In fact, when you put together all the videotapes available for sale—the titles I'd licensed and all the big movies from the studios—it still wasn't enough to really fill the whole store. It was literally a boutique business: The Wizard of Vid sold movies to well-to-do customers, usually at around fifty dollars a pop. There was a lot of profit in that, for sure, but people were still, well, kind of unclear on the whole concept.

It was a weekday afternoon, and I was visiting my Beverly Hills store, making sure things were running smoothly. I didn't visit very often—day-to-day retail operations really didn't interest me. Which, in hindsight, is a pretty clear indication that this wasn't the best business for me!

Anyway, two kids were working the counter, Chris and Lana. No, I don't remember their real names, but neither do you! Point is, I remember I thought of them as kids, even though I was only twenty-nine or thirty. And I remember they were actors and absolutely beautiful, because this was Beverly Hills, and in 1980 a job at a video store meant you were kind of working in the movie industry! We were hanging behind the counter, checking the stock, when a well-dressed woman walked into the store and plunked a bag down on the counter.

"Excuse me," she said in the commanding voice of one of the true, original Real Housewives of Beverly Hills. "I need to exchange this movie."

I stepped in, all charm. "Of course!" I said. "What's the problem?"

"It's defective," she declared.

This happened, I knew. The industry was just ramping up. "I'm really sorry. Did it get stuck in the machine?"

"The machine? What? No. Look. We put this movie right on top of our TV. Right on top. And nothing happened."

There was a brief silence. "So . . ." I said finally, "you didn't put it in your VCR?"

"My *what*?"

I'm not kidding.

As Chris and Lana watched, I patiently explained the concept of the videotape machine, and how such a thing was necessary to view the modern marvel known as the videotape.

"Really!?" She was outraged. "I need to buy a whole new machine?" Although she could clearly afford a few dozen of the things, I regretfully confirmed that this was the case and offered to refund her purchase. The exchange was performed in perfect, icy silence—if there's one thing that Beverly Hills dwellers hate more than bad service, it's being made to look ignorant or behind the times.

She left. I exhaled. We all had a good laugh. "Wow," I said finally. "*That's* a new one."

They stopped laughing. "No," Chris said. "That happens all the time."

"What? No way."

"Yeah," confirmed Lana, nodding. "Like—All. The. Time."

Uh-oh.

So The Wizard of Vid didn't last very long. But one great thing came out of it. The name. I would soon name my new business after it: Wizard Video.

"Wait, Charlie, hold on," you say. "What do you mean? You already had a home video business! You told us about in that last chapter! Meda Home Entertainment."

Oh yeah. About that . . .

I never liked to dwell on failures or setbacks. Maybe I should've, because then I might have learned a little quicker. But I was a creature of forward momentum, so I'll explain what happened quickly:

The business had internal troubles. I wanted to keep acquiring movies. Even before people were saying it out loud, I knew that Content was King. The Wolfs, though, the father-son legal team I'd met through Irwin Yablans, disagreed. They wanted to invest in a lab, to make the duplication process easier and quicker. As we took on debts, the Wolfs bought more and more of the company. Eventually, they made their move, which must have been pathetically simple for them. I'm not saying they weren't bastards about the whole thing—they were. But I was an easy mark, and when they saw an opportunity, they bought out my 40 percent remaining share of Meda Home Entertainment for four hundred thousand dollars.

Sounds like a lot, doesn't it? Well, not too long afterward they sold the company for twelve million dollars.

In fairness, the Wolfs did make one revolutionary change when they took my baby. They added an "i." It became Media Home Entertainment. Genius. Anyway . . .

I lost Meda Home Entertainment. And I was about to lose Meda. Or rather, we were kind of losing each other. But to tell that story, I need to tell you about *Parasite* and me bringing back a lost Hollywood technology and the original Valley Girl and Demi Moore. So grab some popcorn and put on your 3-D glasses. Here we go.

Stan Winston and I were talking about 3-D. Back when we were little kids, 3-D had been huge. Throughout the mid-fifties and early sixties its popularity had waxed and waned. But by the seventies, it was essentially dead. Still, Stan and I thought there were possibilities there.

To be honest, I wasn't a huge fan of 3-D. I thought it was mostly a gimmick. I like it even less today, because now it's basically just a lame enhancement of already spectacular explosions for those big "tentpole" movies. At least back in the day it was a *fun* gimmick. It was used sparingly but *intentionally*, to occasionally poke things right out at the audience, to make them duck or gasp or laugh uproariously, making the experience of seeing a movie more of a social event. That's the kind of thing that interested Stan and me. Plus, while nobody was looking, there'd been some real advances in 3-D technology—it had moved *way* beyond the red-and-green cellophane specs of yesteryear. There was a new company called StereoVision that not only made the movies look better, but allowed you to show the movie with a single projector instead of two, and that eliminated a whole bunch of problems, including having to take intermissions and pauses to "resynchronize" the films. So that seemed cool.

I should say that at this point, Stan was becoming super successful. Back in the seventies we'd both had a lot of highs and lows. I'd watched Stan buy an astoundingly beautiful Jaguar, living the Hollywood high life . . . and then have to sell it, flat broke, a year later. I could relate. But at this point Stan was well on his way to becoming *the* Stan Winston. Still, we were buddies—I knew if I had the right idea for something cool, he'd help me out.

I had an idea.

I went to Irwin Yablans. He knew I wasn't going to release through Compass anymore, that I was moving on, but we were still interested in working together. Even though he'd saddled me with the Wolfs, I *liked* Irwin. He was an irascible, hot-tempered, fast-talking Hollywood type, yes, but at least he wasn't a crook. Irwin listened to my idea, and within a day or two he was making phone calls, finding me the money to make the first genuine 3-D horror movie in twenty years, *Parasite*.

This was going to be fun. I felt like my own man again. I would direct *Parasite* and have more control of the production and distribution. Hell, I'd have to: 3-D was complicated.

Johanna Ray was my casting director. I really liked her and her assistant, a bright-eyed young woman named Debi Dion. Remember that name for later, okay? Anyway, I asked Johanna for something very specific for the lead actress role. *Raiders of the Lost Ark* was huge at the time, and I was totally taken with its female lead—pretty, yes, but also smart, aggressive, ready to take on anything that was thrown at her.

"Find me the next Karen Allen," I told Johanna.

She found me Demi Moore.

Look, to some extent, directors are always in love with their movies' love interests. That's inevitable. You're casting and directing someone that you can imagine falling in love with, someone who sort of rings your bell. I guess there's often a kind of unspoken flirtation with your lead actress, but in my case it always remained unspoken. I never wanted to be a creep; I wanted to keep my sets happy, safe, and comfortable, so I'd never think of ever *acting* on one of those director-actor crushes.

Demi was an exception.

She was young, just turned twenty, I think. But married already, to a rock musician named Freddy Moore, a guy around my age who I grew to like. In fact, when Freddy got a new band together, I suggested he cut an EP, helped set up a recording session, and even shot the cover photo, which featured Demi.

So yeah. Demi and I were both married. I didn't say I was proud of this!

There were other things to think about. Shooting *Parasite* was a thrill, but there were a lot of balls to keep in the air. My director of photography was Mac Ahlberg, an older dude from Sweden who was a dream to work with. Here's a tip for would-be producers—if you find a good, interested, easygoing DP, hold on to that guy and never let him go. He'll always make you look good no matter what your budget. Mac and I worked together for the next twenty-five years.

We had an absolute blast experimenting with 3-D on *Parasite*. Learning how to poke stuff at the camera, how to paint stuff for maximum effect, how to rack-focus just right . . . I won't bore you with the details, but it was fun. Stan Winston was there a lot, too. I told him that because I didn't have a huge budget, I needed the creature itself, the horrifying wormlike parasite from space, to be . . . perfect. Disgusting. When it popped out of its human host and right out at the audience, I wanted everybody in the house to recoil in revulsion.

Stan calmly took all this in, nodded, went off to his workshop in the Valley. He called me a few days later: "Charlie, I got someone I want you to meet."

The *thing* he ended up bringing to the set was pure Stan Winston. Organic and gooey, a fat, eyeless, wormlike monstrosity whose entire being seemed to exist in service to the wicked, razor-sharp teeth that made up most of its horrific head, the part we were about to shove right out at the audience in glorious 3-D.

So that was cool.

One fun story from the production: Early on, we got a bunch of people together to look at the dailies (which are exactly what they sound like—footage that you'd just shot, before even getting to postproduction): me, Stan, Mac, Irwin, etc. This was super important because of the 3-D—we needed to see how things were looking.

So we set things up in a small screening room, put on our 3-D glasses, and rolled the film.

We were thrilled. Stan's creature looked great, Mac had shot it just right, this thing was gonna *work*. Until we heard a voice from the front row.

It was Irwin Yablans, and he was enraged, standing up in front of the screen, screaming. "Stop this fucking thing! What are you fucking doing? What are you trying to sell me!? This is SHIT! It's SHIT! I'm shutting this down! This is *my fucking money* . . ."

I told you he was temperamental.

We turned on the lights so we could try to calm Irwin down. But now that I could actually see Irwin, enraged and purple faced, I noticed something crucial:

The left lens had fallen out of Irwin's 3-D glasses and was dangling there over his cheek. Which, obviously, really did make the film unwatchable. There he was, raging and ranting about the "shitty 3-D" in a pair of broken glasses, the busted lens bouncing ludicrously on his cheeks as he hopped around like a foul-mouthed little Rumpelstiltskin with a Brooklyn accent.

It was a delicate situation, but I stepped in and smoothed it over, pointing out the problem—*our* mistake really, I assured him, not his—and getting him a new pair of glasses. The production went on.

I don't know when it happened, but it was slowly dawning on me that Demi and I were. . . . happening. A part of my mind was always aware of where she was on the set. And she was everywhere: clever beyond her years, endlessly curious about absolutely everything, befriending everyone with her boundless enthusiasm and quick wit and those dark smoldering eyes and that low, gravelly, sexy voice.

I had it bad.

And it was mutual. Our eyes would connect from across the set and it was obvious, unmistakable, magical. In fact, the way I remember it, she was the one who grabbed me, pulling me behind a set and bringing my face down to hers. But who knows? It could've been me who initiated it. But there we were, on set, passionately making out, thrilled by the atmosphere, each other, and the high-risk situation.

It was a short affair, but intense. We'd meet at a bar on Sunset, right near the Beverly Hills–West Hollywood line, and have a Grand Marnier. Then we'd repair to my office across the street . . .

One detail about the first time we did that: On the wall of my office was a giant, lurid poster of a movie I'd just licensed, the cult classic *I Spit on Your Grave*. The poster depicts the back of a woman in a forest. She's dirty, barely clothed, incredibly sexy, holding a hunting knife. The text is equally lurid. Across the top:

THIS WOMAN HAS JUST
CUT, CHOPPED, BROKEN, AND BURNED
FIVE MEN BEYOND RECOGNITION . . .

BUT NO JURY IN AMERICA
WOULD EVER CONVICT HER!

And then, lower down, just below the anonymous woman's inarguably perfect derrière:

I SPIT ON YOUR GRAVE
. . . AN ACT OF REVENGE!

Subtle stuff, right? I loved that poster. So amazingly crude and effective—perfect grindhouse thinking: put the movie's title *exactly where you know they'll be looking*.

As soon as Demi got into my office, she looked at the poster and froze. Gasped, "Oh my god!"

I assumed she was offended. The movie itself was *hugely* controversial. The protagonist is, after all, exacting her revenge for a horrifying gang rape. The movie still generates strong feelings (as have all the recent remakes and sequels).

"Look," I said gently, "it's just a film I licensed for my—"

"No," she said, turning toward me, and I could see that she was smiling. "It's just that . . ." She pointed at the poster, laughing now. "That's my ass!"

Yup. Turned out that when Demi was just starting out in Hollywood, she did some modeling to earn a little cash, and the producers of *I Spit on Your Grave* found her for their poster. They put her in makeup and an outfit—more like one-tenth of an outfit, really—drove her to a nearby forest . . . and a few photos later she made film history, a full three years before getting her first starring role. And now here she was, coming face-to-face with her own life-sized butt.

It was weird. It was hilarious. It was *very* 1982.

We didn't last long, a few weeks at most. It was Demi who broke it off—at twenty already more practical and mature about stuff than . . . well, than I guess I'll ever be! We remained friends, though, meeting for lunch every month or so, laughing, catching up on our increasingly complicated lives. Both of our marriages were ending, both of us were meeting new people, both of our careers were moving forward in weird, wonderful ways. The friendship didn't last all that long, either—we stopped hanging out (for reasons that I'll get to), but I will always have nothing but affection for her.

One side note: In recent years, one of my kids, Zalman, has become close with one of Demi's kids. In a lot of ways Hollywood really is a very small town. Sometimes when we talk, Zalman will mention that he was just over at his friend's place, and he always remembers to tell me, "Tallulah's mom said to tell you hi."

Hi, Demi.

There was no time to pause after *Parasite* hit. Suddenly, 3-D was back and people knew that I was a guy who could deliver it. I'd learned a lot on *Parasite,* and I wanted to go bigger, to make a real sci-fi epic.

Also, when it came to finding the money to make the movie, I had a new producer in my corner: Albert Band.

For us Bands, making movies had always been as natural as having a family dinner. My brother Richard had just written the score for *Parasite* and was happy to do it again for my new epic. Meanwhile, my dad's film career was starting to wane a bit, and he happily—no, *joyfully*—hopped onto his son's brand-new bandwagon. He joked that it was "reverse nepotism," and he became a mainstay in my productions and on my sets for the rest of his life. He made some calls, visited a few old friends, and quickly found me the money to start production on *Metalstorm: The Destruction of Jared-Syn.*

At the same time, I too had discovered an exciting new source of income. I was suddenly making hundreds of thousands of dollars selling empty cardboard boxes.

The porn guys thought of it first. Of course. Throughout human history, from cave walls to the Internet, when it comes to new media, the porn guys think of *everything* first.

In this case, I'm talking about big boxes. Back when videotape sales were becoming a huge market, it suddenly struck the porn merchants that the standard VHS tape was too small to really grab attention on a shelf. We're talking about a product that was costing consumers fifty to seventy-five bucks (you paid a premium for porn back then)—it should feel *bigger.* So the adult shelves started to fill with VHS tapes in giant, colorful, oversized boxes. The rest of the video industry soon followed.

This was just a passing fad. In a few years the rental business would take off, and video stores needed to cram as much product on their shelves as humanly possible, and the boxes shrunk back down to normal size again. But that was still a couple of years off. Not only did I have some ideas about how to box movies for my brand-new company, Wizard Video, I had a clever idea for what to put in those boxes:

Nothing.

Let me break it down for you. I might not have had Meda Home Entertainment anymore, nor did I have the Wolfs' business acumen, but I still knew where the bodies were buried. I was a real film buff, and I knew what people wanted to see. Also, I'd been taking trips back to Italy now and then, just to clear my head and breathe the Italian air (and get a fantastic meal or two!), and I started meeting people and licensing—for almost nothing—horror and exploitation movies that I knew I could sell to an American audience. They just needed completely different packaging and new titles. So I commissioned some truly eye-catching cover art and brainstormed new names. Soon Wizard Video had established itself as a purveyor of fine cult cinema for the home audience.

But I wasn't done—I wanted to change the business model. Duplicating all those tapes had been a true pain in the ass for Meda Home Entertainment, as was shipping out that product and then waiting for the distributors to collect the money for the tapes and reimburse me. Sure, they'd eventually pay me thirty bucks per tape, but it was a long, cumbersome pipeline.

I found three distributors—guys who could cover the entire continental U.S. between them—and offered them this deal: I'll send you the master of the movie, plus a buttload of big, beautiful boxes. You only have to pay me ten bucks per box, but you have to pay it up front. Then you duplicate the tapes yourself and sell 'em.

It was win-win. My partners leapt at the chance. In no time I'd shipped one of them a master of some movie and three thousand boxes, and a few days later I received thirty thousand dollars in the mail. Ka-bam.

As I said, the business changed pretty quickly after that. But in those couple of years, I made a pile of money. There was almost no overhead—just tiny licensing fees, the cost of the poster art, and the cardboard boxes. And one paid assistant. I let go of the rights to those movies years ago, but to this day, they are still sold with the titles and poster art that I attached to them.

I have to confess, I always loved, during that time, rolling up to a party or a premiere in some ridiculously expensive car, talking to people, and waiting for the conversation to wend its way around, in that inevitable Hollywood way, to "So, what do you do?"

"Oh," I'd say, "I'm in the box business."

Of all the movies I've made, *Metalstorm* is one of the ones that fans mention to me the most. For some reason it just resonates with them. It's a lot of fun, and it emerged from the maelstrom of madness that was my life at the time. Fortunately I had my dad and my brother on hand to help me land the starship, and I had the boundless energy to make a ridiculously ambitious sci-fi epic.

I also had Johanna Ray, who once again found me some fantastic unknowns for the cast. Opposite the wonderful Tim Thomerson, we had an unknown actress named Kelly Palzis. She was sweet and clever and extremely dedicated—a true pro right out of the gate. About halfway through the production she told me she wanted to change her name. "No problem," I said, and it wasn't—we hadn't done any publicity or made any titles yet. "What's the new name?"

"Preston," she said. "Bill me as Kelly Preston."

Another cast member was a gigantically tall, friendly young actor named Richard Moll. I wanted him to play Hurok, the leader of a tribe of nomadic warriors. Once we cast him, my effects guy told me that because of his elaborate makeup, it'd be much easier to shoot the big guy if he was bald. That was an easy sell for me—I mean, every six-foot-eight-inch nomadic warrior chieftain oughta be bald, right?

It wasn't an easy sell for Richard. "Oh god, this is going to devastate him," his agent told me. "It's pilot season." Like every actor in Hollywood, Richard had high hopes for TV's pilot season, and he also had a nice head of jet-black hair.

I had sympathy, but I also had a movie to make. Plus, as I told Richard, being a tall bald guy was kind of an awesome look. I threw in another five hundred bucks, and Richard took the role and shaved his head. A bird in the hand, after all . . .

Well, during the shoot Richard did indeed get a good audition for a new sitcom. And wouldn't you know it, the producers actually loved him *and* his big bald head. To this day Richard is still best known as the bald, intimidating-but-gentle bailiff named Bull on all nine seasons of *Night Court*.

I'm glad I had pros like Tim and Kelly and Richard on set, because it wasn't a picnic. It was a hot Los Angeles July, and we were shooting most of the movie in what was essentially a sand-pit, amid all these tricked-out futuristic cars. Worse, this was a 3-D movie, which meant you had to blast every scene with tons of light in order to get it bright enough for the 3-D. We spent the month suffocating, sweating, sweltering . . . and still having a pretty great time. One of the things I love about film sets is that pretty much everybody is happy to be there. Still, it was rough.

In the middle of all this, I get a call from Bob Rehme, the head of Universal. We'd met a few times, and Bob liked me. Bob had heard I was shooting another 3-D movie, and as it happened, he was getting ready to go out with *Jaws 3-D*. He wanted something to send it out with. Back then, it cost a lot to outfit theaters with 3-D—you needed a special lens for the projectors and a special screen, so it made sense to follow one 3-D picture with another.

"So," Bob said after the pleasantries, "can I take a look?"

"Of course," I said. "I'll send you a reel on Monday morning."

It was Friday. There was no edited footage.

My poor editor. He was already working his butt off. But we had to do it. *Metalstorm* was the most expensive film I'd ever made, and we had burnt through almost all of the nine-hundred-thousand-dollar budget my dad had somehow managed to raise, and we had no guarantee that anybody was going to distribute the thing! With a flick of the pen, Bob and Universal could make our lives a *lot* easier. We somehow cut a decent-looking assembly of material over the weekend and messengered it over to Bob by Monday morning.

Late Monday, while I was on set, Bob called. He liked what he saw and wanted to buy the movie.

For three million dollars.

So that was cool.

One other notable thing happened during the shoot. I was so busy, so frenzied with the process of producing and directing and getting the whole thing done in just a few weeks, I couldn't afford to waste a minute. Even the time spent ferrying back and forth from my house to the set, why, that was an hour or so *wasted* every day—an hour I couldn't afford! I needed a driver.

Somehow it was made known to me that my casting director's assistant, Debi, had thrown her hat in the ring, because working on the movie would give her a credit at UCLA's film program. So she became my chauffeur, picking me up in her yellow VW Bug every morning and dropping me off in the evening. I won't lie to you—as soon as I'd met Debi, I'd instantly felt that spark with her. Just as I had with Meda and Demi and basically only one other woman in my life. So even though I was working my butt off in that little car, I was also getting to know a bright, fantastic person who I definitely felt something for.

At that point Meda and I had moved to a house on Woodrow Wilson Drive, still in the canyon. It happened to be right across the street from Frank Zappa and his family, and I'd see them all the time. There was a lot of hubbub around Frank and his fourteen-year-old daughter Moon Unit in 1982, because she'd just scored a major hit (and cultural touchstone) with a song she and her dad had written about a particular kind of teenager she was noticing at the mall after school: "Valley Girl."

Anyway, there was Debi Dion every morning—picking me up and driving me off, waving to the Zappas as we went. Behind us was Meda, and I'm sad to say that our relationship, which had burned so brightly from the time we were fourteen and fifteen in Rome, was starting to flicker out. Ahead of us was the set, and fun and chaos and madness.

Things were about to get messy. Or, to quote my neighbor's daughter, *grody*. Like, gag me with a spoon.

This story comes to a head with the single most awkward moment of my life.

It was a couple of months later, at the world premiere of *Metalstorm*. I usually love premieres. There's all that energy and optimism and red carpets and flashbulbs, yes, but it's also a reunion for us, the happy film warriors who'd been in the trenches together making the movie all those months before.

On this night, however, things were different. As I've said, my personal life had become way more complicated than I wanted. I do *not* thrive on that kind of chaos. I like my drama to remain on the screen.

I remember that I'd brought my friend Stefano down from Northern California for moral support. I do not remember, however, *why* I though a constantly stoned Italian princeling (who'd almost killed me with his brilliant "five-gallon drum of nuts" idea) would be great moral support. But whatever. I liked Steve.

In the glittering lobby of the theater, Meda and I, looking fantastic, took a seat on a cushioned couch that encircled a large pillar, every inch the Hollywood couple.

Moments later, Debi Dion strolled by, and someone—Meda, I think—asked her to join us. This was normal, I guess—it would've been weird not to say hi to the woman who'd picked me up for work every morning and driven me home, right? But by now Debi and I were becoming . . . like . . . a *thing*. I've been married twice in my life, and here I was sitting between my present and my future wife, two wonderful women whom I care for deeply to this day, trying to make casual conversation in front of everyone who was there to see and review the movie I'd just produced and directed. Jesus, I thought, it could not possibly get more awkward than this.

"Hi, Charlie. Congratulations," intoned a husky, sexy voice. I looked up. There, smiling down at me, sparkling like the Hollywood star she was becoming, was Demi Moore. We were no longer a thing, but we were still close friends, having lunches and catching up on each other's lives every month or so.

"Hi, Demi," I stammered, getting up, sitting back down, re-introducing Demi to Meda, Debi to Demi, Debi to Meda to . . . Christ, I thought. What's next? Is Jan Miracle going to come by with a tray of spanakopita?

I don't know what we talked about, but it went on for too long. Finally, somebody called Demi away. I needed air, so I offered to get Meda and Debi drinks. I made my way to the patio, pushing through the people and their cloud of awful cigarette smoke. Someone tapped me on the shoulder. It was Stefano, smelling of a smoke that definitely wasn't cigarettes. He'd followed me out after seeing the scene in the lobby.

"Wow, Charlie," he burbled, grinning like we were still kids in Rome who'd suddenly fallen through a wormhole to the future. "You, my friend, at your movie premiere . . . with your three ladies!? I think that is quite possibly the coolest thing I have ever seen in my entire life!"

I smiled weakly. I did not agree. I couldn't wait for the night to be over. I know there are people who are okay with this kind of thing, even those who enjoy it. But I'm no Svengali. And I'm not a puppetmaster, either, not when it comes to the lives of people I care about. Every choice I'd made had been out of love, yes, but too much love and not enough consideration. So I'd made a mess of my personal life and the lives of people I loved. Well, I resolved that night, that is *over*. I'm going to sort myself out and focus on making some smarter, more responsible choices.

A month later I decided that Meda and I absolutely *had* to buy Liberace's mansion.

Coming Right Atcha

From the beginning, 3-D movies have been controversial. Beloved, hated, often sickness inducing, and frequently dismissed as a gimmick. For me, the gimmickry is the only part I'm interested in. The rest leaves me cold. I'll explain that in a moment.

The 3-D movies I made in the early eighties were the beginning of the big resurgence, and technology led the way. Before then the theaters actually needed two projectors, synchronized perfectly, projecting two images on the screen simultaneously. That meant taking an intermission to resynchronize between reels. It also meant that you couldn't repair a broken film haphazardly; you had to make the exact same repair on the film's mate, or things would come out of sync and make the whole thing unwatchable. Even a little out of sync would induce horrible headaches for the audience.

So when StereoVision came along with the brilliant technology to put the two images side by side on one film, it made things a *lot* easier. It was still expensive: you still needed a special lens and a silver-painted screen and stuff, but it was an improvement.

And you needed light. Lots and lots of light. Even today, 3-D movies look a little dimmer than their flat brothers. That's because those glasses are polarized; each of your eyes is getting exactly half the light that's being projected on the screen. Because if your left eye can see the picture that's meant for your right eye, the whole effect is ruined.

So on set I needed three things: a metric shit-ton of light, dual cameras with special lenses from StereoVision, and the Guy with the Stick.

Okay, he was technically called a "convergence expert." He'd be on set every day with his "convergence stick," which was a thing on a tri-pod that helped calculate where the cameras should be to make the shot look best without overdoing it. There's a point in 3-D where things get wonky and literally headache inducing. Mac Ahlberg and I paid a lot of attention to Stick Guy and learned how to push the envelope even beyond his recommendations, to give people just a little bit more. See, today's 3-D movies focus on adding depth to each shot. But I'm not into depth. I'm into gimmickry: that moment that makes the audi-ence gasp and duck and scream and then laugh their heads off.

Here's an example. In *Parasite* there's a scene where a guy gets im-paled. Not a gentle, polite impalement, either; we literally see him with a six-foot metal pipe sticking out of his chest. And then, horrifically, the camera *moves in* on the guy, so that the pipe comes right out at the audience, sticking as far "into the theater" as 3-D will allow.

And then, at that moment when we are as close as we can be, blood spurts out of the pipe! Coming out toward you just a little bit farther, virtually splattering your face. Are you nauseated because of how gross it is, or because I've pushed the 3-D too far? My answer . . . is yes!

To me, *that's* what 3-D is for.

I did a similar shot in *Metalstorm,* only with a dude's arm instead of a pipe. After that I was more or less done with 3-D and the Stick Guy and all the *figurative* headaches involved in making it work. Plus the stuff just looks silly when you flatten it out for home video, which was where my business was headed.

But for those two films, seeing the audiences react to those mo-ments made it totally worth the headache.

5

In the Toilet

(1983–1985)

Yes, you heard me: Liberace's mansion.

Was I a huge Liberace fan? I was not. I was a rock 'n' roll guy.

Did I think a mansion might rescue my floundering marriage? I did not. We were doomed.

But I heard from someone that Liberace's mansion was up for sale, and when you're possessed by madness and devils and made of momentum, you go for it. I went for the mansion.

It was huge. But also a mess—it hadn't been lived in for a while. Liberace actually had two Los Angeles mansions—this one, just up the hill from the Sunset Strip, and another one on the other side of the hills, in Sherman Oaks, where his mother had lived. By the early eighties, though, Liberace had long since relocated to Vegas and Palm Springs, so the house I saw was the world's most fabulous fixer-upper. Extravagant gardens. Elaborate high terraces. A living room with a giant stage—a genuine raised platform with an apron, big enough, well, for a grand piano (and covered, like the rest of the floor, with an impossible-to-ignore pink shag carpet). All for the low, low price of four hundred thousand dollars.

Yes, my marriage was falling apart, and I didn't think Meda and I could last, and I was completely in love with Debi Dion. But I had kids to think about (yes, plural—Meda had given birth to my son Alex in 1981!). Somehow, I thought this *might* work. At least it would definitely be cool, right? We moved in.

I lived there for exactly one night.

But it was a hell of a night.

Although we'd done a fair amount of painting and repairs after we closed escrow, there was some kind of beehive situation in the master bedroom. So Meda and I had rigged up a sleeping accommodation on the stage in the gigantic living room. Come to think of it, if we'd been getting along better that would've been kinda hot.

Somehow we'd gotten the kids to sleep, which is no small feat when it comes to the first night in a new house. Everything was still in boxes, but I'd managed to get my stereo hooked up. That's always my first priority wherever I am. I need my music. Full disclosure, though, it was more than a stereo—I had these four big Tannoy speakers and I rigged those bad boys up for quadraphonic sound! I remember putting on Pink Floyd's majestic, trippy *Atom Heart Mother* and kinda dancing around my new home, a glass of wine in my hand. My immediate world might be ending, my personal life might be fucked, I thought, but this was *cool*!

I stepped out on the gigantic balcony, overlooking the Sunset Strip. You could see why the place had appealed to Mr. Showmanship, a palace like this, perched above the epicenter of Holly-wood nightlife, all the clubs and restaurants and hotels glittering beneath. It was intoxicating. I took a moment, inhaled, breathing it all in. It smelled like success.

No, I thought, reconsidering. It actually smelled like *smoke*.

Uh-oh.

Maybe you've heard of the famous fire at the Piazza del Sol, one of Hollywood's most historic buildings. The place had started life in the twenties, a beautiful Mediterranean building that im-mediately became known worldwide as the House of Francis, a.k.a. the classiest brothel on the Sunset Strip. Years later, Rod Stewart bought the building with dreams of turning it into a luxury hotel. But in 1982, Rod the Bod was robbed at gunpoint in the middle of the day, right outside the building. The assailant drove off in Rod's Porsche while Rod clutched his three-year-old daughter. The Strip was *rough* back then. Rod soured on the project and got himself into a protracted legal battle with his partner. One year later—and I have no idea if this was related—the place burned nearly to the ground in a suspicious fire. It happened right down the hill from the mansion I had moved into. That very day.

And I mean *right* down the hill. My new home sat high atop the Sunset Strip, and the Piazza was literally the nearest build-ing *on* the Strip. We were perched directly above the spectacular fire, Meda and I, out on the terrace, drinking wine, watching the world burn. There were sirens blaring. There were helicop-ters right overhead, shining spotlights and dumping water on the blaze. It was beautiful and terrible. We knew there was a chance it would spread, igniting the brush on its way up the hillside, and we'd have to grab the kids and flee our new home. But thankfully, that didn't happen. We watched, and watched, as the spectacular flames beneath us were controlled, beaten back, and eventually extinguished, leaving only smoke rising in the quieting night.

The metaphor wasn't lost on either of us. I moved out the next day.

I know, it seems crazy. But some couples take a big vacation when their marriage is on the rocks. Others throw a Hail Mary and have another baby. Meda and I bought an absurd, gigantic mansion. But when that didn't fix things, neither of us wanted any part of it, and we packed up and sold the place immediately. If you think that seems nuts, imagine how our real estate guy felt!

We made it work. For the kids, obviously, but also for ourselves. It's a weird extended clan I've built up over the years, but we all manage to get along. Once you're in the Band, you're in the Band!

I got Meda a place in the Valley, where she wanted to be. Debi and I moved in together, renting a house on Kings Road, not far from Liberace's mansion. Not a huge place, but big enough for the kids to be comfortable during the part of the week that they were with us.

Oh, and I should tell you about our landlord. Our landlord just happened to be a man named John Branca, an entertainment lawyer and legendary rock manager. He's represented everyone from the Doors to the Bee Gees to Alicia Keys to Dr. Dre. Jesus, it's a long list. At the time when Debi and I moved into his house on Kings Road, John was obsessively working on the music videos and documentaries and tour arrangements surrounding the release of his client and friend Michael Jackson's new album, a humble set of ditties named *Thriller*.

Almost instantly, John became more than just the dude who collected our rent. We had tons in common, Debi and I got along great with John and his wife, and we began a friendship that has endured nearly forty years and led to lots of cool stories, including a very surreal visit from Michael Jackson himself. But that was all in the future. For now, he was my friendly neighborhood landlord. And me, I was busy with another property. Right down the hill from my new abode, I was building an Empire.

Within a year or two, Empire International Pictures would own a sprawling, six-soundstage movie studio, housed on one hundred beautiful acres just outside Rome.

At this point, however, it was a second-floor walk-up office just south of Santa Monica Boulevard. Oh well. Rome wasn't built in a day.

It was an exciting time. My dad and I hung up the Empire shingle on Fairfax, and threw ourselves into the business. I was determined to escape the clutches of big movie studios and shady distributers and all the other nonsense that weighs down independent filmmakers. I wanted more control, soup to nuts; I wanted to make, as Steve Jobs put it, "the whole widget."

I started attending the Big Three film markets: one in America, one at the Cannes Festival (in May), and one in Milan (in October). The trick I was trying to pull off was getting people to fund my movies *before I made them*. Radical concept, huh? I had some natural advantages over every other schlub setting up a table, though. For one, I spoke fluent Italian. Also, I was cute. Okay, well, mainly I had something most of the other hopefuls didn't have: a track record. People knew I could actually deliver movies.

I'm happy to report that it worked. With nothing but a couple of posters to show (*nice* posters, though), I was able to presell a few movies right out of the gate. Notably one called *Swordkill* (which eventually was renamed *Ghost Warrior*) and another called *Ghoulies.* Triumphantly, Debi and I headed back to the States, all set to make movies on my own terms. Things were about to get good, even if they were also about to smell very, very bad.

Swordkill is a fun little movie: A mighty sixteenth-century samurai warrior falls in battle—but into icy water, instantly freezing him. Four hundred years later, he's thawed out by scientists in Los Angeles, and he proceeds to rampage through the streets. You know, *that* old tale. Rip Van Terminator. The whole thing is really held together by the star, Hiroshi Fujioka, who knew his way around a katana and could genuinely move and battle like a samurai.

But in order to shoot that amazing opening scene, the battle in the snowy mountains of feudal Japan, we needed a lot of stuff. Like mountains, yes, but also sixteenth-century warriors and horses and armor and gear. There really is no faking that kind of thing, so I arranged to have it all—the dressings for the horses and the warriors—sent over from Japan. It arrived quickly, and it was pretty impressive looking. Great.

We hired the actors, found a location in the mountains, and I sent everyone and everything off with my director, Larry Carroll, to shoot the fateful opening sequence. Larry called soon after— the shoot went fine. If you get a chance to watch it, you'll see—it really does look fantastic.

The next Monday morning, I arrived at the building that housed Empire Pictures, walked up the stairs, opened the door . . . and was immediately knocked back into the wall behind me.

That *smell.*

Imagine if a thousand hoboes forced their way into your

house, drank fifty kegs of Heineken, peed on every single square foot of your home, and then left. Okay, now imagine that one of them actually didn't leave, but instead curled up in a corner and died. And then imagine you left the house sealed up with no air-conditioning in hundred-degree heat, and then returned a week later and opened the front door. How would that smell?

It would smell *almost* as bad as my office that day.

My dad walked in and quickly covered his face with a hand-kerchief, his eyes instantly reddening and tearing. We looked at each other, like, What the hell?

It didn't take long to locate the source. All those leather items from Japan, covered in melting snow, had been thrown into the truck after the shoot and unloaded in the Empire offices. But why *that* smell? I called my contact who'd arranged for the rental.

"Oh, you got 'em wet?" he asked grimly.

"Yeah, why?"

"See, those pieces, they're treated the traditional, old-fashioned way to keep them supple."

"What's the old-fashioned way?" I asked, already suspecting.

"Horse piss. They're soaked in horse piss."

I took a reluctant sniff. Yeah, that tracked.

We boxed up and shipped that stuff back to Japan in record time. But as gross as it sounds, even with several thorough rounds of cleaning and sanitizing, the smell of *Swordkill* lingered in those offices for weeks. No, it was even worse than that: I remember going to a nice restaurant with Debi, and for the first time in my life, I couldn't charm the waiter. He hated us. No, not exactly hated—he was *disgusted* by us, like genuinely recoiling. Slowly we figured it out. That smell had clung to everything, including *us*. It felt like we would never be clean again.

It's a pretty good movie. But it also truly stank.

As great as my timing had been in getting into the home video business, there was another burgeoning industry that I ended up jumping into *too* soon: video games.

See, I thought I saw a niche there, something cool to exploit. Video games were huge at the time; games like *Ms. Pac-Man*, *Donkey Kong*, and *Star Wars* were packing people into arcades, and just about every house, especially the ones with kids and/or stoners, had an Atari 2600, the first massively popular home console.

A lot of people were dismissing video games as a juvenile fad, but I saw a ton of potential there. I mean, this stuff was *fun*. Why limit the content to G-rated fare? What about the teenagers? What about the fun-loving, slightly twisted twentysomethings? In other words, what about *my* fans? Wouldn't they want something a little more adult?

I never go halfway. I made something a *lot* more adult.

I found some programmers, spun off a business from Wizard Video, and Wizard Video Games was born. Next, I licensed two properties that I was sure would stand out from the crowd in the home market: *The Texas Chain Saw Massacre* and *Halloween*. And because something like this had never been tried, the rights only cost me a few thousand bucks.

No, I'm not kidding. I brought slasher film content to an industry dominated by a cute, hungry yellow dot.

The graphics were ridiculously crude (this was, after all, the first Atari console), but the ideas were sound. In *Halloween* you played a babysitter, heroically herding kids to safety as a deranged killer stalks them (and you). In *The Texas Chain Saw Massacre*, you actually got to *be* Leatherface, slicing up victims all over the countryside until your chain saw ran out of gas. In no time the cartridges were manufactured and stuffed into cool, lurid boxes, and I released my hideous progeny on an unsuspecting world. Muahaha!

I never had a chance. Parents were Outraged. Retailers were Concerned. Most stores refused to put my games on the shelf. Instead, if you wanted to buy *The Texas Chain Saw Massacre* for your Atari, you had to ask for it by name at the front counter, and the clerk would pull it from its hiding place and stuff it in a paper bag for you, like it was some pervy girlie magazine.

Despite all that, I might've stayed with the project, but there was another bad break in store: I'd launched my video game business in the same year as the great Video Game Crash of 1983. Bored with the glut of lame titles, people stopped buying cartridges, and the industry went dormant for a few years. I moved on.

A decade later, adults were happily ripping out each other's beating hearts in *Mortal Kombat* and shooting their way through the bloody depths of hell in *Doom*. Oh well. Sometimes being ahead of your time can be a bitch.

You think horror movies are scary? You know what's scarier? Making and distributing a horror movie—All. By. Yourself. But as I said, I wanted it. It was time. As with the video games, I was consumed with the idea of doing it myself, being in control of both the product and how it gets to the public. But unlike video games, I had a pretty good understanding of the movie business. Or at least I thought I did.

I'd been tossing around ideas for *Ghoulies* for a while. I wanted all these nefarious little creatures, nasty li'l demon guys, making trouble for regular humans. Stan Winston and I had been discussing a similar idea, which we called "Beasties," and he'd even made a few sketches for me. But by the time I was ready to make it, Stan was working on a never-ending string of multimillion-dollar studio films. Still, Stan recommended someone he thought could handle the job, a fantastic young dude named John Buechler, who set about creating all the vicious little imps that populate the movie.

The shoot was uneventful—we had a talented cast, Mac Ahlberg doing the cinematography, and John Buechler's slimy, awful super-puppets littering the set. We also had a young actress named Mariska Hargitay, the daughter of Jayne Mansfield, in her first screen role.

My focus, though, was increasingly on the giant, expensive task of getting the movie out into the world. I didn't know much about distribution, but I was confident I could learn fast.

Somehow I got hooked up with this hard-bitten old operator from New York. I wish I remembered his name, but I'll call him Sammy. Sammy was 150 percent pure New Yawker, a fast-talking, back-slapping, chain-smoking, lemme-tell-ya-kid, old-timey showbiz vet.

"Look, kid," he said, and I swear I could smell the cigarette-and-pastrami breath coming over the phone lines. "If you wanna do this, just hit one area: New York and the immediate suburbs. You gotta book a hundred theaters, so maybe it'll cost a hundred twenty grand to make the prints. And then you gotta drop at least four hundred grand to buy the media."

"Four hundred thousand dollars?" I asked, hoping I'd misheard.

"Definitely. You need newspapers, radio, local TV—daytime, prime time, whatever. Eye-catching, too. You gotta get people's attention in a market where every asshole and his mother are tryin' to get attention."

"Okay, so, let's say I do that. Then what?"

"Well, that's the gamble. If you get noticed and you open big in New York, all the doors open up. You go nationwide and you make a pile of money."

"Okay, let's say it *doesn't* open big. Let's say it opens . . . medium-sized," I suggested, looking for an option that would let me scale down or be ready to do damage control.

"Then you're dead," Sammy said immediately.

"Dead?"

"You're fucked. The movie's dead. It'll never play anywhere, nobody will ever see it, and you're left standing there with your dick in your hand. Plus everyone knows you're the schmuck who's out half a million with fuck-all to show for it."

"Wow."

"Eh. That's how it's done."

It sounded horrifyingly risky. I went for it, of course.

Immediately I had to compromise. Believe it or not, I'd shot half of *Ghoulies* in 3-D. My idea was cool, kind of an epic gimmick; whenever the characters on the screen put on their glasses to see the ghoulies, that would be the cue for our audience to put on their 3-D glasses. Great idea, right?

Well, it *seemed* like a great idea, right up until the moment when I found out what it would cost to equip a hundred theaters with special projector lenses and 3-D-ready screens. Put it this way—remember how Universal had paid me three million dollars for *Metalstorm* just to make *Jaws 3-D* worth the investment? Well, Empire was no Universal. Remember, we were run out of a second-floor office that currently smelled of ancient Japanese horse piss.

We recalibrated. Fortunately, Mac had lighted the thing well enough to survive the conversion back to 2-D. So I had a movie. What I didn't have was a killer marketing hook. For that I decided to pay a visit to Gary Allen.

I told you a little about Gary already. He's my stoner friend who edited the *Star Wars* trailer and let me take a peek. Gary had a knack for promotion. He was the genius behind a late-seventies campaign—both a poster and TV commercial—for a B horror movie *that had already failed*: a movie called *It's Alive*.

The poster depicts a beautiful baby carriage, turned away from the viewer . . . with a terrifying claw hanging out of it, almost casually. The header: THERE'S ONLY ONE THING WRONG WITH THE DAVIS BABY . . .

And then, under the carriage: IT'S ALIVE!

And then: THE ONE FILM YOU SHOULD NOT SEE ALONE

Genius. Three years after its failed release, Warner Bros. made millions on the rerelease of *It's Alive,* with the help of Gary's campaign.

Gary was happy to hear from me. I told him I needed a trailer that would just play like crazy, grab everyone's attention. Make or break.

"No problem," he said lazily. "Just come over, man, and we'll smoke a bone. We'll come up with something." I agreed, though I wasn't going to smoke the aforementioned bone. I'd smoked pot a few times, but it really wasn't my thing. And I was pretty sure Gary would smoke enough for both of us.

I was right. He greeted me at the door with bleary red eyes and a goofy smile. He beckoned me in.

"I got it, Charlie man, I got it. I *love* these ghoulies."

"Thanks."

"So . . . like . . . what if, for the poster, get this, what if you had one of these fucking ghoulie guys coming out of a toilet!"

"Okayyy . . ."

"Amazing, right?! And then you could have the caption, like . . ." His hands made a banner in the air as he pitched his brainstorm: "Ghoulies—They'll Eat Your Ass!"

No. Just . . . no. There were a thousand reasons why not, I thought, not the least of which was that this ad was going to run in the *New York Times*. There would be no ass-eating in the *New York Times*. I'm pretty sure that policy remains in place to this very day.

But as we tossed around other ideas for the next hour or two, I found myself warming up to Gary's original inspiration. We kept, um, circling back to the toilet, if you will. Maybe it was a contact high from Gary, who was smoking a truly prodigious amount of ganja, but it was actually starting to sound like a good idea. Somehow, we found ourselves back on it, but with a new slogan:

"Ghoulies—They'll Get You in the End."

We laughed and high-fived. Then I froze.

"Wait a minute, man," I said. "It's great, but Gary, there are no scenes like that in my movie."

"Right?" said Gary, already cutting the trailer in his mind. "Dude! You are going to have to go and buy a toilet, my friend."

I went and bought a toilet. I got Mac and John Buechler to meet me on a set. We had to hastily build a platform so our puppeteer could get under said toilet. We had to light it, and pop that gooey little bugger out of the toilet a few times . . . and so help me, we got the shot and threw it into the movie. In no time Gary had cut me a kick-ass trailer, and we produced a print ad, a TV ad, and our now-iconic poster.

So, *that* happened. And the premiere date was approaching.

But I still had one mountain left to climb. Janice from the MPAA.

Yes, you guessed it—I don't actually remember her name. But "Janice" became vitally important to my movie's fate. See, back then, the MPAA was not very kind to us independent film guys. We had to fight for our stuff in a way the big studios never had to. And the MPAA controlled everything—not just the movie's rating, but also the trailer, the TV ad, everything. I needed to get my material approved, with the added degree of difficulty that all of my material—the trailer, the ad, everything—contained a monstrous, grody little demon emerging from a toilet.

I did catch a small break, though. Because we finished prepping our stuff in the nick of time, right before a holiday weekend, after some desperate begging and pleading the MPAA allowed me to drop my stuff off at the house of one of their board members so she could review it. I drove all my materials up the hill, into Topanga Canyon, to the house of . . . Janice.

Luckily, she was home, and she let me in. Janice was a middle-aged woman, attractive and well-maintained in that Hollywood professional way. Like everybody from the MPAA, she was a little conservative, her hair pulled back in a tight do.

No, I didn't seduce her.

But in a way, I guess I *did* kind of seduce her.

I've always looked a lot younger than my years. Nowadays that's a good thing. Back then, it was a mixed bag. But in that moment, being able to pose as the "gee-whiz choirboy just looking for a break in a cold world" came in handy.

Janice was great. She let me make my whole case, and I really turned on the charm, reassuring her that I had a long track record despite my tender years. Telling her how badly I needed my first solo flight as a distributor to work out, how I'd bet the farm on it. Yes, that monster-in-the-toilet image was a little rough, sure, but it was meant to be *funny*, see, a play on the ridiculous trashiness of *other* exploitation movies.

By the time I left, Janice had promised to get the film to her colleagues and get me an answer first thing Tuesday morning. I had done all I could do.

Janice was as good as her word: on Tuesday she called me first thing in the morning. Unfortunately, she opened by telling me that she and her two colleagues thought my movie was a little . . . rough.

"It's right on the edge, Charlie," she said somewhat scoldingly. But then I heard a smile creep into her voice. "But we understand that it's all in good fun." I could hear how happy she was to give this charismatic young scamp a break. Wherever you are, I love you, Janice!

The movie got an R rating, which was the best we could hope for. But the real win was the other stuff. The trailer got a green band, for General Audiences! The ads, toilet monster and all, got the green light. Hell, I could show that ad during Saturday morning cartoons if I wanted to!

I showed it during Saturday morning cartoons.

Much like a ghoulie, *that* one would come back to bite me on the ass.

New York felt so far away. I'd done everything I could do: the theaters were booked, we'd saturated the papers and airwaves and billboards to the best of our ability. I hadn't lied to Janice—I had spent *everything* on this bet. Now I just had to sit in Los Angeles and wait out opening weekend to find out if I still had a career or if I'd have to start from scratch. Again.

Sammy was my man on the ground in New York, managing things. "All right, kid," he said, "Call me first thing Sunday morning. Five A.M. I'll be up. By then we'll have the first two days of receipts. That's when we'll know for sure if you're fucked."

"Or not?"

"What? Oh, yeah. Sure. Fucked or not. Five A.M."

He hung up. Wow. Sammy was a trip. If he's still alive today, he'd be about 105. I wouldn't put it past him.

Anyway, it was a tense weekend. I was hearing a few good things from friends in New York, things about crowded theaters, long lines at the box office, but that didn't mean much.

My friends were in the trendy parts of Manhattan. I was in a hundred theaters in the area. I'd never been so dependent on an audience before. I needed them all. I needed the suburbs—Long Island, Westchester, North Jersey—to come out for me. I needed the snobs and the mooks, JAPs and Guidos and nerds and dirtbags, white kids in Members Only jackets and Black kids in shiny tracksuits, the entire *Breakfast Club* generation, an army of big-haired, leg warmer–wearing eighties New Yorkers . . . to show up, pay their five dollars, and scream their way through my movie. It seemed like a heavy lift.

I didn't sleep Saturday night. Why bother? At 2:00 A.M. Pacific time, I called Sammy. He picked up on the first ring and didn't even say hello.

"Hey, kid," he said, "you have a huge fucking hit on your hands."

Yes! Sammy let me celebrate for a minute. Then he added:

"But there's a problem."

"What?"

"Look, right now it looks like you're gonna do a million dollars in your first week. Everything you coulda wanted. People are jamming the theaters. But like I said, there's a problem."

"What, Sammy? What's the problem?"

"The problem is that theaters are getting a tremendous amount of complaints about the campaign from parents. They're saying their kids are freaked out. They're not going to the bathroom because they're scared of that fucking *thing* coming out of the toilet. They're scared, their parents are pissed off, and your theater owners are already hearing about it, which is not good. This *will* hit the press, and you are gonna take a ton of shit."

"Oh god." I was bummed. Why couldn't there ever be news that was just *good*? I sighed. "Okay, Sammy, now what?"

"Well, kid, you really only got two options. Option One is you change the campaign. Get rid of that toilet. Make the poster one of those ghoulie things, I dunno, on a shelf, or peeking around the corner, or whatever the fuck. I dunno. Problem is, what if that toilet is what's bringing the people into the theaters? You'd be killing the golden goose."

"Wow. Okay, what's Option Two?"

"Option Two is 'Fuck it.'"

"Fuck it?"

"Yeah. You just say 'Fuck it' and keep going."

We were so far away from each other, separated by both a giant continent and a massive generation gap. But in that moment I really felt like Sammy and I were brothers.

"I think I'll go with 'Fuck it,'" I said.

"Atta boy."

It didn't take long for Sammy's prophecy to come true. The next morning, I strolled into the Empire offices and was greeted by our strange receptionist, an odd little woman who was sometimes cross-eyed and always disapproving. She tapped on some papers on her desk. It was a stack of Telexes, the eighties version of email.

I read a few. Phrases jumped out at me. "You miserable Hollywood douchebag." "My son." "My poor daughter." "Won't go near the bathroom." "I'll *kill* you, fuckhead . . ." Stuff like that. I grabbed a few and walked past my scowling receptionist, buoyed by one thought: Gary Allen was going to *love* this.

Ghoulies did something like thirty-five million dollars in domestic box office, which basically funded everything I wanted to make with Empire over the next couple of years. There were three sequels. But the Fuck It option had other consequences. In the early 2000s, when I was touring the country with my Full Moon Horror Roadshow, whenever I told the *Ghoulies* story, inevitably there would be fans, usually drunk dudes in their thirties, standing up in the theater and yelling, "Yo, when I was a kid, that movie *fucked me up*! I didn't go to the bathroom for a month!" Even today, when I'm doing autographs at a convention, there will invariably be some people, now in their forties, who want to tell me about the toilet terrors brought on by my movie.

Getting Too Much Information about Gen Xers' bathroom struggles. I guess that's the price of greatness.

6

The Italian Job 2: Roman Boogaloo

(*also* 1984–1985!)

As crazy as the previous chapters may have seemed, this is the one where I take an innocent trip to Europe and end up owning a movie studio and a castle. So give me a second. I need to organize my thoughts.

Okay. So. It was still 1984, around the same time I made *Ghoulies*. These were busy times, crazy times, and it seemed like whatever I thought of I could make into reality. And one thing I was thinking of was this: I wanted to make a movie in Italy.

I missed the place, the dollar was doing great against the lira—it just seemed like it was meant to be. Plus, I had an idea. At the Milan film market, I'd managed to sell a sci-fi/World War II epic called *Zone Troopers*. It stood to reason that it ought to be shot in a place where World War II actually happened, right?

Oh, I should confess: Whenever I say I "sold a movie" at a film market, that sale came from a quick pitch line and a very flashy-looking poster. I'd have a dozen or so posters made for the catalog at a market, and whichever sold, I'd make. So that was my process: title, then poster, then sale . . . and then I'd figure out what the hell it was about. And *then* get a script.

Is that a conventional creative process? It is not. Did it work? Hell yeah.

It was pretty neat. I clearly remember standing behind that table in that dumpy little room in Milan. In Cannes we got to occupy suites in a beautiful hotel. Milan was way more downscale, but it served the same purpose: at both, prospective buyers would drop in, flipping through their splashy, ad-laden copies of *Variety,* peering at my posters. It's not the part of the business I like best, but when you land a couple of sales and reel 'em in and you realize that you're going to get to make all these crazy posters into actual *movies* . . . I have to admit, it's a pretty great feeling.

After making preliminary arrangements for *Zone Troopers,* though, I flew back to the States. I had another movie to make, one that I was really excited about. See, I was producing a ton of films at this point, but I was starting to get jealous of my own company: everybody was having so much fun on my sets, and I was too busy playing mogul to be there for all of it. Unfair! So I put my foot down and committed to directing the next Empire film, *Trancers.*

When you're making movies, you get scripts. Lots of scripts. Everybody has an idea, and in Los Angeles, those ideas come with fully written screenplays. I doubt there's a car trunk in town that doesn't have a spec script in it, right next to the spare tire. And often that spare tire would make a better movie. Still, you never know who's got junk in the trunk and who's got gold.

So when my second assistant cameraman from *Ghoulies,* Danny Bilson, asked me to read the screenplay he and his writing partner, Paul De Meo, had written, well, I didn't say no. Danny was a good guy, and besides, you never know where the next great screenwriter is coming from. Also, I was vaguely aware that Danny and Paul had been conspiring with Tim Thomerson, whom I had a great time working with on *Metalstorm.* Still, I was super busy. So I did the forthright, leaderly thing. I had Debi read it.

Debi has always been more selective than I am. Which, admittedly, is not saying a whole lot, because at that time I could be talked into making *anything.* Frank Perilli could come up to me and say, "Hey, kid, I think we should make a flick where two chicks with huge knockers wrestle for eighty minutes in a giant bowl of soup on the moon," and my only question would be, "What kind of soup?"

But that's not how Debi Dion operates. When she came to me less than a day later and said, "Charlie, you have *got* to look at Danny's script," I listened. And man, was she right. I didn't buy the script, but I immediately put Danny and Paul to work drafting a script for an idea I had: a cop from the future comes back to present-day L.A. to hunt down a crazed time-traveling killer who is set on eliminating the ancestors of the future's leaders, all done in a Raymond Chandler, film noir style. Danny and Paul quickly delivered a truly terrific script. And, not coincidentally, it featured a hard-boiled cop protagonist named Jack Deth, a role that was conspicuously perfect for Tim Thomerson.

But Tim wasn't done pulling strings behind the scenes—for our leading lady he suggested a twenty-one-year-old he'd worked with on a few sitcoms, and she absolutely nailed her audition.

Well, that's how Tim remembers it. I remember my dad suggesting she audition, because she was the daughter of his old buddy Gordon. Possibly both stories are true. Either way, that's how I ended up giving Helen Hunt her first starring role.

Trancers **was probably the** funnest set I've ever been on. Maybe part of that is because I was delirious most of the time—more on that in a minute—but also, it was just a fantastic vibe: great cast, great crew, great script. Tim Thomerson is a truly hilarious human being—he'd started his career as a stand-up comic, playing clubs nationwide and making multiple appearances on *The Tonight Show*. By the late seventies his dear friend Richard Pryor started tossing film roles his way, and Tim reinvented himself as a dramatic actor.

On set, the guy was still completely hysterical. And Helen was a buoyant, funny delight. You can see their genuine friendship on the screen (they are friends to this day), and all two and a half weeks of the shoot were awesome for everyone.

Except occasionally for Charlie Band, who was in fact falling apart.

So yes, I insisted on directing. But I never put down my job as studio head. I would work all day and shoot all night (the movie takes place mostly at night) and then grab an hour of sleep, chug down an espresso or two, and head back to work. I was trying to get things going in Rome, too, which was nine hours ahead of Los Angeles (it still is, in fact!), so I'd start calling there around

3:00 A.M. It was a little nuts. Something had to give, and one night, on set, it did—in the most hilarious way.

We were on location in Chinatown, on the roof of a building, shooting the climactic final battle between Jack Deth and the nefarious Whistler, which took place at night. Because of my schedule, this meant I basically hadn't slept in thirty hours and then had to pull an all-nighter, because obviously we had to get everything before the sun rose.

It was something like 2:00 A.M., maybe 3:00. We were setting up a shot, and I was standing behind Mac Ahlberg, answering the occasional question. Tired . . . so very tired . . .

I guess people must have thought I was deep in thought, but the reality is that standing there, I fell fast asleep. And not just a momentary nod-off—I was asleep, like, for reals. Total, deep sleep. Just, like, standing up.

I remember feeling comfortable, so comfortable, strange thoughts, dreams I guess . . . and then, I don't know, maybe I lost my balance and swayed a little, jarring me. But I became aware, suddenly, that I was sleeping . . . I needed to wake up . . . had to . . . work . . .

"ACTION!" I bellowed, using my giant Voice of Command, demonstrating to everyone that I was totally with it and ready to go.

Everybody froze and looked at me. My eyes started to focus.

Nothing was ready. Nobody was in their places. We were still setting up the shot, and everything was going smoothly except for the lunatic director nonsensically screaming "Action!" for no reason in the cold predawn silence.

Tim had a field day with that one. So did Helen. For the rest of the shoot, whenever anything got too quiet, whenever there was a lull, Tim would bellow "ACTION!" and we'd all fall over laughing. But there was a serious lesson that I learned that night, on that roof, a lesson about myself and my body and what it could and couldn't do.

Holy shit, I realized, I'm in my thirties!

I don't like to brag, but I'm going to anyway: *Trancers* is really good. It did well, too, and featured a great poster tease: "Jack Deth is back . . . and he's never been here before!" Appropriately enough for a time-travel movie, it did even better in the far future—around the time I started writing this book in 2020, I got an email from a friend telling me that I needed to check out a podcast where Quentin Tarantino had just name-checked me and *Trancers*. I love Tarantino—let's face it, the guy basically figured out how to *exploit the exploitation movie* and turn it into art! How could I not love him? So I clicked the link and listened.

He did more than name-check. Here, indulge me:

> Then there's this movie that does a fantastic job when it comes to world-building: and that is Empire Productions, Charles Band, *Trancers*. . . . The setup of the story is kind of effing amazing, frankly, to tell you the truth. The whole concept I think is one of the most original concepts of time travel that I've ever seen in a movie ever. . . . Of course you physically can't travel in time, your body stays here. But your consciousness can go back in time, and you take over the body of your closest ancestor from that time period? That's kinda brilliant. That's a really genius idea. And then the whole concept of Whistler and the Squids? That's a pretty fantastic idea. The fact that you have this *Blade Runner* character Jack Deth . . . showing up in his sleazy swinging single ancestor [*laughs*] is the guy he's stuck be-

ing. And Whistler is in 1985 Los Angeles, but we have one problem. Okay, what's the one problem? Whistler's closest relative is the chief of police of Los Angeles. [*Laughs gleefully.*] Would you call that a little problem? . . . And the concept of the Long Second. It's just one great idea after another. I've actually always thought that *Trancers* would be great as just a big-budget movie. Could totally do it.

So that's cool.

While I was shooting *Trancers* I had my new star writers, Danny Bilson and Paul De Meo, transform *Zone Troopers* from a poster into a script. They nailed it. Danny's assistant cameraman days were over. But those days came in handy: when he hinted he might want to direct *Zone Troopers,* I agreed instantly. I liked him and trusted him, and he'd already proven he knew what was what on a set. Danny and Paul, by the way, would soon go on to create lots of things, including the TV series *The Flash* (the '90s version) and Disney's *The Rocketeer.*

After I nailed down the details of another Los Angeles movie or two, we all jumped on a plane and headed off to Rome. It was mostly the *Trancers* gang, including our star, Tim Thomerson, who brought his wife and kid. The mood on the plane was riotous: me, Debi, my dad and mom, my crew, all laughing it up, psyched, for all the world like a sports team heading for an away game. A very faraway away game.

Looking back, how weird was that? My dad and I obviously had a deep connection to Rome, and Mac Ahlberg was a well-traveled Swede (back in L.A. we'd drive people nuts by conversing in Italian on set). But the rest of the gang? They were just blindly following me across the ocean to live and work in a foreign country. If I had any sense at all, I would have felt a heavy burden of responsibility.

I didn't, of course. I just knew it was going to be awesome. And it was.

Rome had changed a lot since I was a teen entrepreneur—although in some ways, it hadn't changed at all, because Rome is always Rome. But *I* had changed. For one thing, I had money. *We* had money. Money was everywhere now that Empire had had a couple of successes. We stayed in a fantastic hotel, ate at amazing restaurants, and worked our butts off on the movie, which also cost money, but that was fine—after all, I had a brand-new million-dollar line of credit, which was about to become five million and then ten million!

I should probably explain that. Let me rewind a bit.

Remember that day at the Milan film market I told you about, when I was selling all those movies? Well, let's go back to that, me standing behind the Empire table, chatting with prospective buyers. Okay? Got it? Good. And . . . ACTION!

"Charlie? Charlie Band?" a voice called in Italian. I looked. A well-dressed older man ambled toward me, followed by a young woman. He was a fat little man, delicately mannered, with an affected little lisp. I knew that voice, and that face.

"Signore Sarlui?" I said automatically, flashing back twenty years or so. Which means you're going to have to as well. Sorry. Here we go. And . . . ACTION!

The neighborhood where I grew up in Rome is called Vigna Clara, and I guess it was sort of analogous to Beverly Hills—prosperous, protected. Our tiny community was behind some gates, and inside those gates were six or seven large buildings, one of which housed the Bands on the top floors. The penthouse contained Dad's offices. It was a pretty sweet setup. There was also a piazza and a swimming pool that was perfect for those hot summer days. We all knew each other. Renato Rascel, the acclaimed Italian actor-singer-songwriter (his song "Arrivederci Roma" was a massive international hit) was a neighbor. And so was Eduard Sarlui. His daughter, Helen, was a lot younger than Richard and me, but our parents were friendly. In America you might forget about such neighbors after a few years apart.

In Italy, though, close neighbors were your family for life. At least when they saw you.

Let's flash forward to Milan. ACTION!

"Charlie!" said Signore Sarlui, clutching my face between his hands, looking me over, insisting I call him Eduard. I was, after all, an adult. Arguably.

We caught up. By some outstanding coincidence, Eduard had become an independent movie producer, aided by the young woman at his side, his daughter Helen. Small world, huh? Within a year or two his Continental Motion Pictures would be the third biggest studio in the film market catalogs, right after the Cannon Group (with their power duo of Golan and Globus) and Empire. You might not have heard of many of his movies, but I'm particularly partial to *Killer Klowns from Outer Space*, if only for the title.

At that point, though, Eduard didn't have much of a company.

But he had something I didn't: connections. And he was happy to share.

"Charlie, you are funding all these movies just from these markets?"

"Yes," I admitted.

"And if you run out of money . . . ?"

"I stop until I can find some more," I admitted.

"No no no no no. I am going to introduce you to the king of all lenders. Frans Afman. From Crédit Lyonnais."

Well, I'd heard that name. Frans Afman essentially invented independent film financing. In fact, back in the seventies he and Dino De Laurentiis *literally* invented the presale to distributors—*my* racket—so that Dino could make 1976's *King Kong* (starring Jeff Bridges and Jessica Lange).

That said, I didn't love the idea. I'd only borrowed lump sums of money once before to make a movie, and if you remember, I got burned. Literally. But a big ol' line of credit? That *would* be helpful. A line of credit, especially from Dino's bank, let buyers know you were legitimate, that they're safe because there's a completion bond in case you fuck up and don't deliver. And more than that, if you *don't* fuck up, a line of credit can be increased. I let Eduard set me up for a date with Frans, and a week later I was on my way to Rotterdam to meet the king. Ready? And . . . ACTION!

Frans was a great gentleman, I'd heard, and a true movie lover. All I had to do was befriend him. And bribe him.

Yuck, it sounds awful when I put it like that. But as in so many industries in so many places—especially Europe—everything ran like that. All the wheels were greased with a little bit of what certain Italian Americans called "a taste," and my Semitic ancestors called a *schmear*. There's two kinds of schmear—the kind you spread on a bagel and the kind you spread on a business relationship. Frans Afman didn't want cream cheese.

But we hit it off in Rotterdam, enjoying a dinner spent babbling on about movies and Rome and Los Angeles, the Charlie Band Charm Offensive in full force. And he charmed me, too—a clever, funny, well-dressed, perpetually smiling man with sharp features and an elegantly bald head.

Well, that's how I thought of him. I mentioned him to Debi recently, and this is how she described him: "a fat pink mean German guy. Awful." I suppose I tend to see the best in people.

Anyway, within a day of that dinner Frans had gotten his schmear, and I had gotten a million-dollar line of credit.

Why have we taken this detour through time and space just to talk financing? Because it's about to become really, really important. Trust me. And now we're done with the flashbacks and we can go back to the present (of 1984) and Rome. Thanks, everyone. *That's a wrap!*

Zone Troopers was coming along nicely. Danny Bilson was getting what he wanted. And I was getting what I wanted. Just as I had hoped, I was doing what my dad had done in Europe when I was a kid: using great people and a strong dollar to put a ton of value up on the screen.

All the location shoots had gone wonderfully, and there were a lot of them. After all, this was a flick about a bunch of plucky American GIs who get caught behind Nazi lines . . . and then stumble across a crashed alien spaceship. And an actual alien, whose friends soon come for him. We spent a lot of time with our GIs tromping across fields, through the woods, sheltering in caves and behind farmhouses. There was a lot of traipsing through the Italian countryside, and when it comes to Italy, to paraphrase Springsteen, baby, I was born to traipse.

But toward the end I realized we still needed a bunch of stuff that would be best shot on a genuine soundstage. It was then that someone advised—and I don't remember who—that I check out Dino Citta.

"Dino Citta?" I asked, as though I'd seen a ghost. "It still exists?"

I knew Dino Citta. When I was ten years old, Dino de Laurentiis launched an audacious project—to construct a film studio to rival Rome's legendary Cinecitta, at that point the largest studio in Europe. It was an insane venture.

And he made it happen. The De Laurentiis Film Center, instantly nicknamed Dino Citta, was a sprawling movie mecca, with six soundstages and a massive backlot set on one hundred acres in the southern suburbs of Rome. I'd been there: I remember visiting with my dad when I was like fourteen years old, because his old pal John Huston was directing an epic with the humble title *The Bible: In the Beginning*.

The atmosphere was . . . almost indescribable. This sprawling production filled the soundstages and the lot. It starred Richard Harris and George C. Scott and Ava Gardner and Peter O'Toole and a two-hundred-foot-long ark for Noah, played by John Huston himself. Hundreds of extras, herds of animals, dozens of sets. My head was on a swivel as I took it all in, the entire Book of Genesis being created around me, with no expense spared. No exaggeration: it cost eighteen million dollars, making it, at the time, one of the most expensive films in history.

A few years after that, I learned that there was a new movie shooting at Dino Citta. It was a sex comedy named *Candy*, starring Marlon Brando, Richard Burton, James Coburn, Walter

Matthau, and, by coincidence, John Huston. I didn't care about any of that. The only thing I cared about was another famous cast member: Ringo Starr.

I begged my dad to pull all the strings he had available to arrange a visit to the set. Naturally, he came through. My brother Richard and I soon found ourselves there on set, impossibly, talking to one of our heroes. It was early 1968, post–*Sgt. Pepper* and pre–*White Album*. Ringo had that great shaggy mane of hair and the mustache he wore during the psychedelic era. He could not have been nicer. I could not have been more awestruck.

Yeah, I knew about Dino Citta.

But I also knew that things had gone sour, financially, for Papa Dino's baby in the seventies, and he had shut down the studio and fled—er, *relocated*—to the United States. I don't think he took a financial hit for the spectacular implosion of the studio. That's not how a European like Dino did business. His name was on *nothing,* at least not once he took down the sign at the studio gate. The real ownership was lost in layers of bank papers and murky deals, and the property was just left there in limbo to rot, the forest reclaiming the back lots, the paint flaking away, an abandoned wonderland destroyed by excess, like a Jurassic Park without dinosaurs, an ancient world now forever lost.

So when I was told that the place was still there, that some enterprising young filmmaker might be able to fix it up and maybe shoot a movie there . . . I just had to go take a look.

It was as advertised: a glorious, sprawling, beautiful shithole. It had been a decade since the maid had quit, and it showed. Only an idiot would want anything to do with that dump.

I immediately fell in love with the place. I have a tendency to fall in love with places, especially places with history. But this was no Liberace mansion, this was an actual *movie studio,* just sitting there, waiting. I sat there awhile, remembering what it had been, and when I got up to leave, my head was buzzing with potential schemes. Somehow I knew this wasn't over.

We continued to have a ball shooting *Zone Troopers,* and once we wrapped I was genuinely sad to have to return to L.A. Already I was making plans, placing phone calls, so I could shoot another movie or two there. And through those calls, and through casual conversations with the locals, I came to hear a persistent rumor: Dino De Laurentiis was still attached to Dino Citta.

It sounded like a ghost story, like an episode of *Scooby-Doo* where you capture the old caretaker who's been haunting the place, pull off his mask, and *gasp*! It's Dino De Laurentiis!

"And I would-a gotten away with it-a, too, if-a notta for you a-meddling bambinos!"

Ridiculous. But people seemed sure of it. Hmm, I thought, as we began the journey back to L.A. Interesting. I filed that information away for some far-flung future day.

That day came a couple months later.

It was 1985 and I was back in Italy, prepping a new slate of films to shoot there. Things were good. I kept the films a-selling, and the schmear a-schmearing, and in no time my line of credit with Crédit Lyonnais had swelled to five million dollars. Frans Afman was vocally proud of his new maverick producer. But although we spoke frequently, I didn't expect the call I got from Frans one afternoon, when, after a few pleasantries, he asked out of nowhere:

"Charles, my boy, do you know Dino De Laurentiis?"

"Um, well, I met him once, at Cannes," I said. Beyond that, not unless he remembered a certain obviously talented fourteen-year-old aspiring filmmaker visiting the set of *The Bible.*

Frans continued, "Are you returning to Los Angeles soon?"

I told him I was, and he responded immediately, "I think you should meet Dino when you return. You will like him." It was more of an order than a suggestion.

In his incredibly friendly but careful manner, Frans let me know that although it was not common knowledge, De Laurentiis still owned Dino Citta.

Well, not *owned*. Not in an official way. Please—this is chapter 6. Have you learned *nothing* from your time in Italy with me? But yeah, in another way . . . Dino was *involved*. He controlled the place. In fact, he controlled it—get this—through Crédit Lyonnais.

Small world, huh?

Back stateside, I had another project to produce. Through my dad I'd met a director named Stuart Gordon, a dude about my age who'd led Chicago's legendary Organic Theater Company and had just come to Los Angeles in the hopes of getting into movies. He wanted to adapt an H. P. Lovecraft story, and naturally I green-lit the thing before we were done with lunch. I mean, Lovecraft? A cool theater guy? Absolutely. Plus, I was still amazed that a kid like me actually got to "green-light" things!

But when I got back to L.A. and looked at Stuart's dailies, I was appalled. Suddenly I felt like Irwin Yablans, transformed into an irate old Brooklyn guy, jumping up in the front row, screaming, "What the fuck is this? This is shit! I offer to distribute your movie and you give me this shit!?"

Okay, I didn't do that, of course. I was cool. But suddenly, I could relate.

The dailies were unwatchable. Dark, muddy, awful. It was obviously the fault of Stuart's cinematographer. Though I hated doing it, I fired the guy. I brought on Mac Ahlberg to fix everything. For good measure, I made sure my brother Richard scored it—it was a cool project, and Richard was fast becoming a really great film composer.

[Okay, full disclosure, I think I actually had my dad fire Stuart's cinematographer. Dad was great at that stuff: kind, caring, but firm. You almost felt like he was doing you a favor by letting you leave the project!]

Then, after putting out that fire, a few weeks later I finally got to take a look at the first cut of the film. I'd been right. Thanks to Mac, it looked great!

And it was . . . well . . . awful. I almost went full Yablans once again.

The cinematography may have been fixed. But the pacing was glacial, the plot disjointed, and the thing was over *two hours* long! It was obviously the work of a first-time filmmaker, in love with every frame he shot. There was, however, some good stuff in there. So once again it was Albert Band to the rescue. My dad had a fantastic eye for pace and story, and he sat with our editor and Stuart for hours on end, doing the necessary surgery, trimming the film down to a tidy, freaky, and terrifying eighty-six minutes.

To this day, *Re-Animator,* starring Jeffrey Combs and Barbara Crampton, is by far the most critically acclaimed movie I was ever involved in. Pauline Kael of *The New Yorker* loved it. Roger Ebert loved it. The *New York Times'* Janet Maslin loved it. It made everybody's top-ten list for the year. I'm not exaggerating. It was one of the few films I ever took to Cannes for an actual screening, and the sweaty, overpacked house (a fire marshal's nightmare!) lost their minds, screaming and shrieking and howling and giving us a five-minute standing ovation when it was all over.

Even before all that, I knew we had something fantastic. And some*one* fantastic. Stuart could be a little irascible, sure, and stubborn as hell. But it came from a place of real passion and drive. I wanted him to make more movies for me. When we wrapped *Re-Animator* I basically patted him on the back and told him to meet me in Rome.

Me, I would follow soon. First, I had a date with Dino.

By the time Debi and I hopped in the car and headed up Doheny Drive toward the De Laurentiis mansion, I'd already received word through the grapevine that I should be prepared to buy Dino's studio lot for about fourteen million dollars. This seemed completely doable. All I needed was Dino's approval. And fourteen million dollars.

The mansion was very . . . mansion-y. Something like twenty thousand square feet of Los Angeles splendor, terraces and gardens and sunlight and unbelievable views. A butler escorted us in. Dino and Martha, his right-hand woman (and soon-to-be second wife) greeted us warmly, and I was instantly comfortable. Like I said, I didn't know Dino, but I *knew* Dino. I'd grown up knowing Italian men cut from the same mold—expressive, warm, clever old guys, with just a hint of scoundrel underneath. My kind of people.

Dino bragged about the dinner he was cooking for the four of us—pasta primavera with homemade penne—and I was impressed that a man of his age and stature would go to these lengths. However, as soon as we got into the kitchen, it made sense: all the vegetables and herbs had been expertly prechopped and laid out, cooking show style, by Dino's sous-chef. I should've known—Dino was in fact executive producing the meal!

Still, he threw it together beautifully, an old hand making a delicious-smelling sauce as the penne cooked, and then the four of us repaired to an elegantly set table on the terrace as the sous-chef took over to finish and serve the meal. I swear, the man could've had a cooking show. He'd leave that to his granddaughter Giada.

By the time we'd finished the excellent primavera (although I probably would've used a tad more garlic), I was Dino's protégé, a second son to him, at least for that evening. Certainly we were kindred spirits, eternally in love with movies of all kinds.

"Charlie," he said to me in Italian, "I can probably make this happen with the bank. But there will be payments, obviously. Can you afford it?" He looked at me with concern and repeated himself. "Can you afford it?"

Absolutely not. But I could make movies, I thought, lots of them. And I could rent out soundstages. But still . . . absolutely not. But then again . . . all I had to do was say yes, and for better or worse, Charlie Band could actually own his very own gigantic movie studio . . . for no money down! It was so tempting, but I also knew I was completely unprepared to actually do this.

Two weeks later Debi and I were driving south out of Rome, holding the keys to the studio.

The trades reported it as "Independent American Filmmaker Purchases De Laurentiis Cinematografica for $20 Million." As I said, I hadn't yet spent a dime. But I was about to spend many, many dimes.

There were renovations, contractors, landscapers. A ton of work to be done, but it was all done with amazing amounts of joy, both on our part and that of the local workers, who were thrilled to see the place come back to life. But this time with a new sign over the Hollywood-style studio gate: EMPIRE PICTURES.

I rehabilitated the studio, fixed it up inside and out. I renovated Dino's unbelievable office, a sprawling, luxurious suite that took up the entire top floor of one of the main buildings and included a hidden staircase to the rooftop, where Dino met his mistresses. A soundstage, built for *The Bible,* was the largest on the continent (second in the hemisphere only to the "Albert R. Broccoli 007 Stage" at Pinewood Studios in England). I rebuilt the bar, which quickly became a gathering place for all the actors and crew. I established a Hollywood-style Walk of Fame for the big stars I'd be importing from America. The lights were moved in, the cameras started rolling . . .

But wait! I can't really produce this chapter of my life, I can't shoot this reel, without establishing one of my life's most important locations:

The castle.

We hadn't even rented a villa. Instead, Debi and I were staying at an ultra-luxurious hotel near the famed Spanish Steps. As I said, money was no longer an object, or at least it didn't *seem* like one. So I started buying art.

My taste in art has always been similar to my taste in movies: dark, grotesque, sinful. Reminders of our mortality. Good art is expensive, though; I never dreamed I'd be in a position to *buy* the stuff.

Well, now I was. And that's how I met Rolando.

I was walking down a street full of cool art shops, and something beautiful caught my eye. A sixteenth-century painting of a perfect, cherubic baby . . . holding a skull. I don't know who owned the shop, but the guy who arranged the sale was Rolando, a friendly, knowledgeable young man from a good family, exactly the sort of guy whom art dealers employed to lounge in front of their shops and make it easy for visitors to find what they wanted. Rolando could tell you the price of everything, and in this case, this beautiful four-hundred-year-old painting was a mere eight hundred bucks. Rolando wrapped up the sale, arranged to have it framed at a place down the street, and I suddenly had a painting of one badass baby—*and* a new friend.

A friend who was about to get me involved in something huge. Literally.

Whenever I was in Rome (I was flying back and forth constantly), I dropped by the store and saw Rolando. And it was during one of my visits, one afternoon, that it began. Rolando was out in front of the store, as usual, and we sat down for some coffee.

"Have you heard about the Castle Giove?" he asked me. Rolando said it casually, but I could tell he was excited. I hadn't heard anything about it.

"It's not far. The largest castle in Umbria, dating back to the twelfth century, and full of beautiful pieces. And see, the Aquarone family owns it, but they are almost all gone now. The heir, the family's last daughter . . . she just wants to party and hang out in Acapulco, and she is going to auction off everything— *everything*! You and Debi must come see."

We came to see. We had our limo driver (yes, we were doing *that* now) take us up the autostrada between Rome and Florence, then off into the hills and up a mountain, high and steep. The entire top of the mountain was dominated by this incredible structure, a real, honest-to-god castle. There was a medieval wing, yes, dating back to the twelfth century, but an even cooler sixteenth-century half. Seven floors. More than a hundred rooms. We were going to find some *stuff* there!

We did. *So* much cool stuff. Rolando, who had met us there, breathlessly explained the process. The auction would take place over three days, and although I was going to be back in the States,

Rolando would be my proxy. I chose three items for him to bid on for me, and named my top price. He smiled and agreed, but Rolando had bigger ideas.

"You should buy the castle!"

"*Buy* the *castle?*"

"Yes yes yes yes yes! Charlie, on the third day of the auction, when all the other pieces are gone, comes the very last phase. They sell the castle itself. You need this castle!"

I did not need a castle. Also, I couldn't afford a castle. My name was already in the newspapers and magazines as the rich young American maverick who'd somehow bought Dino Citta, but that was all smoke and mirrors. I had money, but not castle-buying money. That was another weight class entirely.

I tried to explain this to Rolando, but he didn't accept my answer. I needed to be clear and firm.

"I can't buy this castle, Rolando," I said definitively.

"I'll look into it for you," he replied.

We flew back to the States, clutching the massive catalog of the treasures of Castello di Giove. We hadn't even unpacked when Rolando called, in a frenzy. The auction was being run by friends of his.

"It's crazy, Charlie, crazy! You know how they're selling this thing, the castle?"

I didn't, so Rolando explained. They were going to employ an old Italian auction ceremony from hundreds of years ago. It involved lighting three long matches in sequence. While the first match burns, you tell the history of the place you're auctioning. While the second match burns, you describe the property as it is now, detailing the amenities, the PR stuff. And when the third match is lit, the bidding starts. And this is where it gets interesting. If there are no bids before the match goes out, the auction is over and the property goes unsold. If there are a couple of bids before the match goes out, the auction continues.

BUT . . . should the match go out when there is only *one* bid, before a second bid has been made, then that's it. It's over. The property goes to that first bidder.

The Castle Giove's bidding was going to start at a million lire (approximately $550,000), Rolando said.

"That's great, man," I said. "But we both know that place is gonna go for five or six million, minimum." I mean the castle was just a shell, but *come on*!

"No no no no no! Charlie! Listen—I know what matches they are going to use!"

"What?"

"The . . . brand. I know it. I saw them. Look, Charlie, you have to send me the money for the deposit! You gotta get me the money!"

This was insanity. But I couldn't talk Rolando down, and I wasn't worried he was going to skip town with my money—I'd get the cash back as soon as we lost the auction. So, I did it. I wired him a fifty-thousand-dollar down payment through the Italian consulate and signed the papers necessary to delegate him to be my proxy.

That evening, Debi and I went to an Italian restaurant "for luck." It was a hilarious thought, owning a castle, though not one we took all that seriously. We called it an early night; not only was the auction the next morning, so was my son Alex's fourth birthday party. That, we were sure, was the bigger event.

Anyway, the day was upon us, the party and the auction happening simultaneously, and as much as I love a robust round of Pin the Tail on the Donkey, at some point I snuck out of the birthday party and went upstairs to listen in on the proceedings in Italy.

Remember, we're talking about eighties technology. I didn't Zoom the auction. But somehow Rolando used his connections to get a telephone line run into the back of the room, three hundred feet from the auctioneer in the giant, cavernous hall. He called me at the appointed time, left the phone off the hook, and took his seat.

I could hear the auctioneer doing the match thing: He told the history of the castle. He stopped abruptly, and then, I assume, lit the second match. He described the castle and its grounds. Then there was a pause—the second match had burnt out!—and I ran out of my room and yelled downstairs, "Debi! Pick up the phone! It's happening!"

The auctioneer lit the third match. He opened the bidding.

Silence.

More silence.

Rolando, I should point out, had been up late the night before. Timing his matches again and again.

More silence. This was excruciating.

Then, out of nowhere, Rolando yelled, "A million lire!"

A split second later, the match went out. A voice intoned, in Italian, "Sold!"

Finito. The castle was mine.

Pandemonium erupted. Shouts and screams of confusion and rage. There had been a lot of people there. Rich people. Royalty from Sweden. Big money from Monaco. A lot of people were there expressly for that last auction, for the castle itself.

The thing is, though, unlike Rolando, these people didn't understand the ceremony. They assumed there'd be lots of bidding, and that they'd get in at around the five million mark, when things got serious. But now it didn't matter how much they yelled and protested, they just had to watch while Rolando proudly strode forward, my noble proxy, claiming my prize.

A few minutes later, Rolando came back to the phone to check in. We were both laughing almost too hard to even speak. But in the back of my mind, I did have to wonder:

Now what?

One more thing I should mention, but this is kind of embarrassing. See, I didn't think I was buying a castle. It was just an idea, just another wild fantasy, a scheme I agreed to in principle, mostly to appease Rolando. Debi barely thought it was real. It was the ultimate long shot.

Which is why I didn't even bother mentioning it to my dad.

Which is why, that afternoon in Rome, where he was staying as he produced some of our Italy-based movies, my dad had no idea why he was suddenly besieged by reporters and paparazzi as he tried to exit his hotel. See, the Italian media *freaked the hell out*. Some American film person had swept in and purchased Umbria's biggest castle. Who was it? Spielberg? Lucas? They researched, found their answer, and descended on my dad, the only Band in Europe, like a swarm of bees.

To save face, Dad pretended like he was completely in on it all. But he wasn't, and he was really, really angry with me, almost the angriest he'd ever been.

And he was right to be angry. But that changed amazingly quickly.

Somehow, I got the half million together. Flew back to Rome. And on a bright Saturday morning, we all drove out to the castle: Debi and me, my mom and my dad, Rolando and his wife. We tried to take it all in. I think my dad spent the entire day laughing.

We met the new custodian of the castle (the old one was in his eighties and in no mood to keep tending the place under the regime of the crazy young Americans). He walked us through it all. Seven floors. Something like a hundred thousand square feet. The medieval wing and the "modern" wing (*sixteenth-century modern!*). Astounding. Jaw-dropping.

I put in fourteen bathrooms, a bunch of bedrooms, better electricity. Started to decorate, which was tough, because this was a job for Bed, Bath, and WAY Beyond!

But we made it habitable and completely glorious. I was not yet thirty-five years old, and I was suddenly the owner of a giant motion picture studio and the lord of a frickin' *castle*. The stage had been set and dressed for my epic Italian adventure.

Aaannnnnd . . . ACTION!

PX I Love You

As soon as Debi was introduced to the Sarluis in Milan, the instant we sat down for a drink, Helen Sarlui immediately complained to her (smiling) how when she was a girl, "Charlie used to shoot home movies of us kids . . . and then charge us a ton of money to see them!"

Well, that's not true at all! At least, it's inaccurate. The actual story is cooler.

It was Rome in the mid-sixties. I was thirteen years old and already full of dreams and schemes. And one of those schemes was to run a movie theater. At my home.

I roped Stefano into my plot. Yes, that tall, blond, affable, perennially stoned goofball. He was not as tall back then, and not yet a stoner, but all the other ingredients were there. He jumped onto my scheme, which was simple: We move all the furniture out of my parents' gigantic living room and show movies. For free. But here's the beauty part: we sell the audience American candy at a huge markup!

See, we had a friend in school whose dad was in the military. So he had access to the American army base, and thus he could shop at the PX, where he could get deeply discounted American candy. Now, you and I know that European candies are unbelievably delicious, SO much better than the junk from the States. But these were (mostly) American kids. They pined for the taste of their Snickers and their Milky Ways and their Hershey bars and M&Ms. And they couldn't get them in Rome, so they were stuck eating European chocolates, the poor li'l lambs.

Steve and I set it all up. We grabbed excerpts from old horror movies—*Dracula* and *Frankenstein* and stuff. We picked up some war films—old 8mm World War II stuff—and we wrote narration, recorded Steve reading it, and attached it to the film as a soundtrack. It was a lot of work. But finally we were ready, and we opened our doors to the public.

Only like eight kids showed up. The second show was no better. Oh well, at least they bought *some* candy.

Like any producer, I knew I had to make some adjustments or we'd be sunk. The business model seemed sound, but we just weren't getting enough asses in seats. That's when I had the idea.

Steve and I started roaming the little neighborhood with a camera, filming our friends in the neighborhood doing . . . whatever they were doing. It didn't matter. What mattered was that they were *aware* they were being filmed.

And then we let it be known that our new films from the neighborhood would now be part of our big Movie Nights . . .

The next weekend we opened our doors . . . and packed the place.

Something like forty kids showed up, as many as my parents' living room could hold. And they all bought our candy at a huge markup, munching happily and watching themselves up on the big screen. We made a killing.

Not bad, huh? Now, you might be tempted to take away from this the lesson that mankind is a self-regarding creature, motivated by vanity, and that all they want to do is see themselves on-screen, whether literally themselves or by proxy in the person of a sympathetic protagonist. Okay. But if this is the lesson you're drawing, you're kind of missing the larger, deeper point:

In the movie business, it's all about the concession stand.

7

La Dolce Vida

(1986–1987)

The next couple of years were a giant, messy, stressful, glorious blur, as I ran my Empire on two continents, threw money around like a drunken billionaire, negotiated deals, threw parties in my castle, and got married for a second time.

Oh, and during those few years, I made something like forty movies. The soundstages at Empire Pictures were constantly buzzing, the movies were coming out at a crazy pace, and although they didn't make a ton of money theatrically (they never did), they were crushing it in the home market through my deal with Vestron Video.

That's a truth about my end of the business. With the exception of *Ghoulies*, most of my movies never made a dime in theaters. But running them and promoting their theatrical release enhanced their value tremendously in the home market. "Straight to video" wasn't really a thing yet—I was going to help invent *that* market in the nineties. In the meantime, Empire was a movie studio that just so happened to make most of its money through video rentals. The video stores were where all the indie filmmakers were making their cash by then, but we were better at it than most.

In my mind I tend to separate that period of my life into the Good Times, from 1985 till early 1987, and the Desperate Times, from 1987 to 1989. But in reality, I managed to have a lot of fun and make some decent movies during the Desperate Times. And the Good Times were loaded with their share of desperation. So how do I tell you all about all this? I guess I'll do it the way I do it in my head: movie by movie. Let's start with a weird and wonderful one that you may have heard of, starring a heroic young lad who fights evil magical creatures, a boy named Harry Potter . . .

. . . **no, not *that*** Harry Potter. I'll explain

I'd promised my effects guy, John Buechler, that he could direct a movie, and it was one of the first that we shot at the brand-new Empire Studios. John and I had been talking about it ever since *Ghoulies*—a flick where he could create a menagerie of bizarre fantasy creatures and put them on custom-built sets where he could really turn 'em loose. And at Empire he got the chance.

I'd been turned loose, too. The dollar was so strong that it made sense to fly in talent from the States, put them up at luxury hotels, and let them enjoy Rome. So the cast of *Troll* is kind of amazing. We had Michael Moriarty and Shelley Hack (from *Charlie's Angels*) and Sonny Bono and Julia Louis-Dreyfus and her husband (and fellow *Saturday Night Live* alum) Brad Hall and June Lockhart (from *Lost in Space*) and her daughter Anne Lockhart. Amazing, right? And then there was our protagonist,

Noah Hathaway, the kid from *The NeverEnding Story,* as the embattled Harry Potter Jr.

Now, for years there's a been a lot of chatter about this in the press and online, and there have been a lot of lawyers who've offered to go to bat for me, so I want to be clear here: Are there similarities between *Troll* and the Harry Potter series? A few. After all, *my* Harry Potter is a kid who discovers a magical world full of witches and warlocks that exists right alongside his real world. And he asks a witch to teach him wizardry, in part so he can battle an evil creature—a former wizard—who has taken possession of Harry's little sister and aims to rule the world.

So yeah, there's a similarity or two.

But I've never accused J. K. Rowling of plagiarism or infringement or anything like that. Her world is her creation, and as I said years ago when I was asked about this, life's too short to fight over stuff like this. Plus, if she *had* seen *Troll* and consciously been inspired by it and secretly plotted to steal some of the ideas, I'm pretty sure she would've thought to change the hero's name!

Moving on . . .

So yeah, the cast was great. Sonny Bono was between his third and fourth marriages and was enjoying Rome as much as the "swinging single" character he was portraying. Michael Moriarty was fantastic, and he turned in one of the best, weirdest dancing-alone-in-the-living-room performances since *Risky Business.* Just imagine if Tom Cruise was middle-aged. And dorky. And possibly epileptic.

Julia and Brad had both just left *SNL,* and they were a lot of fun on set. Julia's character ends up turning into a giggling malevolent forest sprite, sprinting through the trees clad only in vines and greenery. And she was a great sport about it—in fact, she was probably the best giggling malevolent forest sprite I've ever worked with.

The movie itself was ambitious. Not only did we build a giant three-story interior of a San Francisco–style apartment building *and* an exterior on the back lot, but the sets had to accommodate John's insane menagerie of slimy, evil creatures, which meant building and concealing hidden spaces for the operators and puppeteers. Add to all this the stop-motion animation I insisted on—I wanted to show the dark, enchanted forest aggressively creeping into our dimension and taking over entire apartments—and it was quite a production.

At the heart of it was our Troll.

Phil Fondacaro is one of my favorites to work with. A good actor, and a thoughtful guy. But because of his stature—he's a dwarf—not a lot of roles come his way that really show off his talent. Except in my movies. For *Troll* I had something special in mind.

"Absolutely not," he said when I asked him to be our nefarious title character. He had just spent weeks in a full-body costume for George Lucas as one of the Ewoks in *Return of the Jedi,* and he had no desire to sweat to death on another hot film set. But then I told him about the *other* role I wanted him to play, English professor Malcolm Mallory, and he couldn't say no. He sighed and agreed to do both, to take the good with the badass.

He still considers it one of the best roles he's ever had, and if you see his touching and tragic scene with the little girl who befriends him, you'll get it—it's probably the best scene in the movie, and one of Phil's favorites ever.

But that troll costume was murder. In fact, it literally almost killed someone.

See, a couple of months later we were at Cannes, promoting our first batch of movies and selling the next. I don't generally go for stunts, but this one was irresistible: we still had John's costume, and I figured our amazing-looking troll could hand out flyers on the outdoor strip where all the action happens. I called Phil.

"Absolutely not," he said. And this time he meant it. There was no way he was getting back into that thirty-pound latex monstrosity, certainly not in the smoldering late-spring sunlight of Cannes.

But I was undeterred, and I soon found a replacement, a young French woman named Tinou, a circus performer who was about exactly Phil's size. But when I called Phil for a few pointers, he was concerned.

"Has she ever worn anything like that before?"

"I don't know," I told him. "But she's in the circus, so . . ."

"Charlie, this is important: Keep her hydrated. Trust me. Let her know what it gets like in there."

I promised Phil that I would. And I did. When the day came, it was something like a hundred degrees. I was a little worried, but my new troll seemed confident. I don't know. I guess Tinou got really into the part, carried away, maybe, skipping around and joshing with the delighted crowd on that hot strip of pavement in the brilliant French sunlight—right up until the moment she went rigid and collapsed with an audible THUNK and just lay there, unmoving. You know that moment at the beginning of *Star Wars,* in the desert, when R2D2 gets zapped? This was that.

We ran over and somehow got the giant troll head off her and got ice and the paramedics came and the giant crowd of onlookers got to watch my troll being carted off on a stretcher, which I guess *did* leave an impression. But for us it was scarier than anything in the movie. And for Phil it was an opportunity to spend the next few decades saying, "I told you so." And he has.

Troll **actually ended up** making a few million in theaters, which, as I said, was a rarity for my pictures. And the whole experience was a pleasure. At the same time, I had my friend Ted Nicolaou on another set shooting his feature film debut. *Terrorvision* was a loony, energetic comedy-horror movie that has become a cult classic in recent years. It also features Jon Gries, who would one day attain cult status of his own as Uncle Rico in *Napoleon Dynamite.*

Great times. At some point I put everyone up at Corsetti Mare, a beautiful Italian beach hotel, and our nights and occasional off-days were spent partying, swimming, laughing, recharging our batteries for those loooong summer days back at the studio.

When those movies wrapped and my first magical summer as an Italian studio head had drawn to a close . . . well, that was the first time I ever threw a wrap party at my castle, and it was pretty amazing. Sure, these were B movies, but imagine finishing your shoot in Rome to find a limousine waiting for you in front of your hotel, ferrying you north, out of the city, into the surrounding hills, up a steep mountain road to your castle . . .

Well, it was even better than that: Candles and dramatic lighting and dancing on the parapets overlooking the gorgeous valley below. Multiple bars and outstanding catered food. Live music. These were fantastic events. Nobody would ever regret getting involved in an Empire picture.

Well, eventually the bank would. But that was still a few years off!

Speaking of banks, I should mention that somewhere in there I secured a deal to fund all these movies and get them distributed. And it took a lot. I've done a lot of questionable things in my career, but this one I'm truly not proud of. But these are my confessions, so I'll be straight with you. In order to get the money we needed, Debi and I had to spend a few days . . . a week, almost . . .

. . . in Connecticut. Don't judge me!

Okay, it's a perfectly nice state. It is not the fault of Connecticut or my friend Austin Furst, whose house we were visiting on our way back to Los Angeles from Cannes. It was this simple: Austin ran Vestron Video, and I needed a distributor. And I needed money to make the movies he'd be distributing. So we put our lives on pause, visited with Austin and his wife while staying at a nearby hotel, and began a days-long dance of wheeling, dealing, and socializing with the Fursts. Austin loved us, and he wanted my movies. I needed to project the aura of a successful wunderkind with infinite resources, but one who also couldn't leave Austin's house without a done deal and a check in his hand. I had to let Austin know I was desperate without seeming even remotely desperate.

It took days, our nonstop life suddenly stopped cold in in its tracks as we hung out doing nothing in Connecticut. It was so completely pleasant and yet so completely not our scene that we started whispering to each other that we were stuck in "hell on earth." Which is only hilarious when you consider how *nice* it all was.

Eventually, though, it ended. Austin and I struck a deal, and Debi and I hopped the next plane for L.A., with me carrying a check for a little down payment . . . of $3.6 million.

As we touched down in L.A., *Variety* was already running a headline about the deal on their front page, touting Charles Band and Vestron Video's "$50 million deal"!

I guess if you did all the math and incorporated all the potential, there is a way to call this a fifty-million-dollar deal. But all

I cared about was that first check, which kept my Empire humming on two continents.

Meanwhile, in Rome, while we were shooting *Troll* and *Terrorvision,* I had also imported Stuart Gordon from the States. He came to shoot his second Lovecraft-inspired movie, *From Beyond.* But then I had an inspiration—I could shoot *another* movie first, on the same set we were building for *From Beyond.* The *From Beyond* set was going to be amazing—all these areas to hide the operators of the massive Lovecraftian creatures we were flying in from the States. But this other script was a creepy little movie written by Ed Naha, who'd just done such a good job with the *Troll* script, featuring a kind of evil creature that would one day become one of my trademarks. It was called *Dolls.* I asked Stuart if he'd direct it before his Lovecraft opus.

"Absolutely not," he said. I was hearing that a lot in those days, and like anyone with an Italian background, I considered that an opening offer. Somehow, I persuaded him. I think one of the perks that sold it was that the poor guy and his family ended up having to spend a few extra months in a fancy hotel in Rome!

Dolls was meant to be a quickie tossed off before the "big movie." But Stuart being Stuart, he became obsessed with it, and it started to grow. And grow . . .

In no time, my dad had to be deployed to rein in Stuart's ambitions so that we could wrap things up and get to the movie he actually came to Rome to make.

Years later Stuart would say that he actually preferred *Dolls* to *From Beyond.* For me, *Dolls* was thrilling because I got to rope in Dave Allen to make me some fantastic stop-motion animation.

We built all kinds of terrifying little toys, plotting and scheming how to use them for maximum terror.

With Stuart and his crew ready to go on their soundstage, I knew they'd make great stuff. The only risk was them going over budget. But I had bigger problems on another soundstage, where yet another movie was shooting, one that featured an actor who was threatening to flat-out, real-life *murder* his director.

David Schmoeller, the wonderful sicko behind *Tourist Trap,* was going to direct for me in Rome. I'd given him the poster for a movie I'd sold, called *Crawlspace,* and he came back to me with a script about a twisted Vietnam vet. I thought that might be a tough sell for an American audience, so I suggested making the guy a Nazi. At first David wasn't sure, but then I uttered the magic words:

"I could get you Klaus Kinski."

He jumped at it.

We would both come to regret that. Especially David.

Klaus Kinski was an intense dude. He'd already brought his brooding, intimidating presence to over a hundred films, and I couldn't believe how fortunate I was to find him available for *Crawlspace.* I was about to learn *why* he was available.

It was a typically disturbing Schmoeller idea: An older man (Kinski) rents out apartments in his building to young women, but spies on them through a network of crawlspaces that he's installed throughout the building. And then he starts kidnapping them and torturing them and . . . yeah, the fun never stops. It was dark. But Kinski was darker.

To hear David tell it, the problems started immediately. And you *can* hear David tell it. Years later he made a documentary short about the experience, happily entitled *Please Kill Mr. Kinski,* which, he says, is something the entire crew was begging him to do.

Anyway, according to David, Klaus was difficult from day one, ranting and screaming over things as small as wardrobe choices, getting into multiple fistfights with the crew, and generally behaving like a madman. He wouldn't let David yell "action" or "cut," so they just had to shoot him doing his thing whenever he chose to do it. It got harder and harder to manage him, and soon there was an actress that David kept on the set even when she wasn't in scenes because Kinski seemed to like her and her presence calmed him. Somewhat.

Me, I was only tangentially aware of all this stuff. I knew there were problems, but I was running an entire movie studio *and* readying a bunch of productions back in L.A. I was working constantly. I was sure if anything got too bad, it would be brought to my attention.

And it was.

It was a chilly day, and my new Empire was bustling. From Dino's gargantuan office I could look down and see three or four of our massive soundstages all humming along at once, scenic backdrops and carts with equipment being rolled in and out through the gigantic "elephant doors." Exteriors being shot on our tremendous hundred-acre back lot. The renovated bar was always hopping—you could get alcohol there, sure, but the place was more of a café where all the productions would congregate during breaks, grabbing their coffees and pastries in the morning, little sandwiches in the afternoon. People flowed in and out of there constantly, chatting and laughing as they returned to their sets. At that moment, it truly did feel like an empire.

I was sitting behind Dino's absurdly gigantic desk, working, multiple space heaters at my feet, because there was no other way to keep the cavernous office warm. I'd just hung up the phone when my assistant came running in. And I mean it—she was literally running.

"You need to come to the bar," she panted. "Kinski and David Schmoeller are fighting again, and I think Klaus is literally going to kill Schmoeller."

"Come on, he's probably just blowing off steam."

"He's got a knife and he's screaming, 'I'm going to kill you!'"

I got up and started running.

Now, understand—this was Italy. Fights broke out all the time, but it was generally just chest-thumping, performative posturing. The craziest, most passionate threats got made, the combatants squared off, and then generally nothing happened. The would-be brawlers were happy to be held back by their friends, and within an hour or so everybody would be having a drink together. That's how it worked.

This . . . wasn't that.

My assistant wasn't lying. By the time I got there, Klaus had a fistful of Schmoeller's shirt in one hand and a large kitchen knife in the other, and he was ranting and screaming and working himself into a spittle-spraying frenzy. Now, Klaus wasn't a big man, but if you've ever seen him on-screen, you know that he can be completely terrifying. In this moment, it really did seem like murder was a possibility.

I started talking to Klaus. Softly. I'd seen my dad do this kind of thing on sets all over Europe when I was a kid. He was great at it. As every police negotiator knows, the key is to get them talking and keep them talking. And you want them to know you take their concerns seriously. I gently asked Klaus to explain why murdering Schmoeller was necessary at this particular moment.

"I keep telling him to get me like *this* . . . but he has me like this. LIKE THIS!!" Klaus was now gesturing with his knife hand, and he released Schmoeller with the other so he could demonstrate, raising and lowering the knife and his other hand to demonstrate his dissatisfaction with the way Schmoeller was framing a shot. He was literally going to murder his director for framing a shot "wrong."

I spoke softly, forcing him to quiet down and strain to hear me. I made him feel his concerns were being heard, for sure, I mean, what artist *wouldn't* want to cut open their director for bad framing? But I also made him take in the scene—the bar, the crowd, the weapon in his hand. Soon he was nodding sympathetically, his addled German brain starting to process my position— which was that if he killed his director I was not prepared to give him another one. He never admitted fault, but he calmed down.

So now I had a genuine assault and a public threat of murder, right there in the middle of Empire Pictures. Certainly, I could've had Klaus arrested right away, or I could have sent David to the police to record a statement, or at the very least had Klaus removed from the premises. I looked at Klaus and David, both still breathing heavily, and I weighed all these options, and then did what I think any young studio head might have done.

I sent them both back to their set to finish the movie.

And that's what they did. Nowadays, *Crawlspace* is remembered for Kinski's strikingly convincing performance as a twisted, murderous fiend. He didn't have to dig too deep for that.

Most of those early Empire films did pretty well, and the overall vibe was fresh, positive, and often giddy. We kept the studio bustling all week long, and on the weekends, I would retreat to my dark medieval castle atop a mountain.

Inside the castle, it was anything but dark. We had great food and wine and long dinners with my dad and mom, my brother Richard, and friends. I'd hired some trusted old pals, too. Remember Tamara? My high school friend who helped me with my nightclub? She came to work for me, and was a frequent visitor to Castle Band. So was our caretaker, my friend Rolando, who was busily making sure that room after glorious room got furnished, electrified, and brought up-to-date from its sixteenth-century condition.

My kids would visit from Los Angeles, too: this place made for killer games of hide-and-seek. We started a family tradition: every July, all the various members of my weird, expanding family would head to Italy and spend two weeks living it up at our Umbrian retreat.

I'm sure the whole arrangement would've seemed amazing and ridiculous and dizzying if I considered how far I'd come in a couple of short years. But I didn't. I enjoyed the moment while asking myself the same question that has animated me forever: *Okay. What's next?*

8

The Fall of the Roman Empire

(1987–1988)

As all that stuff was going on in Rome, I was also constantly flying to Los Angeles and Rotterdam, securing credit, putting movies into production, making all sorts of questionable decisions. Rome wasn't built in a day, and it didn't fall in a day, either. That took *work*.

I made some good decisions, too. For instance, putting Linda Blair in a movie she wasn't, in fact, in.

It was Eduard Sarlui, always finding angles, who approached me with an offer. He had two unreleased "women in prison" movies from South America. He had no idea what to do with them (Eduard wasn't really an idea man), but he thought he might be able to fob them off on me for fifteen grand apiece. He acted like he was doing me a favor, but we both knew he was pressuring me into buying something that otherwise would've been a total loss for him.

I looked at them. They weren't my cup of tea—far too brutal, women being beaten, running around the jungle, boobs flying everywhere. Wall-to-wall torture, breasts, and bandits.

I bought 'em.

See, I had two things I'd kept in the back of my mind: (1) I was under pressure to make an action movie or two, which I really wasn't interested in, and (2) I'd been told that if said action movie featured Linda Blair (and what horror fan didn't love Linda Blair?), I'd make a lot of money.

Turned out Linda was available. For exactly one night. For fifty thousand dollars. So I came up with a silly, quick idea:

One night in Los Angeles, a woman (played by Linda Blair) walks into an office building. They let her upstairs, and she proceeds to kill a lot of people. But as she does so, she tells her tale of revenge . . . which is chronicled in the exploitation flicks I'd just bought from Eduard Sarlui. And *Savage Island* was born.

The shoot took only one night, and Linda was a total pro. Also, there were two guys, a comedy team, I was told, that a casting director begged me to put in the movie because they were trying to break into the business. At the very least, they needed SAG cards, and a movie appearance would get them into the union. One of them let Linda into the elevator on the ground floor, the other greeted her upstairs. And that, friends, was the first on-screen appearance of Penn Jillette, soon to become known as the more talkative half of Penn and Teller.

[It wasn't the first time I'd done that, by the way. A couple years earlier I'd done a similar favor—throwing an aspiring young actor-comedian into *Metalstorm* so he could get his SAG card. And for years after, long after he'd joined the cast of *SNL* and become famous, whenever he saw me at a party or a restaurant, Jon Lovitz always made it a point to come on over and thank me for that small favor.]

Anyway, Linda Blair ended up winning a Golden Raspberry Award that year for Worst Actress, but to be fair, *Savage Island* was only one of three movies named that earned her that honor. As for me, while the movie was being Frankensteined in the edit room, I went off to Cannes with a fantastic, lurid *Savage Island* poster featuring an impossibly long-legged Linda Blair. I presold the thing for a million dollars.

I don't know if that chafed at Eduard Sarlui, who'd basically handed me a million bucks in exchange for thirty thousand. To be honest, he was just an old family friend who weirdly happened to be in the same business that I was, and beyond that I didn't pay a lot of attention to him.

Maybe I should have.

Meanwhile, in our Los Angeles offices, I was about to come down with a severe case of the Yablanses.

It was Irwin who came to me first, my old boss-man from Compass International Pictures. Despite the success of *Halloween,* Irwin's company didn't make it very far into the eighties. He approached me about coming on board my new ship, maybe producing some stuff for Empire. Despite his volatile, irascible side, I liked Irwin. And he'd given my career a big boost.

"What kind of movies do you want to do?" I asked him.

"A ton of fucking stuff, Charlie. Bring me on to Empire and I will bring in great stuff. I just need an office and a phone."

I realized that this likely was . . . not entirely true. But he'd come up with something. I took him on.

It couldn't have been more than a month later when I took a call from Irwin's brother, Frank Yablans. Back in the day, Frank was actually a much bigger deal than Irwin. He ran Paramount in the early seventies, bringing in gigantic hits like *The Godfather* (parts 1 and 2) and *Chinatown*. You might remember him as a key player in Robert Evans's *The Kid Stays in the Picture.*

Frank himself had been edged out of the picture—losing Paramount to Barry Diller in 1974. Since then, he'd independently produced some real hits, including *Silver Streak, Mommie Dearest,* and *North Dallas Forty.* But when he called me, he too was looking for a ship to climb aboard. I soon discovered why he'd selected mine—Frank loved Italy and all things Italian as much as I did, and the idea of my Roman studio absolutely thrilled him.

"What do you have in mind?" I asked him.

"So much stuff, kid. Just give me an office and a phone and I'll make it rain." No, really—the identical pitch that his brother had just thrown me.

Well, he had a track record. And any friend of Italy was a friend of mine. I welcomed him aboard. So now I had two Yablanses joining Empire, filling out the third floor of our new L.A. offices, joining me and Debi up there, along with my dad (when he was in town) and the head of our theatrical division, Mike Ridges. [Side note: Also up there with us was Mike's assistant, an aspiring actor named Greg Kinnear.]

It was a pretty nice setup, except for one factor I hadn't been warned about:

The Yablans brothers fucking hated each other.

Mom and Dad with Uncle Joe and Aunt Marilyn.

Mr. Universe himself (Steve Reeves) and me on the set of *The Avenger*. This is also my last known picture with my appendix (not shown).

The membership card for the modestly named Ultimate ChaBa Club.

Opening night at the club. That's Meda behind me, and my mom offering the traditional Band family salute.

The proprietor of GODSIN, just turned seventeen. Near-death medical emergencies kept me fashionably slim.

RIGHT: Meda Home Entertainment, and the real Meda, at the dawn of the home video era.

With Roddy McDowall on the set of *Laserblast*, about to begin our life of crime.

Shooting *Trancers II* with Helen Hunt. Nearby, our dads were preparing for their cameos as Mustard Man and Chili Man.

On the set of *Parasite* (in 3-D!), here's Demi Moore and me in 2-D.

Megan Ward and Tim Thomerson and me, enjoying a non-quiet moment on *Trancers II*.

With actor, athlete, and blaxploitation legend Fred "The Hammer" Williamson, enjoying some downtime on the set of *Bada$$ Mothaf**kas!*

Gary Busey with his title character, the Gingerdead Man. Gary's the taller one.

The men responsible for more than 500 movies! At a signing event with the legendary Roger Corman.

The rise of my Roman Empire.

My dad and his friends on the set of *Ghoulies II*.

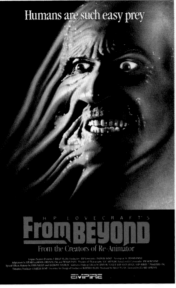

Movie posters throughout the years.

It's true. They'd been born one year apart in the mid-thirties, two headstrong, movie-loving, fast-talking Jewish guys from Brooklyn who'd both moved to Hollywood to make cinematic magic. And they hated each other.

Every day or two, the peaceful top floor of Empire would erupt into incredible Yablans-on-Yablans violence. Not physical violence, but it was pretty raw. It didn't matter whose office the fight started in, it would inevitably spill out into the main office, as these two red-faced fireplugs screamed and paced and stomped away from each other, only to whirl around again, waggle their fingers, and launch another stream of truly astonishing profanity. It was like having a little slice of Depression-era Brooklyn imported into our offices. But not the cute part with the newsies and the apple sellers.

Anything could touch them off—a lighting guy they both wanted to hire. Something as big as their mother's funeral or as small as a lunch order. Anything. For instance, one day I had to hang up on a call because of an unbelievable ruckus in the hall. I went to investigate.

Irwin was losing his mind: "A prison flick? A PRISON FLICK!? You goddamn motherfucking prick! *I'm* making a prison flick!"

"Shut your goddamn mouth and calm the fuck down. It's nothing like your shitty movie!"

"Shitty movie? You . . . I'm going to go to prison for real, because I'm going to rip your dumb head off and fuck your neck-hole!"

"Yeah, you'd like that, you miserable little fairy. But you won't, and you know why? Because you're a fucking pussy! And you know I'm right!"

"Right? What are you right about, you ugly pile of shit? You fucked me. You fucked me!"

At this point I could see that Mike Ridges had also hung up his phone and was waiting for me to do something. Young Greg Kinnear kept his head down, waiting for the storm to pass. I tried to get their attention, but they were too far gone.

Until Debi stepped between them. She started speaking softly, explaining to Irwin that his prison drama was in fact nothing like the screwball prison comedy that I had green-lit for Frank, that nobody was fucking anybody here, that it would all be okay. She put her hand gently on Irwin's arm, and he yanked it away. But she put her hand right back on him, smiling, understanding, undeniably pretty—a leading lady soothing a savage swamp monster.

Debi turned out to be adept at talking the brothers down and making peace. So now my beloved girlfriend had a new title to add to her growing résumé of production work: Yablans Wrangler.

Fortunately, those days didn't last for too long. Irwin would soon head to the middle of the country to produce *Prison* for me and spend too much of my money. And Frank couldn't wait to get to Italy and produce *Buy & Cell* and . . . spend too much of my money.

But let's be fair. I didn't need much help spending too much money. I was pretty good at that myself.

Making a sequel to *Ghoulies* was a no-brainer. Building an entire amusement park indoors . . . that was a different kind of no-brainer.

The studio in Rome was still a-humming, but things were changing. The lira, which had been so weak against the dollar, was rebounding fast. It didn't make as much sense to fly everybody and everything in from the States and rent all those hotel rooms, but I kept right on doing it. And I wasn't going to skimp on *Ghoulies II*—partly because it was such a valuable property, and partly because *Ghoulies II* was being directed by my dad. Incredibly, my dad hadn't yet directed a movie for me. This was going to be the one.

The movie takes place almost entirely at night at a giant carnival, the kind that pops up at homecomings and county fairs. It would've been pretty simple to rent such a place for a week or two, but for some reason I thought it'd be even better to rent all the equipment and build the thing from scratch. Indoors.

I have to admit, whether or not it was a good idea, it was *fun*. After all, we had one of the largest soundstages on the planet, the Big One upon which Dino de Laurentiis had filmed the hugest scenes in *The Bible*. Why not use it? I procured everything—a carousel, a Ferris wheel, bumper cars, a Tilt-a-Whirl, game booths—*everything*, and built a giant, fully-functioning carnival. Inside, on the big stage.

Was it a good idea? Maybe not. But once the lights were hung and the rides were powered up and the extras took their places and we suddenly had our own little monster-infested fun-house world contained in that vast Roman jewel box, there was no denying that it was extremely cool. I remember standing there with my dad, once it was up and running, watching the guys set up a shot, John Buechler fussing with one of his slimy little monsters, the Ferris wheel turning . . . just looking at this stupid, ridiculously expensive world we'd built.

My dad smiled. "This," he said. "This is crazy."

That moment alone made it worth every penny.

Back in the good old USA, Irwin Yablans was breaking out some major new talent for his first Empire feature. And alienating them as fast as he could.

Me, I was ping-ponging back and forth between Europe and

Los Angeles, and I was in L.A. to take a look at the auditions for Irwin's ghost-in-a-penitentiary revenge flick, *Prison*. One look at the tapes and it was obvious who Irwin's leading man should be—a young Danish American actor with almost no experience named Viggo Mortensen. He was a nice kid, and I was sure he'd do great with the no-name director we'd chosen: an ambitious kid from Finland named Renny Harlin. Also, I threw in Mac Ahlberg as their cinematographer, because as long as we had a Finn and a Dane, why not add a Swede? They were all ready to head out to Wyoming to shoot at an actual prison location when one afternoon my assistant told me that our young star wanted to have a word: "He said he wants to speak to you personally."

Uh-oh, I thought. Viggo got a better job. Or maybe his wife had talked him out of it. Had Irwin alienated him already? It couldn't be anything good. I picked up the phone.

"Mr. Band?" he asked tentatively. Another bad sign. Nobody called me "Mr. Band." I asked him what he wanted.

"About the movie . . ."

"Yes?"

"I'm being paid like fifteen hundred dollars a week, right?"

Okay, so that's his game. I started to ask myself how much more I could afford. I replied cautiously, "Yes, that was the deal, wasn't it?"

"Yes, but . . . Can I . . . can I get, like . . . a one-thousand-dollar advance?"

Awww. I was only a few years older than Viggo, so I knew where he was coming from. I wrote him a check. After all, it had only been a few years since I was an industry newcomer, pounding the pavement for work (while fleeing all contacts from the DMV!).

At around that exact same time, Debi found out that Renny Harlin and his housemate, who was writing *Prison,* didn't have a couch in their apartment. She immediately gave them one from the Empire offices. This was just how Hollywood worked—at least *my* Hollywood. I knew what it was like to be broke.

In fact, I was about to learn what that felt like all over again.

With my three Scandinavian wonders and Irwin Yablans safely sent off to their prison, I scrambled around L.A. for a while, making connections, prepping sales, starting projects. Financially, I felt like I was constantly trying to stay one step ahead of a looming tidal wave, but I tried to fight through it the only way I ever knew how, my personal mantra: "Keep making stuff."

Whenever I felt stressed or uninspired, I'd head for my Idea Room. It was right next to my office, and it was filled with stuff to inspire me: posters, knickknacks, art I'd bought or commissioned. A lot of the images were by artists I'd discovered in "Artist Alley" at Comic-Con, which I loved attending every year. So my Idea Room was full of amazing pictures, often grotesque or lurid, that the world had never seen. I'd try to pair up the images with the craziest, most eye-catching, most ridiculous exploitation titles I could dream up, and then bring 'em to my crew.

That's how we got *Slave Girls from Beyond Infinity.*

And *Sorority Babes in the Slimeball Bowl-O-Rama.*

And one of my personal favorites, *Assault of the Killer Bimbos.*

Those movies are all pretty silly, but they did well and continue to do well, oddly enough. *Bimbos* is particularly interesting, because it is often compared to a movie that came out three years later, *Thelma & Louise.* In fact, B-movie aficionado Joe Bob Briggs once devoted his entire TV show to the subject, screening the two movies back-to-back.

Listen: *Nobody* thinks Ridley Scott's film was stolen from mine—least of all me. But there are a lot of fun similarities. Both movies are about women in the American West hopping in a car and fleeing from the law, desperately trying to make it to Mexico. Both have scenes with our heroines getting revenge on men for treating them like bimbos. There are actually some lines of dialogue that are the same. But that's about it.

But—and I don't like to analyze this stuff too much—there's a reason why my movies often resemble stuff that came out years later, and it's not plagiarism. We exploitation filmmakers don't have the power or money to tell you what you want to see, to saturate you with ads, to fill the screen with A-list stars. No, the only advantage we have is immediacy. We have to put things on the screen that you want to see *right now*. Cultural moments are just that—moments. By the time a big studio finds a script and a director and a cast and works the principal photography into its schedule and agonizes through postproduction and prods the giant beast of its marketing department to find room on its release schedule and mobilize a campaign . . . that literally takes years. But if you want *me* to make a movie about what you're thinking about right now? Well, how's next Thursday? Just tell me what you want to see.

And what do you want to see? Well, boobs and blood and monsters and mayhem, of course! But it's more than that. To succeed, we have to give you stories, stories that satisfy something that's in the wind.

I'll give you an example that doesn't involve me: When I was a teenager and just arriving back in the country, suddenly "blaxploitation" films became a huge thing. This wasn't random. Martin Luther King Jr. had just been assassinated, and more of white America was beginning to wake up to the horrors of racism, to the nuance and power of Black culture. A dialogue was starting to happen. It'd be easy to say that cheap, violent movies full of stereotypes and bad acting were not a vital part of that dialogue, but they *were*. There was a hunger for communication, for getting things out in the open, for justice. And so, mixed in with all the kung fu and gunplay and ridiculous dialogue and bouncing boobs, there, on the screen, was a Black hero or heroine, kicking serious ass, being cheered by Black *and* white audiences. The major studios wouldn't touch that stuff for years.

That's as much of a sermon as you'll ever hear from me. But you can't tell me those movies weren't important.

Note: I'm not making an impassioned argument for the "importance" of *Assault of the Killer Bimbos*! After all, this is a movie that the *Los Angeles Times* called "a formidable attack on one's senses, good taste, patience, humor, and leisure time." I wish I had put that on the poster.

Anyway, one more thing about my movie, *Thelma & Louise*'s deformed older sister: I couldn't bring star power like Sarandon and Davis and Pitt. But we were able to bring in stars like Cassavetes and O'Neal!

Okay, it was *Griffin* O'Neal, the son of Ryan, and *Nick* Cassavetes, the son of John. But, hey, I made you look, didn't I? And that fact actually inspired me to leverage a similar trick in a spectacular way a year or two later, for my fine film *Beach Babes from Beyond*. But I can't tell you that story yet; we have to get back to my crumbling Empire.

I flew back to Italy, with a stop in New York along the way to drop in on my concerns in the Big Apple. Yes, I'd taken on a couple more producers, Tim Kincaid and Ed French, who were capable of churning out some videotastic movies for Empire. If mine were B movies, Tim and Ed's took the course pass/fail.

But they always passed. And their stuff was better than the other garbage being foisted on me by Crédit Lyonnais, who had a constant stream of crap that they demanded I release under my banner, which confused buyers and diluted the brand. I founded Empire because I wanted to make movies, but somehow I found myself releasing things I had no attachment to, just to stay afloat.

Market conditions were changing, because market conditions *always* change. The dollar was falling against the lira, and making movies in Italy was no longer a bargain. Still, in that four-year period I managed to make something like forty movies. I didn't fiddle while Rome burned. I *jammed*.

Also, if I'm being honest—and what's the point of these confessions if I'm not?—I am always a bit of a soft touch when it comes to requests for more money. If a little extra cash is going to make a movie better, you can talk me into spending a few thousand more than we budgeted. Now multiply that by the insane number of movies I was making, and what you get is a financial Jenga tower that improbably enough was still standing. For the moment.

Anyway, I was flying over the country when I used one of those newfangled "Skyfones" to check in with Mac in his rented prison, partly to see if anyone had locked Irwin in a cell yet. I wasn't far off.

"Hey, Mac, I was just flying over you and I thought I'd check in!"

"Charlie, it is doubtful that your flight plan would take you over Wyoming." Cinematographers. The good ones are very detail oriented.

"Okay—I was just checking in to see that things are going smoothly."

"Aha."

"So, are they?"

"Are they what?"

"Going smoothly."

"No, Charlie. They are not."

Here's what happened.

As it turned out, Renny Harlin was a young director who was a little full of himself and thought he knew everything. In other words, a young director. And Irwin was . . . Irwin. He kept pestering Renny to let him direct the second unit, to get all the shots that they'd need to cut the movie together. Eventually, Renny agreed, if only to get Irwin—who had an opinion about everything and nothing else to do in Wyoming—out of his hair.

On the morning of the shoot, though, Renny called Irwin in to his office to walk him through the shots.

"You're going to tell me what to do on a second unit?"

"Yes," Renny said. And this twentysomething, completely broke director walked the producer who hired him through each and every thing he needed, in deep detail, literally calling the shots, while Irwin sat there silently. When Renny was done, Irwin got up, thanked him, walked out, and headed off to lead his unit.

That night, they reunited with the rest of the team, including Mac, to watch the dailies. When Irwin's first second-unit shot came up on the screen, Renny immediately noticed that it wasn't right. No way would it match what Renny had already filmed. Then Irwin's next shot came up, and it was also completely wrong. And so was the next one. At this point Renny's looking at Irwin, who's just silently watching the screen, blank-faced in the flickering light, and Renny's wondering how anyone could mess things up so badly, thinking maybe the old guy had lost it, trying to figure out what he's going to say to Irwin and to me.

Finally, another shot comes up on the screen, and to Renny's surprise it's an exterior shot of Irwin Yablans, standing there, smiling, facing the camera. The camera pulls back to reveal that he's holding a sign that reads RENNY. Then the camera pulls back some more, to reveal the full sign:

RENNY—FUCK YOU!

I was happy to leave the chaos in the U.S. and get back to the chaos in Rome. Despite our troubles, Empire was running at a breakneck pace. Frank Yablans had assembled a great cast for his comedy *Buy & Cell,* including Malcolm McDowell, Robert Carradine, and the great wrestling/acting legend Rowdy Roddy Piper. Frank was also keeping Malcolm around for a second film, *The Caller.* Malcolm was a delight, Roddy was a riot, and, naturally, everyone was thrilled to be in Rome.

Around the same time, I was shooting *Pulse Pounders,* a trilogy of sorts—all short sequels to some of Empire's most successful movies. Including a follow-up to *Trancers,* reuniting me and Tim Thomerson and Helen Hunt, and a follow-up to *The Dungeonmaster,* which brought Richard Moll back into the picture. It was amazing to see everyone there, along with so many of the writers and directors that had become Empire's extended family. It felt almost like one of those star-studded series finales, where all your favorite characters come together for one last blowout party.

I didn't realize how close that was to the truth.

But what a party! As most of these movies approached their final days of photography, I threw a full-on, pull-out-all-the-stops bash at the castle. I recently found some home movies I took of the event, and seeing it all for the first time in thirty years brought back to me how fundamentally insane that chapter of my life was. I was working and playing around the clock, making movies and living it up in two of the most incredible cities on the face of the earth.

There on the screen is Tim Thomerson, enjoying some pasta and cracking up the whole table. Helen Hunt is at another table, talking to my mom. Out on the terrace in the afternoon sun my daughter Taryn, then ten, runs up to me and I twirl her in the air a few times. Everyone's dancing to Madonna, all the actors and actresses and crew, but the guy stealing the show is my six-year-old son Alex, who is dancing on a table, shirtless, expertly lip-syncing each word, every inch the genuine rock star he would become in a decade or so. Behind him, Ben Vereen looks on approvingly. If there was trouble in paradise, you'd never know it from the tapes.

Right before leaving Italy, I oversaw one last project, probably the most ridiculously expensive thing Empire ever attempted. It was called *Arena,* a giant sci-fi flick about a galactic gladiatorial wrestling competition, featuring humans and all kinds of monstrous aliens duking it out. It was Irwin Yablans's baby, and I brought him over to Italy to send us even further into debt and to fight with his brother. That said, there's a lot to like about *Arena,* Empire's biggest and last glorious folly.

One other event marked the end of those days. On August 8, 1988—8-8-88—at a castle on top of a mountain in Umbria, Mr. Charles Band married Ms. Debra Dion. We'd started in the Hollywood Hills four years before, and now we were sealing the deal at the top of an Italian mountain, surrounded by flowers and ancient stonework and a giant menagerie of friends and family. It was a beautiful day.

Back in Los Angeles, I threw myself right back into the business of Fixing Everything. I was still new to this whole "studio head," "movie mogul" business, but I could read a spreadsheet. The numbers didn't look good. I had a plan, of course. Maybe if I made another couple of movies, but this time with—

—the phone rang. It was Eduard Sarlui, my old neighbor, the man who'd introduced me to Crédit Lyonnais. He had something he wanted to discuss, and it didn't sound sociable. I went to his office.

As you know by now, I usually think the best of people. And although I have a pretty good memory for most things, I tend to forget the bad stuff, or at least push it to the back of my mind so I can continue to move forward. Maybe that's because of my near-death experiences in those third-world hospitals. I don't know. I consider it a positive trait.

That afternoon, Eduard Sarlui was studied and serious, his pursed lips even tighter than usual. He seemed very sympathetic. He made it clear, in his roundabout way of speaking, that he wasn't really there as Eduard Sarlui; he was representing the bank. And the bank wasn't happy. I told Eduard about the movies I had in development. He dismissed that sort of talk.

"Charlie, it is not about more movies. It is about where we are. And the bank . . . the bank has lost confidence in you. According to their records, you have now personally amassed a debt of . . . one moment, I have it here . . . of twenty-six million dollars."

Oh, shit.

Eduard smoothly continued, though. It turned out that he was prepared to propose a deal on behalf of Crédit Lyonnais. They would forgive my debt—*all* if it, with a stroke of a pen. All I had to do was walk away from Empire—the name, my offices in L.A., my studio in Rome, and every movie and intellectual property I created with them. All of it.

Oh. Shit.

I drove back home. I talked to Debi. I talked to my lawyers. I talked to my dad. No matter how we looked at it, it was clear: Empire was dead. I had to take the deal.

I managed to get a couple of small concessions out of them. I got to keep the movies I had currently in development. And I got to keep *Trancers,* because that was my baby and I still thought there was some value there, whereas to the bank it was just one of forty movies they were about to own.

A few days later I was at Eduard Sarlui's house in Beverly Hills, signing the papers. He radiated sympathy, every inch the refined European patrician, helping bail out an old family friend. It was the only thing that was reassuring about the whole mess—the presence of a man I'd known since I was ten years old. Still, as I drove home, I was suddenly a guy who had . . . well, nothing. A couple of properties, maybe. The ideas in my head. A great family and tons of friends and loved ones. Okay, not *nothing*. Not to me.

Oh, I also still had a castle. Which seemed a little less enchanting now that I literally had no business in Italy anymore.

I tried to start looking forward right away. We took everything we needed from the old Empire offices over the next week, transporting stuff to some new temporary offices I rented in the Valley, a place with no name on the door because there was no company. Friends and colleagues dropped by to pick up stuff and to say goodbye. Stuart Gordon, Ted Nicolaou. I kept it upbeat. I told them all that we would rise again.

Okay, those words sounded slightly less convincing as we were literally being escorted out of the building. But I meant it.

A few days later, news of all this hit the trades, along with an important update: Charles Band's Empire Pictures was gone. Dissolved. All of its assets, its movies, and its studio outside Rome had been sold, through Crédit Lyonnais, to "Epic Entertainment," which would continue the business under the direction of its founder and president . . .

. . . Eduard Sarlui.

The Bachelor Party

Okay, I wanted to set this one aside, because it isn't really my story. Even though I was there. Kind of.

Here's what I can remember. It was a gorgeous Los Angeles spring evening in 1988, and I was just starting to settle in after a long day's work, when two of my closest friends, Gary Allen and Ted Nicolaou, showed up at my door. They'd met through me, but now they were close—a couple of fun stoner buddies. They were excited. "Charlie, you gotta come with us, we'll smoke a bone, get some food, come on!" I was a never a huge fan of pot, and I was tired, but they were unusually pushy that night. I went.

Within minutes I was in the car, and minutes later they were putting a massive joint in my mouth, and within minutes of *that* I was more stoned and disoriented than I have ever been in my life. Before or since. I really don't like feeling like that, so I was glad when we arrived at a really nice Middle Eastern restaurant in West Hollywood where I could sink into a dark booth and disappear while I got my head back together. We were led into the back room, and

"SURPRISE!!"

The room was full of like forty dudes, from around the world, a giant assembly of friends and colleagues. It was my surprise bachelor party.

Oh god.

Actors. Directors. Stuart Gordon. Distributors. Stefano. My dad. I sat down, barely keeping it together. The room was filling up with even more weed smoke, and I was trying not to breathe because I didn't want to get even *more* high, and here's where I have to take other people's word for what went down.

There were belly dancers. Three of them. Incredibly skilled, incredibly sexy, incredibly . . . close to me. They danced and shook and shimmied around the room. Next to me, Stefano was completely stoned (as usual) and loving it all . . .

Meanwhile, at the door, Debi stood and watched with Ted and Gary's wives, Becky and Barbara. They were a pretty tight team at that point, Empire's Angels. They'd paid off the manager to let them invade. And have their music ready.

Also, they had spent the day buying and putting on complete, beautiful, skimpy belly-dancer outfits.

They waited for their moment, the second that the real belly dancers left, and then they charged into the room, veiled, whooping and yelling and gyrating like mad. Naturally, they zeroed in on Ted and Gary and me.

I was barely aware of anything but the fact that this new belly dancer was a little more . . . *aggressive* than the last. Meanwhile, across the room, as soon as Barbara sat herself down on Gary's lap and started moving, he exclaimed: "Heyyyyy! I know that butt. That's either my wife or my brother-in-law!"

Elsewhere, Ted tried to extricate himself from his plight by tipping his new "dancer" a dollar. Becky immediately ripped off her veil and yelled (in her amazing southern accent), "Ted, you bastard, I *saw* you—you gave that real belly dancer FIVE DOLLARS!"

The room was now dissolved in laughter, riotous, choking, uproarious laughter. And I was unaware of all of it. I was still super-duper high, and this anonymous succubus was gyrating in front of me, hypnotizing me, like some kind of weird erotic dream . . .

And then, frustrated by my complete stoned cluelessness, the gyrating anonymous succubus in question ripped off her veil and said, "Charlie! It's me, Debi."

By all reports, I then let out an uncanny, high-pitched shriek and literally jumped into Stefano's lap.

9

Full Moon Rising

(1989–1991)

Believe it or not, I didn't spend much time being angry at Eduard. Even now, as I tell this story, I still can't bring myself to dwell on it for too long. It happened. I couldn't afford to dwell on the bad stuff back then, and I don't see the point of doing it now—even while writing a memoir! I'm just not wired that way.

Debi was not so sanguine. As it became clear what Eduard had done, she launched into several spectacular tirades. On the subject of Eduard Sarlui, she went Full Yablans, as did a bunch of other people in my life. For me, though, it was losing Empire that hurt, and that would've happened with or without Eduard Sarlui. Moving on . . .

Well, wait, I oughta tie up that storyline. I wasn't worried that

Eduard was going to do something great with my studio and take the credit. Eduard just wasn't an idea guy. He lacked the talent, and even with the studio and library I'd so helpfully built for him, I was pretty confident his new venture wouldn't last long.

It didn't. He produced a few movies as Epic Productions, none of which attracted much attention. He and his partner ran into trouble almost immediately, and a couple of short years later, in '91, the bank took over Epic. By '93 Eduard and his partner were suing Crédit Lyonnais, because they apparently hadn't been paid for "their" studio and properties. I don't know what happened to Eduard after that. Early on I'd see him at film markets, and I avoided talking to him, but after he lost the farm he disappeared from the scene.

Crédit Lyonnais didn't fare so well, either. It was plunged into scandal, sued for fraud, its properties were sold off, and it nearly went bankrupt in 1993. It was finally absorbed by another bank in 2003, a victim of years of shady, old-school European financing, as well as something that I like to call the Band Curse. Actually, it was probably more likely the Dion Curse. You do not fuck with Debi Dion.

The downside to all of this is that when Crédit Lyonnais started to circle the drain, they sold off a lot of their assets, including most of my Empire movies, to MGM, where the rights reside to this day. People still rent *Ghoulies* and *Re-Animator* and *Troll,* so MGM really has no reason to sell them back to me. But someday . . . *someday . . .*

I tried not to pay much attention to any of this at the time. Losing Empire was a big blow. It was incredibly sad, almost like the death of a loved one. But I approached it like being released from those horrible hospitals—I stepped outside, took a deep breath, and didn't think about how weakened I was or what had been taken from me. I moved on.

Within a couple of weeks of losing it all, I was already throwing myself frenetically into a new venture that would carry me to new heights, where I would build a new company and a new, gigantic movie studio, literally in an empty Romanian field, and make hundreds of movies and millions of dollars. And I was determined not to make the same old mistakes.

The good news is that I *didn't* make the same old mistakes. I made exciting new ones!

I don't remember exactly how I hooked up with Paramount Pictures, but it was an easy, comfortable fit. I had a track record, and they were putting a lot of money into a business that to me was obviously the future of entertainment: home video. Direct-to-video home video. Why lose money in theatrical releases? All I really needed was great distribution, advertising, and prime placement on the video shelves. Paramount had all that stuff in place, and I had some ideas as to how they could do it better.

At the time, the guy running business affairs at Paramount's home entertainment division was a man named Jim Gianopulos, He was young, energetic, and almost exactly my age, and we hit it off immediately. With his encouragement, I finished the properties I'd walked out of Empire with, and I distributed them through Paramount. Those movies did great, and suddenly I was the entire division's darling. I immediately used that goodwill to pitch them a sweeping vision for my new venture. Before I get to that, one of those first couple of movies is worth mentioning.

Cannibal Women in the Avocado Jungle of Death was a hoot all the way through. Written and directed by an immensely talented young dude, J. F. Lawton, it's a fantastic piece of satire—kind of a loving send-up of B movies while absolutely *being* a B movie, and playing with all the tropes of sexism and feminism and commercialism that were dominating our culture back then (and still are!).

The cast was amazing, too. It featured Shannon Tweed, a former Playmate of the Year, whom you may know as the partner of Gene Simmons, the front man for KISS. They were already inseparable back then. We also had Adrienne Barbeau, whom you may know as Rizzo from the Broadway cast of *Grease,* the TV show *Maude,* or the movie *Escape from New York,* but whom I also knew as the former Mrs. John Carpenter.

To round out the cast we needed a scoundrel, a guy who could exude some of that Harrison Ford energy and also really land a joke. J.F. and I both knew who it had to be—a comedian I'd seen at the Improv who seemed to have all the right tools. His name was Bill Maher.

The movie did really well, and it's still a lot of fun to see today. And despite its somewhat adult themes, it was rated a family-friendly PG-13, which I think earns me the distinction of being the only producer in the 1980s to have Shannon Tweed keep her clothes on. Which, for that era, was just about the most perverse thing you could do!

Right as we were wrapping *Cannibal Women,* J. F. Lawton offered me another script he'd just written. It was a dark, kind of sleazy tale of a Hollywood hooker trying and failing to pull herself out her sad, impoverished existence. It was good, but it obviously wasn't my kind of thing. It was too dark to be a sex comedy, and it was conspicuously devoid of monsters, time travelers, and murderous toys. I thanked J.F. and passed on it.

J.F. did find a home for that script, though. He got it to Garry Marshall, who immediately demanded that J.F. make it lighter, funnier, and give it a fairy-tale ending. Well, *that* worked, and soon J.F. was receiving applause, large royalty checks, and a WGA Award for Best Screenplay, for *Pretty Woman*.

After my first few properties did so well for Paramount, I was their new Golden Boy of home video. It wasn't just my movies they liked—they liked my patter, my spiels, the way I truly understood how to approach the exploding home market. And I didn't waste any time—within a few months I asked Jim Gianopulos to assemble the crew so I could pitch my vision for the next Charlie Band company.

They assembled on the Paramount lot in one of those big conference rooms, and I came in with drawings, posters, paraphernalia. I wanted to project the image of a company that was already in full flower; all they had to do was jump on board. Of course, at the time I just had a few ideas and some really cool artwork, one piece of which was a sketch of a steamer trunk full of extremely evil-looking puppets . . .

After a little glad-handing and kidding around, I took over the room and hit 'em with my pitch. "Guys," I said, "it's called Full Moon Features. And I want it to be the Marvel Comics of the nineties."

One thing I never lacked was ambition.

A decade or so later, of course, Marvel would become the absolute biggest name in blockbuster movies. But this was 1989. I was talking about the Marvel Comics of my childhood. I used to spend hours of those golden Roman afternoons poring over my Marvel comics. I loved the characters, of course, and their wild storylines. But I also loved the world they created. Marvel heroes and villains would cross over from one book to the next, show up in each other's storylines, be part of giant events that would span multiple titles. And I loved the degree of what we now call "transparency." Marvel had a real relationship with its readers; they responded to fan letters in every issue. And there, at the end of every book, you could find "Stan's Soapbox," where the great Stan Lee would write about the process, his writers and artists, or just spout off about the real issues of the day, like the Vietnam War or racism. Marvel gave you an entire universe to live in.

That's what I pitched to Paramount that afternoon. Full Moon would be more than a studio. More than a brand. We'd be a universe unto itself: a vast, creepy, sci-fi-and-horror universe of interlocking franchises where fans could either dip in for occasional stories or immerse themselves in the world. Crossovers. Multiple sequels. A video magazine at the end of each VHS tape, *my* "Stan's Soapbox," where I could talk to fans and let them look behind the scenes, a feature I called the "Full Moon Video Zone." To make it dependable and fan friendly, I set up the implausible goal of releasing a new movie every thirty days!

I literally worked up a sweat spinning this elaborate vision to the guys, then calmed myself down and paused, giving them a chance to react.

They went bananas. Full Moon was born.

For my first Full Moon movie, Jim Gianopulos gave me something I pretty much never got from a studio, before or since: a fair deal. Rather than Paramount's giving me money up front and leveraging that to own a bigger piece of my property, I would fund the movie myself and get a fair share of its receipts. Plus, I'd retain the rights to my movies—I wasn't going to get Empired again.

A good deal was essential, because I knew what movie we'd start with. It was an idea I'd been playing with for a long time.

I pitched it to the Paramount gang with that sketch I'd commissioned, an old steamer trunk, opened, revealing a menagerie of puppets:

Puppet Master marked the birth of Full Moon—and the rebirth of my career as well. They could take Empire from me, but I still had my friends, my collaborators, my family. I got the band back together. The Band band. David Schmoeller directed. My brother Richard wrote a beautiful, haunting orchestral score. Dave Allen signed on to do all the stop-motion animation it would take to bring those nefarious puppets to life.

By this point I was completely over the idea of getting "Name" actors to bring in an audience. That seemed like old-school thinking. If you were in the video store and you wanted to see a movie about killer dolls, the presence of some old star from the seventies wasn't going to affect your decision. But I did want someone special for the beginning of *Puppet Master,* someone to add some gravitas to the part of the old, World War II–era puppet-maker Andre Toulon. And for that I found Bill Hickey. Bill had recently been nominated for an Academy Award for playing the withered old don in *Prizzi's Honor,* with Jack Nicholson and Anjelica Huston. But although he was withered, he was far from old—he suffered from some kind of medical condition that made him look much older than his fiftysomething years. He was perfect as Toulon.

As important as the movie itself, though, was the way it would be released. I had a plan. It involved making sure that all of America's video stores had reason to feature our release, give it prime placement, put up some posters, etc. And the only way to make that happen was to get Paramount's marketing guys excited.

Remember how I said that my Full Moon movies never screened theatrically? That was a little bit of a lie. The movies were shot on 35mm film, and they all *did* have screenings. *One* screening, on the Paramount lot. I made sure it was a real event, with the Paramount team as the guests of honor. At that first one I had the legendary Forrest Ackerman on hand, the man who essentially created sci-fi fandom, editor and writer of *Famous Monsters of Filmland,* a pre-*Fangoria* bible for anyone who followed *my* kind of movies. The whole event was done up Hollywood-movie-premiere style, and then we watched *Puppet Master* in one of Paramount's screening rooms.

It blew the marketing guys away. They were just the allies I needed to make this film big. This might sound like a minor detail, but listen: When video store owners opened their packages from the studios each month, those packages came jam-packed with Stuff. Swag. Display materials. Dolls, tchotchkes, cardboard stand-ups, and a big catalog describing the movies on the tapes within. The packaging of these materials was key, and my Paramount marketing guys made sure Full Moon movies looked slick and legitimate. I was a B moviemaker, sure, but those Full Moon releases became what I called "counterfeit A movies," getting themselves right up there on the shelf with the big theatrical hits. The idea was that the placement—along with the right promotional campaign—would make my movies feel like big-budget A movies that you somehow happened to have missed when they were in the theater.

It worked. To this day, I have fans come up to me and say, "Man, I loved *Puppet Master.* My mom wouldn't let me see it in the theater, but me and my friends rented it . . ."

I usually don't correct them. Why destroy an illusion I worked so hard to create?

It couldn't have gone better. *Puppet Master* wound up being one of the biggest hits of the year, and because of my deal with Jim Gianopulos, I finally got to see a real share of the profits. That movie made me several million dollars.

A year after Empire had been wiped off the map, I was back on it!

Speaking of which, Empire wasn't the only property that had been wiped off the map. Over in Europe, the entire Eastern Bloc was collapsing. One month after *Puppet Master* hit the video stores, the Berlin Wall came down and Germany was reunited. Inspired by that, one month later the Romanian uprising was sealed with the execution of their hated dictator, Nicolae Ceaușescu, and his wife, by firing squad, on Christmas Day. It was televised. Those Romanians, I swear—they do darkness *right*.

Before you accuse me of hyperbole: no, I'm not saying Full Moon was involved in the fall of the Iron Curtain.

But it was about to be.

A couple of months after Ceaușescu met his demise, I was at the American Film Market in Los Angeles (the U.S.'s answer to Cannes and Milan), peddling my new slate of movies. By now I was a full-fledged success, Paramount/Full Moon's wunderkind. The only fly in the ointment was that I hadn't yet seen all those millions from *Puppet Master,* but I needed to ramp up production *now*. Which forced me to make some less-savory deals with Paramount in order to keep things moving through the pipeline. That didn't seem so bad; I'd seen the sales numbers and knew my money was coming. And I was on the lookout for opportunity on the floor of the AFM, shaking hands, talking about the future.

It was then that I was approached by a stranger, dressed all in black, with a Transylvanian accent.

Okay, it wasn't nearly that creepy. And to be honest, I don't think he was clad in black. It was 1990, so he was probably wearing green pleated pants with a matching sports jacket over a T-shirt. And he wasn't scary at all—Ion actually seemed pretty cool.

But he did have *that* accent. And he had what he considered urgent business.

"I vant you to come to Romania," he said. "To make movies."

He laid out his pitch. He knew I had owned a studio in Rome, and he said there was a beautiful movie studio in Bucharest. Ceaușescu was a monster, of course, but he and his wife had also been big fans of the arts, and so they'd maintained theaters, opera houses, and a world-class movie studio. It was still in operation, sort of, and all the personnel were still being paid by the government. All I had to do, said Ion, was bring a cast and a script. He would cover everything else.

"Well," I said, "I do have a vampire movie I was hoping to make at some point . . ."

"Come see," said Ion.

I checked with the State Department to see if any bans or advisories were in effect. No bans. But a heavy warning—things were unstable, and U.S. citizens were advised not to travel there.

Okay. But it wasn't strictly a *ban*. Ion's deal sounded pretty fantastic. I went.

I want to be clear—I wasn't courting danger. I was courting opportunity. I was spending a lot of time in Italy anyway (more on that in a minute), and it wasn't a big deal to hop on over to Romania. And even though things were a mess there, I knew they'd turn it around. It was an educated, sophisticated population. Plus, unlike, say, Hungarian, Romanian is a Romance language (hence the name!)—anyone with a background like mine could get by just fine with the locals. With all that in mind, I booked a flight on their airline, TAROM . . .

. . . straight into hell.

The first thing that would've scared people off was the plane itself. An ancient jet, painted inside with horrifying old sterile colors and lit with cheapo fluorescent lighting, a motley assortment of drinks served on a rickety hospital gurney that shell-shocked-looking attendants rattled down the aisle. The air was thick with smoke, too, because in Romania at that time it was rare to find an adult human without a cigarette in their mouth.

When I landed in Bucharest . . . Jesus. I have to confess that the airport almost made me turn around. It was bad. Like, prison-camp bad. Ramshackle old wooden structures, wire fences, soldiers everywhere carrying heavy automatic weaponry. It was gruesome and depressing. But true to his word, Ion was there at the airport, looking somewhat embarrassed, with what he hoped was an encouraging smile on his face.

We drove in Ion's ancient, sputtering, Eastern Bloc automobile into downtown Bucharest. Despite all the truly terrible fascistic monstrosities Ceaușescu had erected, enough of the beautiful, vibrant old city remained. The people were wonderful. The studio, though run down, was serviceable. It seemed to me that Romania was down but not out.

I told Ion that I thought we could do some business together, and he was overjoyed. As I flew back to Rome, I knew exactly who I needed to make this harebrained idea work. I called Ted Nicolaou.

I haven't told you nearly enough about Ted Nicolaou. He's kind of an amazing character and a big part of my life. He came to me with David Schmoeller and the rest of the *Texas Chain Saw Massacre* guys. He edited a bunch of stuff for me, including *Ghoulies,* and quickly became my jack-of-all-trades, because he could handle absolutely anything. With his cool, sardonic Texas hipster look and his easy manner, he was a dude I could send into virtually any situation. He became—and I mean this in the most flattering way—my test subject. My Man on the Ground. If the situation was going to be weird, it was time to send in Agent Nicolaou. Somebody needed to get back to L.A. to write and direct fifty thousand dollars' worth of Linda Blair to edit into a South American prison flick? Send in Agent Nicolaou.

Need to fly a dude into a dangerous former Eastern Bloc country to shoot a vampire movie with the locals?

Agent Nicolaou.

It didn't take long to convince Ted. I hooked him up with the right people, and we started developing what would become *Subspecies*. It seemed like a crazy idea, but we went for it. At the time, we had no idea what a huge thing would rise from the seeds we planted in that fertile Romanian soil. Ted got to work. I got back to Rome.

Now that Full Moon had risen from Empire's ashes, it was time to get projects rolling again. And Stuart Gordon came to me with an idea. Like all Stuart's ideas, it sounded kind of expensive. He wanted to make Edgar Allan Poe's *The Pit and the Pendulum*. That hadn't been done as a movie since Roger Corman had done it thirty years before, and it seemed pretty challenging: dungeons, torture chambers, witches burning, medieval courtyards. I mean, those were the kinds of giant sets that'd cost a fortune to build, unless you shot it all at some kind of . . .

. . . castle.

Oh. Right.

In truth, I'd been wanting to shoot stuff at my castle for a while. It had come a long way since '85. Entire wings were now habitable. In fact, I had just done some entertaining there. I'd invited my biggest buyers—the Germans, Japanese, and English—to join me at my castle after the Milan film market. They all jumped at the chance.

This was beyond schmoozing. It was megaschmoozing. Their faces as they were driven up the mountain and escorted into the castle were priceless. These men were accustomed to filmmakers taking them to lunch and maybe giving them a key chain with a logo on it.

I led them to their guest wing. I'm not sure if I carried a candelabra in front of me or not, but it was definitely implied!

In the first two rooms I placed my new, dear friend Nigel Greene and his brother, Trevor. Nigel was a pioneer of the British home video industry. Next to him I put Nigel's parents. My two Germans, a couple, went in the next room, and my three Japanese businessmen, traveling alone, went in the final three. Each room, mind you, was cavernous and beautiful and full of treasures, virtually a museum. Debi and I went off to our chambers and prepared for the evening's feast. The Lord and Lady of Castle Giove had to look their best.

We wined and dined our guests thoroughly, and then Rolando escorted them all back to their wing. The Lord and Lady retired, giggling like idiots.

In the morning, I met Rolando in the kitchen and asked him how our guests fared. He said there'd been a problem.

"Charlie, your English friends were fine, and I didn't hear a peep from the Germans, but those Japanese men . . ."

"Oh no. What?"

"They kept running back and forth . . . and then they all slept in the same bed."

I gently asked them about it at breakfast. Here's what I learned: When you're used to the confines of crowded Tokyo, even a modest European hotel room can seem uncomfortably large. These cavernous castle rooms just flat-out creeped the hell out of my Japanese friends. They freaked out. So they crammed themselves into one bed for the night. When I pressed them in the comforting light of day they were hilarious about it, and we all had a huge laugh and enjoyed the rest of our stay. But it was a reminder to me: Holy cow, I own a frickin' *castle*. I gotta use this place.

And so we went to shoot two movies in Italy. The first was Stuart's *The Pit and the Pendulum*. My dad once again came along to produce—as always, Stuart's trusted, more thrifty sidekick. They had come to love each other. Our cast included good ol' Lance Henriksen as Torquemada, who, since *Mansion of the Doomed,* had become famous for his role of Bishop in the Alien movies. And we had Oliver Reed, the renowned British actor, who years before had actually cut his teeth in Hammer Films productions, the great English B-movie mill of the 1960s.

It was really awesome. A trip. We'd all wake up in our palatial rooms, grab coffee and breakfast, and then descend two flights of stairs to our sets—the beautifully lit dungeons and torture chambers—and work a full, long day, only to ascend back to the great dining hall, where at least eighteen of us would feast and laugh for hours, and then return to our rooms to start the whole cycle again.

It wasn't without its problems. Lance was a Method actor, so living inside the role of the monstrous Torquemada wasn't exactly a picnic for him. Or for the crew.

Oliver Reed was a kind of Method actor as well, but his method was constant alcohol intake. He was clearly cut from the Richard Harris–Peter O'Toole mold of British actors. I soon learned that he spent his early mornings down in the village, at the bar, consuming as much beer as possible. On set, though, he was totally lucid and completely professional. Then, at dinner, he would laugh and drink vast quantities and never once get up as he held forth, joking and pontificating for literally hours on end, always the last man at the table as we all retired. It became a joke between Debi and me, because Oliver's routine didn't even seem physically possible, not given the sheer amount of liquid he took in.

A few days later we learned Oliver Reed's dark secret.

It was Rolando who discovered it, learning it from the housekeeping staff. Oliver had rigged up a system where he'd acquire empty bottles, sequester them, and then . . . relieve himself into them all night, right there at the table as he drank and joked and held forth.

Wait, did I say "dark secret"? I meant "gross secret."

My other movie in the castle was more personal. Just as in the Empire days, my constant hamster wheel of developing, producing, promoting, and selling kept me from doing other things. It had been a year or two since I'd carved out a three-week period to just direct a movie. I remedied that situation with *Meridian*.

It wasn't typical Full Moon fare. I mean, there were monsters and magic and mammaries, sure. But *Meridian* was a Gothic romance. Harlequin novels were huge at the time, and some of them were supernatural themed. Why not grow the Full Moon brand into a market that nobody else was in?

Meridian was essentially a Beauty and the Beast story, the tale of an American woman (who happens to be the heir to an Italian castle!) who falls in love with a magician—who is cursed to turn into a beast-man. It starred Sherilyn Fenn, who—soon after the movie came out—found herself on the cover of *Rolling Stone* magazine as one of the stars of *Twin Peaks*. We shot the whole thing in the castle. Except for some of the exteriors, which we filmed at the nearby ancient "Park of the Monsters."

About that . . .

It seems too perfect to be true, but in the nearby town of Bomarzo, there had lived in the sixteenth century a wealthy mercenary who'd met, fallen in love with, and married a noble-woman. When she died, he commissioned a grand garden for her, a place of wonders, a theme park of sorts. Giant stone carvings are everywhere: Hannibal's enormous war elephants, thirty feet high; goddesses; a monstrous gargoyle whose open mouth you could walk into (and out of, dramatically, while lit from behind at night, for instance!). To this day most tourists don't hear of the Parco dei Mostri, but my neighbors were all too happy to point me toward it. It was bizarre, grotesque, and perfect.

The last element I needed was the Beast. But this couldn't be a Buechler puppet or a Dave Allen stop-motion special. In any romantic Beauty and the Beast tale, after all, at some point, well . . . Beauty bangs the Beast. And it can't look like a woman humping a marionette (although now that I say that out loud, it gives me an idea for a movie . . . but I digress!). I needed a costume, a rough, scary, but somehow human-looking and kinda sexy beast.

I called Greg Cannon in Los Angeles. He was at that moment doing effects makeup for Francis Ford Coppola's new horror flick, *Bram Stoker's Dracula,* starring Gary Oldman and Winona Ryder. Yes, big-budget horror was becoming a thing. What chance did I have?

Greg was more than helpful. He told me of a costume that they'd just used on set, Dracula in beast form, hypnotizing and seducing the helpless Lucy. "Charlie," Greg said, "this thing is perfect. But obviously it belongs to the production. I can't . . ." Greg seemed to be struggling with something. He was moving into the big-budget movies, but his roots were in my world. I let him talk.

"I'll tell you what I'll do," he said finally, as though I'd been twisting his arm. "I will steal the costume, dye it, change its look just enough, and you can use it in your movie."

"Wow," I said, waiting for the inevitable other shoe to drop.

"Just one condition, though, Charlie," he said. Here it comes, I thought.

"Yeah?"

"You have to bring me there. I gotta see that castle."

Word had gotten out.

Greg got his wish, and I got my sexy beast-man. It was almost certainly the only monster suit in movie history to be featured in two separate roles . . . and get laid in both.

A couple of years later, Greg would receive the first of his five Oscars for his makeup work on *Dracula,* as would the guy who built that costume. But as I said, we independents have one advantage, and that is speed: if you were a fan of a certain kind of video rental back in the day, you got to see that award-winning monster in action over a year *before* the premiere of *Dracula.*

I've never told that story to the public before, for obvious reasons. But hopefully enough time has passed, so, um, Francis, if you're reading this, er . . . sorry! *Mi dispiace.*

Master of Puppets

Every once in a while a nervous young fan, probably one whose parents let them see *Puppet Master* at too tender an age, will ask me, in a whisper, "The puppets . . . are they real?"

"Yes," I tell them matter-of-factly. And after they gasp I add, "They're real puppets."

And they can be a pain in the ass.

Sure, I've used stop-motion animation here and there, but that's way too expensive to do for more than a couple of shots. Most of the meat-and-potatoes shots of Blade and his terrifying brethren have to be done with good old-fashioned rod puppetry, and that comes with its own set of challenges. Especially back before we had CGI to wipe out our worst blunders, we always had tons of problems to solve for each shot. For instance, those puppets can't really move from the spot you place 'em in, because they're controlled by a couple of rods from below.

"Below?" Yeah, about that . . .

For most of the important locations in the Puppet Master movies, we had to build sets on platforms that were four or five feet off the ground so that our puppeteers had some room to maneuver. It's cramped down there, and it can get pretty chaotic. It takes two people to operate each puppet, so if you've got a scene with Blade and Leech Woman and Pinhead and Tunneler all conspiring over their next bit of mayhem, suddenly you've got eight guys down there, craning their necks to see through cracks in the set, jostling each other, yelling instructions or bitching that they can't see or hear anything. A lot of the time, what's going on beneath is more exciting than what's happening in the scene.

Sometimes you can get a monitor down there so a puppeteer can see his work in real time. That's a technique that Jim Henson pioneered with his Muppets, but it comes with a unique challenge: when you're looking at the monitor and you want the puppet to turn toward the left side of the screen, you have to turn the puppet *right*. That's hard enough for the big movements, but doing the detailed work . . . it can really mess with your head. You basically have to learn to rewire your brain, because you're performing in MirrorWorld.

When we didn't have monitors for everyone, the puppeteers had to resort to either (1) peering through the cracks or (2) performing blind. With enough teamwork (and enough hilarious, frustrated screaming) you can make that work. But you have to have a clear game plan and communicate super clearly, because up on the surface, where the movie is being shot, the director has to make sure the movements are right *and* that the camera isn't seeing those damn rods. So it's not ideal, but hey, it adds just a little bit of extra anger to a demonic puppet's performance!

I still like to shoot real puppets instead of CGI—it feels so much more organic, and to this day I don't think anything can take a viewer out of a movie like bad, unconvincing CGI. But computer effects have made things a lot easier. Nowadays you can put puppeteers right on the set without worrying about the cameras seeing the rods, because the rods can be virtually erased with a swipe of the digital pen. It's still labor intensive, yes, but at the end of the day, if I can make a creepy puppet with a drill bit on his head tunnel through the sternum of a terrified, screaming human . . . it's all worth it.

10

Unreal Estate

I went back to L.A. The nineties were upon us, my business was humming along, and I had entered another of those golden periods of my life where I could do no wrong. Paramount was loving me—they wanted me in on every meeting, pitching, evangelizing about the home video revolution. The one snag was that Jim Gianopulos had left Paramount. In order to keep my business rolling at full speed I had to take increasingly less advantageous deals. At the time I didn't worry; money was pouring in, and I was having a blast.

Jim, by the way, did well for himself. He went over to Fox and turned the company around, cleverly retooling its studios and its business to take on the twenty-first century (no small feat for a studio that had literally been named after the twentieth century!). By 2017, Jim made his return to Paramount Pictures, but in a slightly enhanced role: he's the current chairman and CEO.

So Jim did okay. And it was in every way deserved.

Meanwhile, I was concerned with doing something smart with my money. I started buying up real estate—rental properties all around Los Angeles, but mostly in places where I knew the value would go up, like Silverlake. Over the next couple of years I amassed something like thirty properties. As for Debi and me, we were living in a nice but unspectacular house in the Hollywood foothills, on a street called Camino Palmero. It was a cozy cul-de-sac, really, with maybe six homes, and across from us was the landmark house made famous as the home of TV's Ozzie and Harriet.

For the uninitiated, *The Adventures of Ozzie and Harriet* was a bizarre piece of American radio and TV history, the real precursor to the Kardashians. The Nelsons were a Hollywood family doing a sitcom about themselves. Using their real names. Everything else was mostly fictionalized, but for fourteen years America got to watch the Nelsons grow up and live and change—all on sets built to look like the actual house they lived in on Camino Palmero.

Bizarre, right? And hugely popular (for eight years on radio and fourteen on TV!). So even though it had been twenty-five years since the show had been canceled, our street had its share of gawkers and tourists.

This was exacerbated by the house at the end of the street, right near the entrance to the famed Runyon Canyon Park. It was called the C. E. Toberman Estate, a gated mansion in the gorgeous Spanish Colonial Revival style. Compared to that, our accommodations were pretty modest, and starting to feel cramped. The kids were becoming teenagers (Taryn already was!), and then, in late 1990, came the news: Debi was pregnant. My son Harlan was born the following February. The Band clan was expanding.

Staring at my second son, newborn, helpless in Debi's arms but already active, hearing my son and daughter arguing about something in the next room, all I could think of was that line from *Jaws*.

We're gonna need a bigger boat.

Meanwhile, in Romania . . .

Getting *Subspecies* off the ground was challenging. Ion had mis-led me a bit. The movie studio was gigantic, yes, but empty. They barely had more than a lightbulb, so I had to fly in everything, all the equipment, from Rome. The entrenched, government-paid studio crew was more of a hindrance than a help, too. Not to get political, but if there's one business the government shouldn't be in, it's a fast-paced, dynamic one like the film industry. Imagine if your local post office ran Universal. And then sold off all the equipment to cut costs.

Worse, Romania was still downright frightening. The air-port alone deterred a couple of our actors—one woman took one look at it and just waited near the tarmac for the next plane home. Even Ted Nicolaou was a little rattled. He called and said, "Charlie—I don't know how to do this here. It's scary." But he kept at it.

In fact, to keep himself sane, Ted started keeping a journal, documenting all the impossible delays, the backbiting, the care-lessly missed connections, the desperate and occasionally ter-rifying Romanian shysters and grifters. The diary makes the shooting of *Apocalypse Now* look like *The Love Boat*. Ion turned out to be a bit of a fraud. And paranoid. And divisive, trying to elevate himself by sowing distrust among the cast and crew. Meanwhile everyone was freezing, eating awful food, getting sick, and fighting constantly. Ion was failing at the most basic things, like making sure there was clean water to drink on set. The Americans spent their nights in filthy, cold hotel restaurants, eating wretched meals consisting mainly of gray potatoes and scrawny chicken, drinking huge amounts of questionable wine, bitching, laughing, fighting, screaming at each other, breaking glasses, and stumbling to their rooms at 4:00 A.M. only to start all over the next day, shivering on freezing sets as they waited for inexplicably delayed crew people and equipment to arrive.

Other than that, it was a great shoot.

One more issue: You'd think the Romanian film industry would have *tons* of stuff for vampire movies lying around. Closets full of rubber bats, coffins, stakes, and garlic. You'd be wrong. In truth, Romanians don't share our obsession with vampires. In fact, they're a little insulted by it. To them, vampires are just a silly, weird thing that Americans are into, and Transylvania is a beautiful mountainous area with some cool college towns.

I flew in and tried to help. There were some positives. The locations were astounding. The Romanian actors were serious and skilled. We were building some amazing and gigantic sets— million-dollar stuff—for pennies. In fact, one of those sets was insanely big.

See, I had a concept for *Subspecies,* a twist on the vampire thing. I wanted our vampire, Radu, at one point to cut off his fingers, and have those fingers transform themselves into tiny, devilish minions. Ted didn't love the idea, but I sold him on it. I had to: it was on the poster!

Plus, I figured out a cool way to shoot the minions: instead of paying for time-consuming and expensive stop-motion animation, what if we built a gigantic replica of Radu's lair and had some of Romania's highly trained but newly unemployed dancers dress up as the tiny minions? Use a little forced perspective with normal-sized characters, and BAM! It'd look like a great special effect on the cheap!

Another ray of light was Ted's Romanian director of photography. Vlad Paunescu was young, motivated, skilled . . . everything that the rest of the crew wasn't. Also, Vlad and his lovely wife, Oana (a costumer), knew absolutely everybody. They'd been key figures in the revolution, running through Ceaușescu's underground tunnels filming the dictator's hoarded, stolen riches for all the starving people (and the world) to see. Ted and I realized that if we were going to get this movie done, we'd need Vlad. I offered to put him on a second payroll, on top of the salary he was getting from the government. He jumped at it and immediately set about Making Things Happen.

After cutting that deal I'd been back in Rome for only a few hours, though, when I got a call from Vlad. He sounded uncomfortable. I thought maybe he was backing out. Instead, like Viggo Mortensen before him, Vlad needed an advance. Which is only interesting when you learn that nowadays, Vlad is one of the richest men in Romania. He owns a movie studio.

We'll get to that.

Thanks to Ted and Vlad's work, *Subspecies* came out looking great. With one notable exception. As soon as Ted was back in the States (looking gaunt and ravaged and a little vampiric himself), we took a look at the dailies of my tiny severed-finger-devil minions on their amazing, oversized set.

It was unusable. Like, incredibly, absurdly, laugh-out-loud ridiculous. Those tiny dancers looked like Elton John tiny dancers. I'd wanted terrifying evil imps. What I got was mini-Mummenschanz. Ted had done his best, but when we looked at it, it was obvious to both of us. Ted sighed: "Stop motion it is."

Ted and I agreed on other things, too. I told him I wanted to turn *Subspecies* into a franchise, and shoot it in Romania. His entire body flinched. I pled my case: How could we pass up the opportunity to shoot vampire movies in and around Transylvania itself? After some thought, he said he would consider it, but he had some caveats. "Charlie," he said. "We can't shoot at that studio again. No way. The best thing to come out of this whole mess was Vlad and Oana. They're amazing." I agreed. This time the government wouldn't be involved. But of course there *was* no nongovernmental film industry in Romania. We didn't have any other companies we could work with.

But we had Vlad.

I called a meeting with my Bucharest brain trust. I wanted to shoot *Subspecies II* and *Subspecies III* right away, with Vlad as both cinematographer and producer, throwing money around as necessary to secure locations, find extras, and grease all the rusty wheels of Romanian infrastructure. It felt a little like the Wild West, but Vlad and Ted and I thought we were the right gang of rustlers to make things happen. We smiled at each other across the table. We decided to go for it. Immediately. Agent Nicolaou's Romanian exile would continue.

Back in L.A., I was building Full Moon into the brand I'd envisioned—the Marvel Comics model. We had franchises. We were moving toward a movie a month. And believe it or not, we even had our own version of "Stan's Soapbox."

Paramount was skeptical about the idea. I wanted to put a special feature at the end of every single Full Moon movie. A "featurette," hosted by me, where I could answer fans' questions, tell them our plans, and give them a peek behind the scenes. The bean counters didn't like the idea. Videotape was cheap, but it adds up when you start tacking on minutes to tens of thousands of tapes, and for something that was (in their eyes) entirely unnecessary. But I pointed out that my movies were short, rarely filling up the standard ninety-minute tape. Ultimately, I won that argument, and the Full Moon "Video Zone" magazine was born.

It was around then that I got an unexpected call: the new head of Paramount Pictures, Brandon Tartikoff, wanted to see me.

Brandon was a bit of a rock star, one of Hollywood's rare celebrity executives. He had famously turned NBC around in the eighties, building a dead network into a prime-time powerhouse. He created what would become known as "Must-See TV" with shows like *Seinfeld, Law & Order, Miami Vice,* and *Cheers* (and my old friend Richard Moll's show, *Night Court*!). He was so well-known that he did cameos on his own network's shows, once even hosting *SNL*. But in 1991 he decided to leave the network and take on the movies, becoming the chairman of Paramount.

This was all cool, but what did he want from a relatively unknown director from his largely ignored direct-to-video division?

A lot, it turned out.

I went to his office, and took what was really one of the most positive Hollywood meetings I'd ever had. Brandon had seen *Meridian,* and although it wasn't my biggest hit, he totally got what I was trying to do.

"It's romance, man. And sexy. It's really good. But what if . . . what if we started to throw some real money your way, have you make a couple of Movie of the Weeks?"

I liked the sound of having real money thrown at me. And I liked where Brandon was going with this. His plan was to hook me up with some of the people over at Harlequin (which I didn't even know was an actual publisher—I thought it was the name of a genre!), and see if we could license some of their best supernatural-themed romances. I instantly agreed, and I left there grinning like an idiot, Brandon slapping me on the back. In the coming weeks it became clear that I was now under his wing, and the era of the big-budget Full Moon romance was born!

A few months later, Brandon was fired, making his one of the shortest-lived tenures in major studio history. And the era of the big-budget Full Moon romance was over.

No matter. I had other fish a-frying. The Full Moon franchises were flourishing. I made *Dollman,* about a tough-as-nails Clint Eastwood–type cop from space who lands on Earth ready to kick ass, hops out of his spaceship, and discovers . . . that he's tiny on our planet. Tim Thomerson was perfectly deadpan and hilarious as the itty-bitty enforcer. I was particularly proud of my poster copy: "THIRTEEN INCHES . . . WITH AN ATTITUDE."

At this point we were still screening the movies for the Paramount guys, and the events were becoming a monthly party. *Dollman* debuted for forty or fifty laughing, whooping people, ensuring that it would have a prominent place in the next month's video shipments.

I made *Demonic Toys,* a kind of toy-based cousin of the *Puppet Master* franchise. And then I made *Dollman vs. Demonic Toys,* throwing in a character from Ted Nicolaou's *Bad Channels* for good measure. Franchises! Crossovers! My soapbox "The Video Zone" at the end of every tape! My nineties-Marvel dream was becoming a reality.

One story sticks out from that crazy, mad rush of film production. We were shooting *Puppet Master III,* which a lot of fans think is the best of the series. It was directed by David DeCoteau, who I should tell you about some point.

Heck—how about now?

David came to me in the mid-eighties, a twentysomething kid with all kinds of motivation. I guess he'd gotten a script to Debi for a movie he was self-financing, and Debi thought I should meet him. I liked him immediately.

His career path was a little different than mine: he spent his early twenties writing and directing in the burgeoning gay exploitation/porn industry—which was actually a pretty creative, occasionally hilarious mini-industry in the eighties (*Gayracula,* anyone?). I didn't know about that at the time, but it wouldn't have mattered to me. Movies are movies. All the while Dave was squirreling away cash to fund a supernatural horror movie he wanted to make. And he did it—well, at least he saved enough for the shoot. After talking to him, I offered to take a look at his footage and fund the postproduction if I liked it. Two weeks later, he showed up, film canisters in hand . . . and showed me what would become *Dreamaniac.*

It wasn't a masterpiece. But David showed a lot of promise, and I loved that he had the same approach as me: Just *make* the thing. I funded postproduction, gave him some cash, and released *Dreamaniac* as an Empire film. That money was more of an investment in David than it was in *Dreamaniac,* and that investment paid off. David has directed tons of stuff for me over the years, and he became one of my dearest friends.

He also has boundless enthusiasm and real talent, and I knew he'd be great for *Puppet Master III,* for which I was pulling out all the stops. It would take place entirely in wartime Nazi Germany. Dave Allen was on board for the stop-motion stuff. I even rented out the enormous Universal back lot—something I never did—so that we could shoot convincing exteriors with World War II–era cars and extras.

It was there on the back lot that it happened.

I made it a point to be on set that day, because being on that lot was exciting (and expensive!). If you've ever toured Universal Studios Hollywood in one of those trams, you've rolled through those sets and know how spectacular it all is—those incredibly elaborate, absolutely real-looking city blocks. I hate all the entanglements that come with working for the big studios, but those back lots are pure magic.

We had the place for the day, outfitting the streets with old cars and Nazi flags and all that. Me, I was hanging back, watching all the fun, when I noticed a well-dressed older man, also just watching. I could tell he wasn't with our production.

Look, I don't get freaked out by stuff. I *make* horror, I don't experience it. I've happily spent nights in my medieval castle completely alone, assuming that if ghosts *did* exist, they were probably on my side. Like a magician, I do this because it's fun, not because I believe in it. After all, it's exactly because we make the stuff that we know better than anyone that it's all hocus-pocus.

But this . . .

I wandered over to the gentleman. He smiled broadly. "You're Charlie Band," he said. I admitted that I was.

"I'm such a big fan of yours. Quite a fan."

"Thank you," I said. I was a little surprised that a fan had somehow gotten onto the lot and found me on the set.

"I want to show you something," he said, reaching into the breast pocket of his tailored jacket. "I've been carrying this close to me for years." He pulled something out and handed it to me.

It was an old postcard, a little worn. A beautiful shot of a giant building on a cliff overlooking the ocean, with the words "Greetings from the Bodega Bay Inn."

I froze. My mind did some gymnastics. This was impossible.

"Beautiful, isn't it?" he said.

Let me explain. The Bodega Bay Inn is a crucial location in *Puppet Master,* the place where the old master Andre Toulon conceals his creations before the Nazis come for him, the place where all the mayhem happens in the rest of the movie.

Also, the Bodega Bay Inn does not exist.

I had designed the "inn" myself. Dave Allen built a beautifully detailed model of a famous hotel in Pasadena, far away from cliffs and oceans (but very convenient to my new facilities in Atwater!). Dave then drove that model up the California coastline and positioned it perfectly, using forced perspective, to make it look like a giant hotel on a cliff. But it was never giant, never really on that cliff, and because forced perspective is so hard to achieve, we only had one shot of it, from the one angle that Dave placed it to create the illusion.

The postcard the old man held was not only seemingly older than my movie. It was a beautiful photograph of the hotel on the cliff, from a completely different angle. From the other side of the building.

I don't remember what I said to the old fellow, but I made a motion, holding up one finger, I'd be right back, and he smiled, and I wandered off to find Dave or Debi or *anyone*, really, so they could see what I'd just been shown. When I was ten paces away I turned back to ask the old man a question . . . and he was gone.

I have no theories as to who that man was or how that photo or that moment came to be. I don't attach anything to it, except that it was creepy and inexplicable and I guess I'm a little *grateful,* like a magician who's been stumped by an illusion that he can't explain. A moment had been created in my life like the ones that I try to create on-screen: I'd been shown the impossible.

As the Full Moon vision became reality, I did the next logical thing: expand. We created a Full Moon offshoot brand, Moonbeam Entertainment, my family-friendly label. We launched that with an adorable comedy about a boy who somehow acquires real, frozen dinosaur eggs and ends up with lovable, chaos-inducing baby dinosaur friends. It was light and silly—and a monster hit. See, *Jurassic Park* had just taken over the world, and like any decent exploitation filmmaker, I was all over it.

One interesting note is that *Prehysteria* was directed by me *and* my Dad. I was determined that our first family movie would turn out well, but I was also ridiculously busy. So each morning I'd wake up, call my dad, and figure out a schedule. It became a joke on the set that the actors never knew which Band would be their director. Years later, people would ask me what it was like directing a movie with my dad, and my reply was always the same: "I don't know. I never saw him."

Truth be told, though, even if we didn't see each other on set, my dad and I were never, ever out of touch with each other. We probably spoke on the phone five nights a week, and we were constantly involved in each other's lives. So sharing directing duty without seeing each other was a lot less weird than it sounds.

It seemed to work. *Prehysteria* was a gigantic hit. It made tens of millions of dollars.

But not for me. You've heard this song before, I know, but by 1992 I was taking less-than-awesome deals from Paramount in order to keep movies in the pipeline. Not that I had any right to cry poverty at the time, but I was making thousands where Paramount was making millions.

But hey—Paramount was happy with me. I was probably one of their only producers who was enthusiastically involved with the home video marketing. Because I knew *that* was where the rubber met the road. We were sending out action figures, stand-ups, great splashy catalog content, anything to keep video store managers interested and excited to feature our movies.

To this day I obsess over movie posters and promotional materials, the appearance of not just the film, but all the things that surround it. In the movie business that's known as "key art," the art that defines the look and feel of all the marketing stuff, and—in my case—often the movie itself. All that became a little easier in the nineties when I started working with a talented graphic designer named Ryan Brookhart. We saw eye-to-eye instantly, and we've managed to find ways to work together ever since. Whether you rented a Full Moon VHS tape in the nineties or you just browsed new offerings on my Amazon channel, you've seen Ryan's stuff!

There was one marketing scheme I was particularly proud of. I got the Paramount guys to send out something for a movie, a booklet with the most amazing cover. Imagine opening the box from Paramount in 1993 and seeing a colorful, enticing image with the words: "Travolta. Estevez. Swayze. Stallone. Together for the FIRST TIME!"

You're IN, right? And then you turn the page to find . . .

Beach Babes from Beyond. Starring Joe Estevez (Emilio's uncle), Don Swayze (Patrick's brother), Joey Travolta (John's brother), and Jackie Stallone (Sylvester's mom).

But hey, as advertised, this *was* their first movie together.

The Paramount guys weren't so sure about it. One looked at me and voiced their concern: "I mean, you're basically lying. And then making them feel like idiots for believing you."

I told them I was positive that the nation's video store owners had a sense of humor, and they'd reward us with great shelf real estate.

As it turned out, I was right. It's like every magician can tell you: people don't mind being deceived, as long as they're also entertained.

Speaking of real estate, I had finally pulled the trigger on one more Los Angeles property. The family was having lunch on a bright, sunny Saturday when I made the announcement.

"I found us a new house," I said.

My son Alex, almost twelve years old, looked a little nervous. But his big sister was definitely ready to have a little more space.

"Is it big?"

I smiled. "Bigger than this place." I looked at Alex. "I fact, we might be able to have a room just for musical instruments and stuff."

He brightened a little. "Yeah?"

"Maybe. Let's go see it."

"Now?"

"Now.

We stepped outside—Taryn, Alex, and Debi (holding baby Harlan). As we got in the car, I watched my family look around with mixed emotions at our cozy little six-house street. The palm trees, Ozzie and Harriet's place across the street, that ridiculous mansion at the top of the road . . . they'd really come to love Camino Palmero.

We drove. Down into West Hollywood, then west, into Beverly Hills. They took in the huge houses, watching with interest . . . but then I turned, heading south, then back east through less-glamorous Hollywood, and then into Hancock Park, where the houses grew bigger and more expensive . . . but then I turned again, heading north. The kids were groaning, getting frustrated with me. We drove across Hollywood Boulevard, turned left on Franklin, driving past the famed Magic Castle . . . and turned right on Camino Palmero to our old house.

"Couldn't find it, huh?" asked Taryn.

I drove us past our house, up the street . . . and through the gigantic, open gates of the C. E. Toberman mansion. Our new home.

You don't get to be the Best Dad in the World every day. But this was one of those times.

C. E. Toberman was a developer known as the Father of Hollywood. He was responsible for such humble venues as the Hollywood Bowl and Grauman's Chinese Theater. In 1924 he built himself his dream palace at the base of the Hollywood Hills, in among the movie stars and movie moguls, conspicuously next door to Errol Flynn's estate. You've probably seen the place— it's been in a bunch of movies and TV shows, including as the home and home base of Vincent Chase on HBO's *Entourage* for three seasons. A ten-thousand-square-foot main house, a separate structure for a gigantic tiled indoor swimming pool under skylights (which I restored), tennis courts . . .

It wasn't much, but it was home.

Even better, I didn't sell the old house. I offered it to my mom and dad, who were living in a house I rented for them in the Hills, on Blue Jay Way (yeah, *that* Blue Jay Way. I'm a hopeless Beatle fan!). Mom and Dad gladly took it, and the Band clan pretty much took over that little street, like a fun, latter-day, slightly demonic Ozzie and Harriet.

Eight years later, my son Alex would become a genuine rock star, the lead singer and songwriter of a band called the Calling. If you were young in 2000, you probably had their first album:

Camino Palmero.

Pretty cool, right? But my real estate spree wasn't done. I now had my eye on another nice big patch of land. In Romania.

By now our Romanian venture was really rolling. Vlad and Oana had assembled a rotating crew we could trust, they knew exactly which palms to grease, and now that we were doing things without those slow, corrupt Soviet-era-holdover government drones, things were moving faster. Even Ted, who'd hated the place so much while shooting *Subspecies,* was having fun. He was my own Colonel Kurtz: Agent Nicolaou had gone native!

On a visit in early 1992, Vlad and I started talking—just talking, mind you—about what it would take to buy some Romanian land. And, just hypothetically, what if we did that and *built a giant movie studio?*

As you probably know by now, I was never "just talking" back then. And neither was Vlad. We got moving.

Here was the challenge: Converting from a Communist dictatorship to a Western-style democracy wasn't easy. The government owned all the land, and now that was going to change. But how? You couldn't just put it on the market—with the currency so weak, if you opened everything up to the highest bidder, some big American company would sweep in, buy it all, and suddenly signs at the border would read "Welcome to McRomania, try our Happy Meal!" and a giant pair of Golden Arches would tower above Bucharest.

No. So, to keep Romania Romanian, they passed a rule: Only people who were native to a particular region could buy any particular parcel in that region. And they could only buy two hectares (a little less than five acres). With a scheme like that, Romania would be safe from Ronald McDonald.

But not from me and Vlad.

I won't bore you with how we came up with The Plan. Nah, like a good caper movie, I'm going to cut to the chase. Here's how it went down:

On a cloudy day in 1992, a plane touched down at the airport in Bucharest. Instantly, workers and armed guards swarmed around the cargo hold, and a trunk full of American cash, four hundred thousand dollars in all, was loaded into a car, along with my money guy, Mickey Kaiserman. Mickey was my COO, and maybe the most unlikely bagman in human history: he was a tall, skinny Jewish guy from the Bronx, from a family in the kosher catering business. He didn't speak a word of Romanian. But I wanted him to lead this special-ops mission in Bucharest, and somehow I convinced him to do it.

Escorted by guards with Uzis, in cars and on motorcycles, the car rolled out of the airport, into downtown Bucharest, and came to a stop in front of the giant National Bank of Romania. The trunk was carried in.

An hour or two later, a group of men loaded enormous pallets of Romanian leu (their currency) onto the back of a semi-truck. At this time, remember, the economy hadn't stabilized, and inflation in Romania was out of control. You could buy tens of thousands of leu for a dollar. I don't know how much cash was loaded onto that truck. Tens of billions for sure. Maybe trillions. I know that the traditional local term for that amount of money is "a metric fuck-ton."

The truck pulled out, now surrounded by an honest-to-god motorcade. Some new vehicles, some old and ramshackle—an Eastern European version of *Mad Max,* rolling north, through the city streets and then, gaining speed, through the increasingly sparse suburbs, into the countryside.

The big truck came to a stop on a country road by a field, outside the village of Izvorani, four miles from the highway, twenty-five miles north of Bucharest. In the field a couple dozen locals were waiting. They were being loosely organized, excitedly but politely, by Vlad Paunescu, who'd put on a suit and slicked back his hair for the occasion, projecting Successful Businessman vibes as hard as he could. As instructed, all the assembled locals had suitcases or duffel bags in their hands. Empty.

Mickey Kaiserman emerged and introduced himself to Vlad. The unlikely couple—the hero of the revolution and the kosher caterer's boy—nodded at each other. It was Go Time.

Two armed paramilitary dudes opened the back of the truck, and—somewhat incongruously—offloaded an old-fashioned dark wood office desk and placed it on the ground. A sober-faced accountant in a suit took his seat behind the desk, opened up his briefcase, and started organizing papers there in the field, for all the world like a Romanian John Cleese in a Monty Python sketch.

Eventually the accountant signaled his readiness, and the guards started motioning. The locals organized into a line, and one by one, Vlad sent them forward. The first Romanian approached the desk, presented the accountant with papers, and handed off his suitcase to one of the guards. The accountant examined the papers, nodded, stamped them. Then he attached them to other papers, had the local man sign his name, and then affixed it all with stamps and seals and placed the documents in an out-box. He nodded to the soldiers, and one of them came forward with the man's suitcase, now fully loaded with cash, and handed it back to the local man. Who then walked home with more money than he'd ever seen in his life.

The man was suddenly well-to-do. And Vlad and I suddenly owned two hectares of that field.

Over the course of the afternoon, this process was repeated maybe twenty times. By the end of it, the truck was empty, the guards were paid handsomely, the desk was loaded back onto the truck, and everyone drove away. Soon there was nothing but a vast empty field there in the light of the setting sun, just as it had been the day before.

Except now Vlad and I owned it.

Okay, to be honest, it was mostly mine—80 percent mine, 20 percent Vlad's. But we were partners. Together we were determined to take advantage of the conditions on the ground and turn that unkempt Romanian field into one of Europe's biggest, best movie studios. One hundred acres of soundstages, back lots, and state-of-the-art infrastructure that would serve as both a home for Full Moon Features and a desirable destination for world-class cinematic productions from all over the globe.

It was a crazy, ridiculous, ambitious plan, one that would take years of planning and construction and hustling and scheming. At that moment it seemed both attainable and at the same time completely impossible.

Spoiler alert:

We did it.

The One with Jay Leno

It was a quiet afternoon on Camino Palmero. Probably 1992 or so, because Alex was still a kid. I know this because I remember the phone ringing and hearing his high-pitched voice as he answered it. I was barely listening at first:

"Hello? Hi . . . that's us. I'm Alex . . . What? I don't know . . . Yeah, I love that one . . . Well, we were *gonna* return it . . ."

I was paying more attention now. WTF?

"What? *Cannibal Women in the Avocado Jungle of Death*? Yeah, I know that one. My *dad* made that one . . . maybe you should talk to my dad? Okay . . ."

Alex held the phone away from his face and said, "Dad? Jay Leno wants to talk to you."

Here's what happened. Jay Leno was on the town, shooting a comedy piece for *The Tonight Show.* This was a pretty simple concept: Jay goes to a Blockbuster Video and clowns around, messes with customers and employees, etc. He happened to pick the one on Sunset near Fairfax, only a few blocks from our house.

At some point he asks the employees to find him That Customer. The one with the most outstanding late fees. The one with the most absolutely bizarre rental history . . . In both those categories, we Bands were guilty as charged. And as jaw-droppingly illegal as it was, Jay had somehow persuaded my local Blockbuster to show them my account and rental history, and then to call me, at which point he grabbed the phone and started hassling my son about our late fees and bizarre rental habits!

I took the phone and chatted with Jay. It didn't take me long to figure out that this was an opportunity to reach *The Tonight Show*'s millions upon millions of viewers. So I *might* have steered the conversation to some the fine video offerings available from Full Moon Features.

Okay, I went into full Sales Mode.

It was fun, and we had a ball watching the piece when it aired later that week. But the story didn't end there.

About a decade later, flush with the success of their debut album, the Calling got to play *The Tonight Show.* They crushed it, and after the song, Jay called their lead singer over to the desk to chat. And he let the audience know that he and young Alex Band had actually met before, but not in person. And then he showed a clip of his Blockbuster bit from the nineties.

I'm actually not sure if I ever paid those late fees.

11

Vlad the Finagler

(1994–1999)

While our Romanian outpost was developing, I kept things rolling back in the USA. For instance, I wanted to reunite Tim Thomerson and Helen Hunt one last time for *Trancers III.* My casting people told me that was impossible. Helen had just begun a little sitcom called *Mad About You,* and was well on her way to becoming a household name. "She would cost more than your movie's entire budget," I was told.

That's Hollywood. Everybody just expects people who "make it big" to instantly forget their friends. But I figured we had just made *Trancers II* a year or so ago, and once again it had been a total blast. Fun side note about that one: Once again, Jack Deth finds himself amid the garbage on Skid Row, among colorful, crazy, broken-down old winos and bums. But this time one of those filthy bums was my dad. And next to him, just as filthy, was his old pal Gordon Hunt, Helen's dad. If you watch it, you can spot their faces under all that grime, having the time of their lives.

I told the casting people to ask Helen anyway.

She did it for union scale. A few thousand dollars.

Once again, we had a fantastic time. Helen was obviously going to be very, very busy in the years to come, but this felt like the best possible going-away party, with Tim and Helen clowning around on the set one more time. I still talk to them both once in a while. They're still buddies. My only point here is that Hollywood is frequently wrong about Hollywood.

Speaking of family, here's another interesting movie I made around that time: *Shrunken Heads,* directed by Richard Elfman, brother of Danny.

Richard had come to me through Danny, whom I'd met a few years before. I'd been a fan of his band, Oingo Boingo, but by the late eighties he'd established himself as Hollywood's hottest new film composer, starting with *Pee-wee's Big Adventure* and *Beetlejuice,* and by 1989 progressing to blockbusters like *Batman,* and . . . you know what? I don't need to give you his résumé. You've probably heard of him, and anyway, that's what IMDb is for!

I liked Danny. And at some point he'd called me and asked if he and his girlfriend could spend a few days at my castle. I said yes, of course, and promptly alerted Rolando to expect them. I mean, wouldn't *you* lend Danny Elfman your castle if you weren't using it?

Anyway, Danny's brother showed up and pitched me a movie he wanted to direct. It was called *Shrunken Heads,* and it was definitely up my alley: a trio of teenagers are killed by a crime boss, and then their severed heads are reanimated by a voodoo witch doctor, at which point they fly around seeking revenge.

In other words, a typical Full Moon love story.

Richard also guaranteed that he could get his brother Danny to score the thing. Which would be great. Looking at the script, I started to realize that this might not be as easy as I thought—to make it work, we'd have to fly those heads over cityscapes. The best way to do this was to use a hot new robot cam that Richard was excited about. Also we'd need a city, which meant I had to open my wallet and rent out the Paramount back lot. Fun, but expensive. A movie that was supposed to cost me a few hundred thousand was now running me about $2.5 million.

Still, I had high hopes. It was a great-looking production, a good script, Danny Elfman on board . . . Paramount was talking about giving it an actual theatrical release, which would've been a huge boost.

Somewhere along the line, predictably enough, Danny turned out to be too busy to score the whole film. But he wrote us a fantastic title theme, and my brother Richard stepped in and did a wonderful job with the rest of the movie. It was still headed for the big time . . .

. . . until we screened the thing. And saw the one, completely fatal flaw.

Look, on paper it all worked. The script, the production values, the music—everything. The lights go down and the screen lights up and you hear that gorgeous, insane Elfman title theme. And then you meet the main characters . . .

. . . And they are much, much younger looking than they're supposed to be. They're basically *kids*. Look, we meant to cast teenagers. We *did* cast teenagers. But that's not how they came across on-screen.

Even today, you still can't cheerfully murder children on-screen. Imagine that first season of *Stranger Things* if, during the first few minutes, all those adorable kids playing Dungeons and Dragons got their heads chopped off. Or if instead of just frightening the Brady Bunch kids in Hawaii, Vincent Price had beheaded them. That's essentially what happens at the beginning of *Shrunken Heads.*

At the party after our customary screening on the lot, the mood was more subdued than usual. One of the Paramount honchos, the one who was deciding whether to put the thing in theaters, leaned in toward me and said, "Yeah, we're gonna have to pass on that." I took a long sip of my drink, then exhaled slowly.

"Yeah. I would," I said.

Things weren't great with Paramount after that. But not because of *Shrunken Heads.* It was 1993, and the people who'd been so into Full Moon were departing, one by one (partly because of the division's success—they were moving up!). And although my movies still made money, the relationship was going sour. I was letting them chip away at my percentages, and then working out schemes to get more money up front so I could get the movies made. And when you're tasked with putting a movie out *every four weeks,* brother, that's a lot of scheming! At some point I got called out on the carpet for this, the new head of the department literally yelling that I was cheating them.

Cheating!? Friends, Charlie Band does not cheat! Charlie Band schemes, plots, wheedles when necessary, moves resources around, borrows from Peter to pay Paul, and then convinces Paul to pay Peter back. But *cheating*? No.

Unlike some other filmmakers, I never even paid myself from my movies' budgets. I used every penny to make the movies. And then, if someone needed a little more money to make their movie better, I would simply find them that money . . . from the budget of the next movie I was making. Brilliant, right? In my experience, that kind of thing always works. Right up until the moment when it stops working.

In retrospect, I should've sat them all down and explained that while I was making money for Paramount, Paramount wasn't making *me* anything anymore. That there was no upside to the relationship for me. I should have let them know about these problems long before. But I do not respond well to being pushed around and accused of things. I offered to open my books to them, demonstrating that their money was going only into the movies I was making for them. That cooled things down. Then I packed my things and cut ties with the studio.

Divorces are never easy. But in this case at least I had a prenup: I got to keep the Full Moon name and all my movies. Lots of people offered to help me sue Paramount to get my share of that money, but I had no appetite for that kind of thing. Like Andre Toulon, I was leaving with a steamer trunk full of the things I valued most: my puppets, my evil dolls, my demons and mutants and monsters. The fact that I got to keep all those properties felt like a big victory for me, proof that I'd gotten smarter about my business since the Empire days.

Well, a *little* smarter.

My new movies weren't going to fund themselves. Things were changing. I did what I always do when I need to clear my head. I went to my castle.

Things had changed a little there, too; Rolando had moved on, and my new caretaker was a friendly, hardworking local guy named Enzo. Also, the castle had become more relaxing for me: I no longer had an insane, bustling studio just down the autostrada. For that kind of chaos, I had to go to Romania or Los Angeles.

It was a warm afternoon, and I was having a glass of wine

up on a high parapet with Giovanni Natalucci, my longtime art director. Giovanni was my art maestro, a brilliant, scholarly presence who knew everything about his craft. And he was a historian, which is important because—

"Charlie," he said as we stood there, breathing the sweet, clean Italian mountain air. "Do you see that, down there? Those . . . two turrets." He pointed.

I looked. I'd noticed them once or twice, but never thought about them. Down in the valley below, two old stone turrets from some ancient structure jutted out of a hillside, which was not unusual for Italy. I nodded.

"That land," Giovanni said. "That land is for sale. You should buy it."

"Buy it?"

"Yes. Those turrets are the top of something beautiful. Maybe an old fortress. Possibly a mill. You know, there used to be a river that ran through there, but it was diverted in . . ."

I let Giovanni go on, giving me a capsule history of Umbrian agriculture. And staring down at it, well, it was intriguing to wonder what was underneath that hill. I was almost as curious as Giovanni. Still, I'm no archaeologist.

Then again, it *was* a nice piece of land.

A few days later I bought it. For something like ninety thousand dollars. And I had Enzo start digging.

No, he didn't unearth whatever was buried there. But there was a good, flat field on another part of the property. He hired a crew and dug me a truly beautiful swimming pool, with a patio and a cool little cabana or two.

See, the one thing I lacked in Giove was outdoor space. Old fortresses, after all, are built right into the mountainside, because they're there to keep lookout and protect the village immediately below. We didn't even have a lawn.

#CastleProblems, am I right?

Anyway, from that day on, during my extended family's annual vacation, we had something to do on those swelteringly hot July Italian days. We'd pack up towels and bottles of water and wine and gigantic picnic baskets, hop in a car or two, descend from our mountain lair, and spend the afternoon at the pool. I'd swim, sit back in a lounge chair, eat some grapes, and watch my children splash around for hours on end until we were all happily exhausted. Then we'd head back up to the castle for dinner.

I know, it sounds like a slice of heaven, right? But I need to be completely honest here. Despite appearances, it was . . . even better than that.

By this time I never went to Italy without dropping in to see what was happening in Romania. Even though our studio had no soundstages yet, we were already shooting movies there!

The first thing we had done was build a wall around the property. I'm not saying we couldn't trust our immediate neighbors. No. I'm saying you couldn't trust *anyone* in Romania. Not during those years.

But I figured once we had the walls up, we could quickly throw up some outdoor sets on the land that would eventually become our back lot. We started with one of the simplest and most venerable back lot sets in movie history: an Old West town. Which was perfect for an idea I'd been playing with.

No, not a western. Who do you think you're talking to? A *space* western, wherein a villainous lizard man lands his spaceship on some backwater planet, on the outskirts of town, and heads in to settle an old score with the sheriff.

Oblivion was a lot of fun—a sci-fi western with a campy sensibility. I came up with the story and was lucky enough to get Peter

Allen David—the notorious PAD, a legendary Marvel Comics writer—to do the screenplay. I sent in equipment and some of my best crew people from Italy (remember what I said about department heads? See chapter 1!). George Takei dropped in for a cameo. The producers on the ground were Vlad and Oana.

It came out great, and was successful enough to merit a sequel. For which, naturally, we already had the set. Not a single real building was done yet, but Castel Film Studios was up and running!

I had yet another ambitious project I was launching around then, one that had started almost thirty years before and would stretch all the way into the present.

From the moment I met Dave Allen, from the first time I got him to agree to make those fantastic aliens for me in *Laserblast,* Dave had something special in mind. It was 1977, I think, and he'd already been messing with the idea for a decade.

"It's called *The Primevals,*" he said. "A team of scientists discovers a civilization descended from an alien race that crash-landed eons ago, and . . ." It was clearly a passion project for him, a sweeping epic filled with stop-motion creatures interacting with human actors in far-flung locations, a modern-day stab at making a Ray Harryhausen–esque classic, like *Jason and the Argonauts.* I loved his pitch, his vision, his energy. It sounded fantastic.

I told him no.

I mean, come *on.* It was 1977. I was paying all the money I had to get a few seconds of stop-motion animation for a movie that otherwise was going to cost less than those few seconds. I didn't have the resources, and Dave knew it. But you can't blame a guy for trying.

He kept trying. When I had Empire up and running and Dave was stepping on board to work his magic on *Ghoulies II* and *Eliminators* and *Dolls,* he would always take a minute or two to pitch *The Primevals* again. By this point. Dave was working on big-budget pictures for big studios, like *Willow* and *Ghostbusters II,* but he wasn't going to find the right allies there. He knew that I dug his work, that I was crazy for stop motion, and he told me, honestly, as he always did, "Charlie, I gotta make this thing." He had a script, a plan, and every single moment of the movie was meticulously storyboarded. It was all there.

Still, my answer was no. It was too ambitious. Out of my league in almost every way.

By the early nineties Dave was working for me all the time. He did the Puppet Master movies and *Demonic Toys* and *Prehysteria.* CGI was starting to take over the industry. In 1993, *Jurassic Park* was a cinematic atomic bomb for effects guys, a seamless blend of practical effects with computer-generated visuals that put the entire movie world on notice that Things Were Changing. But Dave kept the faith. He believed in the power and the organic feel of stop motion. Once again, he pestered me about *The Primevals.*

This time I said yes.

I mean, what the hell. I now had some money. It was a gigantic risk, but I loved Dave and everything he did. We'd find a way to make his dream come true.

I brought my dad in to produce and to help Dave improve the script. It was a big project. At that point my movies generally took two weeks to shoot. Three, tops. Dave was going to need twelve weeks of principal photography, with scenes shot in Los Angeles, the Italian Alps, and Romania. And that was just for the human actors! Dave devoted an entire stage in my Atwater warehouse to *The Primevals,* and he and his guys were going to be working around the clock, building miniatures, lighting sets, moving those figures around in that agonizing frame-by-frame animating process. It was going to cost millions.

We went for it.

The shoots with the human actors went off without a hitch. (Well, more or less. This is the movie business, after all.) Dave threw himself into the stop-motion shots, while also joyfully tossing off great stuff for me for *Oblivion* and *Oblivion 2*.

And then, a year or so into the process of animating his dream project, Dave got sick. Cancer. He had to slow down, but he kept working. He was given a prognosis of about five years, and he wanted to get the project done. But less than a year after his diagnosis, Dave was dead.

It hit me pretty hard. Dave Allen was a real friend. We'd been making movies together for twenty years, and even though he'd go away occasionally to do Big Jobs for studios (he'd even been nominated for an Oscar for Barry Levinson's *Young Sherlock Holmes*), he always returned to me and my strange little movies.

Plus, he was the First to Go. Not that there hadn't been any death in my life, but everybody who gets the privilege of living past the age of forty has a First to Go—that friend you think of as "one of us" who dies from a cause you'd always associated with older people, and suddenly you realize you now *are* "older people." Maybe Dave was a few years older than me, and certainly, at fifty-four, his death came way, way too soon. But still. You can deal in horror and grotesquerie, kill off a thousand characters in hundreds of inventively horrifying and grisly ways, and it still won't prepare you to lose a friend.

By the time he died, Dave had completed maybe 150 of the more than 250 stop-motion shots he had planned for the movie. Dave's protégé and successor, a wonderful guy named Chris Endicott, wanted to take Dave's storyboards and finish the movie. So did I, so Chris kept working in the space in Glendale that I still maintained for him and the project. But by the time 1999 rolled around, as you're about to learn, I no longer had the means to drop another million or two on a movie. We took all the film and the models and the storyboards from Dave's uncompleted masterpiece and put them into storage. There was nothing else we could do. I locked the project away somewhere safe.

It stayed there for a very long time.

I was in my office when I got a call from my mother.

"Charlie, you know I'm not a tattletale . . ."

"Of course not, Mom."

". . . but I think I just saw little Alex go by in the Viper."

"That's impossible, Mom."

I was sure she'd imagined it. Alex was fourteen, I think, and obviously wasn't going to be driving my big, attention-grabbing sports car through the crowded streets of Hollywood.

Still, when I got back to Camino Palmero I humored my mom by opening the garage where I kept the beast. There it was, exactly as I'd left it the last time I'd had the opportunity to take it out on the road. Maybe Mom was starting to lose it.

Just to be extra-special sure, I put my hand on the hood.

It was burning hot.

A few minutes later Alex was sobbing, confessing, swearing he'd never do it again. (Years later, I learned that this was not the first time he'd tooled around Hollywood in his dad's Viper—just the first time he'd gotten caught.) Me, I acted as stern and disappointed as I could, but thinking back to my childhood in Rome, well, it wasn't hard to see where that, um, *enterprising* attitude was coming from. Learning how to drive a car like that, at that age, and then actually *doing* it?

Kind of a rock star move.

In 1995 we reunited at the castle to shoot one more movie: Stuart Gordon, my dad, me. Jeffrey Combs and Barbara Crampton. And H. P. Lovecraft, of course. We all reassembled to shoot *Castle Freak,* which Stuart had conceived from one of my posters and one or two of Lovecraft's stories. It's still a well-loved movie, and probably the most gruesome and disturbing film I've ever made. But the process of making it was exactly the opposite: a complete delight all the way through.

Once again, we lived and shot at the castle, building sets all over the place, using our real-life backdrop to its fullest. We'd finish shooting and enjoy long, wonderful, laughter-filled dinners, retreat back to our palatial rooms, and sleep like babies in the cool air of those quiet Italian nights. It was perfect.

But trouble was brewing in the background.

The mid-nineties brought their own set of challenges. I was glad to be out of the Paramount deal, but I was moving forward as a true independent in an era where all the true independents were dying out. Without Paramount's mighty distributional and promotional machine, I had to make the movies, get the word out, and get the tapes out all by myself. For most independents, getting shelf space in the video stores was becoming impossible. We were getting squeezed out. I mean, apart from me, very few indie guys could even get a meeting with Blockbuster. And even the small independent store owners didn't have space or money for us, because the studios had them over a barrel. The studios' basic strategy was this: "You want *Aliens* when it comes out? Great. You also have to take these other nine movies."

Because of my relationships and my track record, I fared a lot better than most of my indie brethren. But I was running giant spaces in Los Angeles and an ever-expanding studio in Romania, so I had a lot of mouths to feed. In fact, speaking of expanding, in 1995 Debi gave birth to our second son, Zalman. Not that our estate on Camino Palmero was getting crowded, but my life started *feeling* crowded.

Faced with the costs of getting my movies out to the public, and with no desire to get entangled with another studio, I made the choice that felt natural to me: I sold off a couple of assets. Did I really need to own *thirty* properties in Los Angeles? No. I put one or two on the market.

And then one or two more.

Still, I was a man with plenty of stuff to sell, and some of my movies—many of my movies—were turning a profit. The best-sellers at that point were my Moonbeam movies—the family stuff had a natural audience. I was also about to get involved in something just as profitable but more than a bit less family friendly.

It was my buyer for Hollywood Video who came to me with the idea. Hollywood and Blockbuster were my two biggest, most all-important chains, so when they spoke, I listened.

"Charlie," he said, "you know what does best in our stores? The soft-core erotic stuff. *Playboy* and *Penthouse* are killing with that kind of thing. If you made movies like that, but maybe with a sci-fi or fantasy twist, we could clean up."

It wasn't a hugely appealing idea to me, but obviously I was no stranger to having a little sexual content in my movies. Plus I'd made those hot fairy tale musicals way back when. And if I could throw in a little sci-fi . . .

The first one was a little erotic fantasy thing called *Virtual Encounters,* an exploration of something that didn't exist at all at the time: VR. An uptight businesswoman hires an exclusive service that allows her to experience all sorts of erotic scenarios virtually, and . . . oh, you get the picture! It did really well. Okay, I thought, this could work.

Then I came up with another idea: An alien race sends one of their own to Earth, and puts it in the body of a ridiculously hot woman to observe human mating habits. She *does* observe, and then gets involved, and also helps a distressed couple . . . ladies and gentlemen, *Femalien* (see what I did there?). And my new label, Surrender Cinema, was born. *Femalien* was soft-core erotica, yes, but with a story and a sense of humor. Weirdly, it's now considered a classic of that genre.

Even more weirdly (to me), it *crushed,* sales-wise.

And that's a truth I learned that still holds true. To this day, as much as I love my horror and twisted comedy offerings, as much as Full Moon Features—on Amazon and my independent app— are obviously horror-oriented channels, it is always the erotic stuff that gets the most streams and downloads. By far.

That might seem unlikely, especially in this age of free hard-core porn that you can stream from any device you own. (Or so I'm told. I myself have only viewed such things for research purposes!) But it turns out that there's still a bustling market for the less-graphic stuff. And there are reasons for that.

Back in the nineties, if a young couple wanted to take a walk on the wild(ish) side and see something sexy, they weren't likely to go behind their local video store's beaded curtain to the hard-core section (yes, kids, those existed!). Those endless close-ups of colliding genitals could be way too much, especially for a new relationship. But rent a fun, silly movie that gives you a little bit of a plot and beautiful, well-lit bodies . . . *now* you had the makings of a fun Saturday night! And that still seems to be the case.

Anyway, this was a bit of a new gravy train for me. Over the next few years we made a ton of the stuff, mostly directed by my friend David DeCoteau. Except for discovering the occasional talented actor or actress to use in other movies (like *Femalien's* Jackie Lovell, whom I immediately put in *Head of the Family*),

I didn't pay all that much attention to my burgeoning erotic empire. I let David run things. Which led to one funny story.

It was a couple of years in, and Surrender Cinema was humming along, the pleasantly lucrative background noise of my otherwise harried existence. It was late one night, and I was just finishing a grueling editing session at my Atwater Village facility. It was then that one of my young editors popped his head out of his room and asked if he could talk to me.

"Hey, Charlie . . . it's about those Surrender Cinema movies I'm editing . . ."

"Yeah? Don't sweat it. You're doing a great job," I said.

"No, it's not that. It's just that, well, the movies . . ." I could tell he was uncomfortable. Maybe the racy content was too much for him?

"What about them?"

"They're just—just . . . getting . . ."

"What? What are they getting?"

"They're getting really gay."

"What?"

"Super gay. And getting gayer by the minute."

What could that even mean? I went in to look at the movie he was putting together. Then I screened another recent offering. And sure enough, the movies increasingly featured these gorgeous young men, running around almost-naked and oiled up, often clad in white jockey shorts. Tighty whities. Which wasn't really a thing that straight women wanted to see, and it made straight men (or at least my editor) uncomfortable, but it was a huge thing in the gay community. Meanwhile, not only were the actresses getting less of a loving treatment from the camera, they were . . . well, let's say they were perfectly good actresses who just didn't happen to be very sexy or sexual. They seemed to spend a lot of time clothed while tying up and torturing these sweaty, perfectly toned boys in silver lamé shortie shorts.

I had to go talk to David.

Full disclosure—David was and is one of my closest friends. Also, for some reason a *lot* of my closest friends throughout my life have been gay men. I don't know what it is—maybe it's my sense of humor or my somewhat European sense of style or my taste in art and architecture, but I would've made a fantastic gay man! If not for that one nagging detail where you have to have sex with dudes. That's not for me, which interfered with my otherwise perfect gay credentials. But my point here is that my comfort level was such that I knew just how to approach David tactfully and discreetly and hint at my concerns:

"Dave, man. Your movies are getting too damn gay!"

"What are you talking about!?" he shot back, offended. I explained, and an animated and kind of hilarious argument ensued. David was insulted as a filmmaker; he knew he was making soft-core erotica for a straight audience, and the implication that he'd lost sight of that mission was an *insult*. Besides, he argued, he wasn't making it for guys. "Charlie, you simply don't understand my untapped market! My 'Tighty Whitey Frighties' are horror movies for *girls*!" Yeah, right. On we went . . .

"All right!" he finally yelled. "This is what we're going to do. From now on, I'll cast the men, and you'll be in charge of casting the women."

I think he meant it half facetiously when he said it, but we paused for a second. Now that I thought about it, to be fair, over the years I'd been guilty of casting a few male leads whom women I knew would eventually tell me were *not* attractive. The word "gross" had in fact been used to describe the male star in at least one love scene. How was I to know?

David and I looked at each other. His idea made sense.

And that, boys and girls, is how the late-nineties Surrender Cinema offerings came to feature genuinely attractive men *and* women. And at least 30 percent fewer tighty whities.

Dave and I have joked about that incident for years. I showed him this section as I was writing this book, and he shot me an email reminding me about his "Tighty Whitey Frighties" line and adding, "Just a few years later *Twilight* opened to huge numbers! Gay Dave was right all along!"

"Charlie, you should take a meeting with Michael Jackson."

Well, first of all, *yes.*

It was my friend John Branca on the phone, rock's original supermanager. It had been years since I'd rented his house, but that rental had led to an enduring friendship. Debi and I always went to his fantastic blowout Christmas Eve parties. So hearing from John wasn't unusual. Being asked to meet with Michael, on the other hand, was.

I wasn't a superfan or anything, but I'll say this: If you weren't around in the eighties and nineties, you probably can't imagine just how *huge* the King of Pop was. If you were a child of the eighties, that fandom bordered on religious fervor. This was 1997, so the offices of Full Moon were *loaded* with children of the eighties. Things were in a constant state of quiet hysteria in the week leading up to Michael's visit.

The offices, by that point, were impressive. We were at the top of the historic Broadway Building on the corner of Hollywood and Vine, the crossroads of the Walk of Fame. The King of Pop's arrival was pretty much what you'd expect for an actual king: bodyguards checked out the place, a path was cleared, and then he emerged from the elevator and glided toward my office. He said hi to everyone he passed (which I'm relatively sure caused some of my employees to lose consciousness), and then I welcomed him into my inner sanctum. We had important business to attend to.

We talked toys.

For real. Michael was a fan, it turned out, and even though his obsession with toys and dolls and miniatures wasn't as, well, stabby-killy as mine, we had a lot in common. At the time Full Moon was doing a lot of business with action figures—Puppet Master stuff especially. Michael liked it a lot, and he happily accepted the Blade figurine I gave him, although I'm pretty sure he already had one. We chatted for an hour or so, talked about things we might do together at some point, and that was that. Nothing much came of it, but it was memorable.

Well, not *nothing*. Later that year, me and the family got the chance to attend Michael's concert in Milan, as part of his gigantic HIStory tour. We joined his motorcade at the hotel and promptly got *lost* by his motorcade—the tour had made the mistake of hiring local security to arrange things, and their approach to arranging a motorcade was like everything Italian: casual and improvisational. Man, I love that country!

But we did make it to the arena, and the kids got to say hello to Michael backstage, which was a thrill, and then we were escorted to some pretty fantastic seats. But what I loved the most about it all happened next. To pump up the crowd, we were treated to a glitzy film about Michael, from the early days to the present, because, you know, "HIStory." Anyway, it was early in the film when my son Harlan, who was six or seven at the time, leaned over with uncontainable excitement to exclaim to Debi and me:

"I didn't know Michael Jackson used to be Black!"

As production ramped up in Romania, I started rotating my best, most trusted people in and out of there. David and Ted, of course, but a lot of other guys, too. And we were starting to notice a growing phenomenon. Guys were coming back with amazing experiences, souvenirs . . .

. . . and brides.

Beautiful, educated Romanian women, made of deep, penetrating stares and high cheekbones and Soviet-era world-weariness laced with unbelievable hope. They were all different, but of a type. Some of the marriages were true love, and others were at least true compatibility. And others . . . well, let's just say that not every Romanian really wanted to stay around and watch their country rebuild if they had other options. One of our directors came back with a pouty-faced, model-gorgeous wife who was *clearly* going to leave him at her first legal opportunity to do so. Well, it was clear to everyone but him. He didn't figure it out until he got the divorce papers. By then all the couple had in common was that neither one would be returning to Romania anytime soon.

Which was a pity, because Romania was thriving. It still amazes me how quickly the Romanians were able to turn their fortunes around. The food improved, the economy took off, the cities started to light up. Just a couple of years after he and his freezing cast had come within a hair's breadth of murdering each other (and possibly *eating* each other just to relieve the monotony of those shriveled potatoes), Ted Nicolaou was watching everything blossom and flourish. Even at its worst, you couldn't help but love that country, but by now he was happily directing movies at our shiny new studio, enjoying the great restaurants popping up all over Bucharest, and living it up with the suddenly successful Vlad and Oana. Vlad was working his tail off—not just tending to the construction and operation of the studio, but also continuing to be the best DP in the country.

I wanted in on the fun, too. I'd been visiting all the time, but much as in my Empire days, I'd been too busy to actually direct a movie at my studio. So I came up with a little something . . .

Just the year before I had shot *Head of the Family,* one of my favorites (remember, with the tongue? See chapter 1!), and I wanted to bring both Michael Citriniti and Jackie Lovell back for another insane romp. And it *was* insane—it's the story of two weird scientists who collect biological oddities, horrifically deformed animal and human specimens . . . until a few of their specimens come to life, burst forth from their jars, and wreak havoc!

I called it *Hideous!,* naturally.

Even when I direct, I rarely have the time to really shut out all the other business and focus solely on one movie, but I made an exception this time, and it was a delight. Vlad was my DP, Oana designed the costumes, and the whole process was incredibly smooth and fun. And gratifying, too: this studio that Vlad and I had built . . . it *worked*! If there was any problem at all, it was that it was the dead of winter, and no economic recovery was going to change the fact that Romania. Was. Frickin'. *Cold!*

Which was fine, mostly, because we shot most of the movie indoors. Except for one scene, which is the one that people remember most.

Early on in *Hideous!,* a fantastic specimen—a grotesquely deformed human baby—falls into the hands of one of the collectors (played by Mel Johnson Jr., whom you may remember as Benny the mutant cabdriver from *Total Recall*). He drives home through the snow with his precious cargo, only to be stopped and robbed by the other collector's batshit crazy and dangerous personal assistant (played by Ms. Jacqueline Lovell), who forces him into the woods at gunpoint, cuffs him to a tree, and then heads off with the specimen.

What makes the scene more memorable is that she does all

this while topless. Nearly naked, actually, except for the fact that she's wearing a giant gorilla mask.

Why? Because *nobody ever forgets that scene.*

Plus, Jackie's hilarious in it, and Mel is perfect as the cultured, affronted millionaire suddenly being exposed to indignity and madness. But to appreciate them you'd have to watch that scene a couple of times, because all you notice the first time is "guy gets tied to a tree by a topless wisecracking chick in a gorilla mask."

But here's the thing. It was *cold* that day. Jaw-clenchingly, ass-bitingly, face-numbingly cold. The kind of cold that instantly breezes through all your layers of clothing and chills your bones. They made me wear heated insoles in my shoes to keep me from losing a toe or two. *That* kind of cold.

And there was Jackie, wearing only a gorilla mask and a tiny pair of black shorts. And boots. And amazingly, you wouldn't know she was cold. She's hilarious, disguising her character's identity with a voice that sounds like a cross between Michael Keaton's Beetlejuice and Mr. T. To call her a "trouper" doesn't even begin. That was the actor's equivalent of being on SEAL Team 6.

We picked a remote road near the studio to shoot it. If you happened to be driving by on that day you would have seen, just off the road, a nearly naked white woman in a gorilla mask tying a well-dressed Black man to a tree. And you would've had questions.

What we hadn't counted on was that Romania really *was* flourishing. There were a lot more cars and a lot more places to go. So rather than the low traffic we expected, we had *lots* of people driving by. There was yelling and horn-honking, and we kept having to pause to usher people on their way. Not only had we created an indelible movie moment, we'd given the northern suburbs of Bucharest some dinner table conversation.

As much fun as I had making *Hideous!,* the late nineties weren't kind to my business. DVDs were coming in. Big studios started doing large-budget versions of the kind of movies I made, squeezing out our market share. In fact, the whole home entertainment business was becoming the kind of thing that only big studios could really do well.

But I stayed optimistic. Probably foolishly so. I did everything I could to keep things rolling. After all, it wasn't just for me: I had four kids now. Also, between Romania and my various facilities in Los Angeles I had something like 150 employees. All those people were counting on Full Moon—counting on *me*—to keep the train a-rolling.

I started selling stuff.

Lots of stuff.

And then I sold some more.

It wasn't immediate. It wasn't a fire sale. It was a death by a thousand cuts. But in a short amount of time I sold off all thirty of my Los Angeles properties, which nowadays would be worth somewhere in the neighborhood of a hundred million dollars. I sold off large pieces of my impressive art collection, some of the best stuff, the medieval *vanitas* and other treasures. But the most valuable thing I sold off was kept in a fireproof safe in a high room in the Toberman estate:

My comics collection.

Multiple Issue #1s, original art, you name it. I'd been a huge fan, as I said. In fact, in the nineties I actually had meetings and developed a character with the great Jack Kirby. Dr. Mortalis was sort of a latter-day take on his Doctor Strange, my favorite Marvel creation. The movie never got made, but I treasure my time working with the Master. Same with Stan Lee, a dear man whom I planned a couple of projects with.

I should mention—Stan Lee and I became friends, which

thrilled the eight-year-old in me to no end. I remember one night when Stan and his wife Joan came over for dinner. We brought them upstairs to meet our son, Harlan, who was incredibly shy at the time. We told Harlan that this was Stan Lee, the creator of Spider-Man and the X-Men and the Hulk . . . and that only made Harlan even shyer.

Stan and Joan knew just what to do. Somehow they ended up slipping off their shoes there in that bedroom . . . and started jumping on the bed. They were in their seventies, both of them, but they loved kids and had never lost touch with that part of themselves. In moments Harlan had joined them, and if there's one home movie I regret *not* taking, it's that one.

Later that night, I found myself alone with Stan for a moment. I'm not good at schmaltz and sentimentality, but I felt like I had to say something. I let him know in as few words as possible how much the world he created had meant to me. The incredible art, the freaky characters, and most of all, "Stan's Soapbox," the way the maestro himself would speak to us, his fans.

Stan got it. We hugged, he gave me a solid "New York guy" pat on the face, and we headed back to rejoin the others.

So yeah, I consider it an honor to have known those guys at all, and I absolutely treasured the contents of that safe.

I sold it all.

Believe it or not, in today's market that safe full of stuff would rival the value of my real estate, and it was infinitely more valuable to me.

Worse, all this stress and madness took its toll on my relationship with Debi. Our family, our life, our beloved street, and everything and everybody on it became yet another thing I was

Responsible For, and the weight of that responsibility was starting to press down on me. Hard.

All these things—the business, the family, Romania, my love of comics—came together in a project that was written for—and would only be seen by—a small handful of people.

It was 1997, and I called my friend Sandu Florea in New York. Sandu had fled Romania right around the time I went in, and by the time we started working together he was an established comic book artist, producing beautiful work for Marvel *and* DC. *Spider-Man, Batman, Buffy the Vampire Slayer:* he had some fantastic credits. But I needed him for a special project. It was a one-off comic book, written by me. A Christmas present for my family about our lives together, an amusing novelty gift like no other. It was the first of three I've commissioned from Sandu over the years. This first one was entitled *GO, MAN, GO,* and when I open it and look through the hilarious adventures of "Man" (me) nowadays, I see . . .

. . . a desperate cry for help.

Oh, it's amusing. But put against the backdrop of my life, it's a portrait of a man who is literally swarmed by his family and his work obligations from the moment he wakes up to the moment he collapses in bed at the end of the day. His spends all his time pursuing and distributing vast amounts of cash in a never-ending cycle. His life is without repose, recreation, or sex, and his dream, at the very end of the book, after he falls asleep, is to one day be recognized and appreciated by those he is providing for.

Look, I'm sure the real-life, three-dimensional Charlie Band *was* being appreciated. And I recognized (and made jokes about) the fact that having to maintain your mansion and your castle is kind of a ridiculous problem to have! But at the core of it, my "hilarious" Christmas gift to my family was me sending a message to myself, even if I didn't get it at the time.

I'm sure Debi did.

One more story from my late-nineties adventures. We shot *Retro Puppet Master,* a prequel, in Romania. It was the story of how Toulon learned the ancient Egyptian secret of animating the inanimate. Fun, right? Even more fun, it was kind of an alternative universe *Puppet Master,* using the puppets that appeared in Lee MacLeod's original sketch. Dave DeCoteau directed, and as young Toulon he cast a beautiful young actor named Greg Sestero.

Shooting that movie was memorable for Greg. Particularly because it was his first starring role, and his only one until a few years later, when he produced and starred in his eccentric friend Tommy Wiseau's independent feature. *The Room* is now thought to be perhaps the greatest awful movie of all time, and Greg later chronicled his journey in his book, *The Disaster Artist,* which itself became a movie, produced by Seth Rogen and directed by and starring James Franco.

I bring this up because of a little-known fun fact. Like the book, the opening scene of *The Disaster Artist,* which was eventually cut from the movie, takes place in Romania. There, young Greg Sestero (played by James Franco's brother, Dave) is shooting *Retro Puppet Master.* They re-created our set there at Castel Films and built some puppets. There was even a cameo by Dave DeCoteau.

While on set, Dave was reminded of something he'd pretty much forgotten about all those years ago—he was reintroduced to the actor he had turned down for the role of Young Toulon in favor of Greg.

James Franco.

And then, all at once, the millennium was drawing to a close. People were panicking about the "Y2K bug," a software flaw that was purportedly going to shut down our entire world, from web browsers to nuclear power plants. People were planning for the apocalypse. Me, I was planning my next movie, and I needed money for it. I went to Romania.

Vlad and Oana were thriving. We toured our studio, which was a beehive of activity—they were shooting the next Highlander movie there, *Highlander: Endgame*. It was one of the first of many high-profile films that would shoot there, including *Cold Mountain* and *Borat*.

We walked around Bucharest, and they showed me their store, their leather goods business, their new home. We ate at a wonderful restaurant, then walked the streets, which were lit up with holiday decorations, festooned with banners welcoming the fabled Year 2000. These people were not worried about the apocalypse—they'd lived through worse and come out the other side, and the streets sparkled with gratitude and hope.

Me, I wasn't quite as starry-eyed. My Romanian adventure was ending for now. The only Full Moon movies that were making money anymore were the erotic ones, and we didn't need to fly to Romania to make those. (In fact, even my operations back home were scaling back, and I no longer maintained that giant Atwater space.)

Over the years Vlad had assumed more and more control of the studio, buying pieces of it from me as I needed capital. The split was still 80–20, but now it was Vlad who owned the 80 percent. And that night, in Bucharest, he was arranging a hundred-thousand-dollar loan for me with his money guy, a loan against my last remaining 20 percent share of the studio.

While talking about the loan, Vlad expressed concern, and he offered me a guarantee. "Charlie," he said, "I know these are hard times for you, but you founded this studio. We built it. You can't lose this. I promise I'll protect you." I took him at his word; I'd always been good to Vlad, and he had always been good to me. The three of us walked on, down the joyously glowing Bucharest streets, talking and laughing.

Not too long afterward, back in the United States, I got a call from Vlad. I'd been unable to pay the money back to that point, but I still had high hopes. He said, "Charlie, they're calling the loan in. It's out of my hands."

"Really, Vlad?" I said. "I thought these were your guys."

"They're not nice guys, Charlie. It's . . . it's out of my hands," he repeated. Moments later, he hung up.

That was the last time Vlad and I ever spoke. He still runs Castel Film Studios, and he's an extremely wealthy man. As for me . . . well, the new millennium was beginning, my prospects were dwindling, and like so much else in my life, my stake in the fantastic, improbable studio I'd built from nothing . . . was gone.

Happy New Year!

Stretching Time: Dave Allen and Stop-Motion Animation

Finishing Dave Allen's magnum opus, *The Primevals,* has been a labor of love for Chris Endicott and me. But make no mistake: it takes a lot of love, because it's a hell of a lot of labor.

You probably know the basics. Or maybe you don't, so: You have to build puppets with a metal skeleton (or "armature") that's posable. That's the most expensive part—an armature could run you twenty-five thousand dollars! Then you cover it with a rubber "body" taken from a mold you created (remember, you might need to make an identical one if it rips!), and then paint it and add hair as necessary. And then comes the painstaking process of moving the puppets in the scene, one . . . frame . . . at . . . a . . . time.

But it's even more complicated than that.

Remember, these creatures have to exist in an environment. Which means you have to build amazing miniatures, which is super expensive, but that's how it was done in the early days, for movies like the original *King Kong.* Or you can shoot it in front of a blue or green screen and add in the background later, which creates its own set of challenges and often ends up looking really fake. Or there's Dave Allen's favorite approach, pioneered by Ray Harryhausen: you make a film for a backplate, then add in your creature, then layer in your foreground. Nowadays you can create those "masks" digitally, but until recently guys like Dave literally shot the puppet in front of a screen on which the backplate was projected. He'd also put a sheet of glass in front of the camera, literally masking off in black the parts of the picture he didn't want the camera to see. Then, after shooting the beast and the background in (stop) motion, he'd literally rewind the film in the camera and use a glass pane that was the opposite of the first one—masking off in black paint the area we'd seen before. That allowed him to shoot the foreground stuff, frame by frame, right onto the same film, exactly in the part of the picture that was previously blacked out! Think of it: the compositing is literally being done in the camera, on the film.

Barbaric, right? But it worked.

It got weird and improvisational sometimes. For instance, we had one scene where we needed an actor to run from our terrifying yeti. But using a blue screen would've looked bad. To make it work, we shot the actor running, and then printed that film out, frame by frame. Dave then had Chris cut the actor out—yes, like with a scissors!—frame by frame, and tape him to glass in front of our Yeti. So we basically shot him in real time just so we could shoot his movements in stop motion later.

Mind-bending? Yes. Dave liked to say, "When you're animating, you're stretching time." I love that, although it leads to problems because the world moves fast, and you need things to not change at all. While we were shooting *The Primevals* we came back from a holiday break to find the set had flooded a little. Although nothing was ruined, the miniature set we'd built, a fighting arena, had warped from the moisture. Just a little, but it would've made a disastrously obvious difference on film. An entire day was lost as we got that arena between some two-by-fours, put it in a vise, and expertly *twisted* it back into its original shape.

Then again, there are perks. For instance, the rains left the ministadium covered in ants as well. But you'll never see them, because in stop-motion terms, they move *way* too fast. Stretching time bailed us out.

12

Band on the Run

(2000–2008)

So the new millennium had arrived, and things were . . . well . . .
terrible.

I'd lost Romania. I'd lost the mansion on Camino Palmero.
And I'd lost my marriage. Truly terrible times can put a huge
strain on a relationship, and Debi and I didn't make it through as
a couple. We separated, and although we remained close, it was
clearly over. A lot of things seemed to be over.

This chapter is going to take us through some very bad years,
a period of time that I thought would be over quickly but then
stretched on and on and on. A chapter that I considered calling
"The Fifteen-Year Suck."

It didn't *all* suck. There were some real bright spots and amazing moments. I kept making movies, and I made some decisions
that set the stage for a bigger, brighter future.

But overall, it sucked.

So, what does a guy do when he's down on his luck and the world is against him and it all seems too much to bear? I did what many of the evil geniuses and vampiric monsters in my movies do: I retreated to my lair, my castle in the European mountains, alone, to brood.

And also I opened a restaurant.

Which admittedly isn't really an evil genius/vampire move.

Also, "opening a restaurant" is one of the few items on the very small list entitled "Businesses That Are Riskier Than the Film Industry." But that's okay. The heart wants what it wants, and my heart has never wanted anything easy.

I can't believe I've gotten this far in my story without telling you about my thing with food and cooking. I'm . . . into it. I fell in love with cooking when I was a kid, and by the time I was a teen I would literally walk into the kitchens of my favorite restaurants in Rome, just to see how they did stuff. The chefs were almost always women, and they were charmed by the skinny American with the audacity to invade a working kitchen, so they'd let me stay and watch for hours.

It was an amazing education. I didn't learn a single recipe. I learned how to *cook*.

Telling my loved ones I was decamping to Italy was hard, but they understood. I'd made almost two hundred movies, supported my parents and my wives and my kids, and I would keep supporting them, as best I could, even through those lean years. But now I had little to keep me in America. Full Moon's output had become largely erotic movies, and that was never something I could get too, um, *excited* about.

I got my life in some semblance of order. I had moved my dad and mom into a nice apartment, gotten myself a slightly less nice pad, moved Debi and the kids into a new, smaller house (one that, weirdly, was owned by Gore Vidal!). By that point I was dating someone, an actress, and it was a tumultuous on-and-off thing, the only item on my relatively short but intense romantic résumé that I am truly not proud of. Meda and Debi, even my shorter affairs with Demi and Jan Miracle: they were all wonderful people with whom I had a real spark, smart and capable women who really *got* me and what I was about. This . . . this was not that.

I went to Italy alone.

If you haven't guessed, the restaurant was *in* my castle. For years people had been advising me to turn the place into an attraction, give tours, make it a destination. This seemed like a great way to make all that happen. I threw myself into it—construction, plumbing, creating a great look and feel and menu. I found the right chef and the right waiters and the right everything. I made connections with suppliers and local media. Within a few short months I opened Castello di Giove.

Opening night was a triumph. Patrons were ushered into a fabulous, labyrinthine palace with elegant tables scattered through several gigantic rooms with roaring fireplaces and crisply dressed waiters hustling everywhere, bringing fantastic food and carefully selected wines. The place was beautiful. And *packed*—every one of those 140 seats was filled with an impressed, happy patron. If this had been a movie opening, that first week would have ensured a blockbuster success and cult classic status for years to come.

Unfortunately, restaurants are nothing like movies.

In retrospect, there was probably a way to make it work, to call people's attention to a glorious establishment on the road from Rome to Florence, to make it a destination from luxury hotels for an enchanted evening. It would've taken a firmer knowledge of the tourist industry, plus a deep understanding of what palms to grease. This was Italy. There are *always* palms to grease, but you have to know which palms. Hell, often you have to grease the palms of the people who can point you toward the right palms! I didn't know any of that, and frankly, I soon found that I didn't have a lot of interest in that world. I'd already made something great, which for me inevitably leads to one thought: What can I make next?

Which is exactly how a restaurant proprietor should *not* think.

Without the support of the industry in Rome and Florence, my restaurant never became a destination. Within a couple of weeks, after the initial promotion and excitement died down, my patrons were mainly local people. And not a lot of local people, either—the place was too fancy and expensive for the locals who I saw every day at the market. By the time we entered our second month of business, the giant dining rooms were sparsely dotted with customers. Having a great meal, yes, but they kind of had the castle to themselves, as it were.

Within a few months, I had to shut it down. And now I really was a revenant, brooding alone in his high castle.

But I don't brood. I went back to America.

Though these were lean times, I still had some fun, and in the process scraped together enough cash to keep everyone supported and keep my kids in their (incredibly expensive!) schools. For instance, I was approached by some guys over at the Sci-Fi Channel about throwing together some kind of show, maybe a showcase for Full Moon movies, a movie night like the ones hosted by Elvira or Joe Bob Briggs. And I knew exactly who I wanted to host it—I had been hanging out with William Shatner, and he seemed like the perfect guy for the job. I called him.

"Bill, it's Charlie," I said. "I want you to be my Elvira."

"I don't know," he said without missing a beat. "I don't think I have the figure for it."

William Shatner's Full Moon Fright Night only ran for a season, but it was a decent success (Sci-Fi pulled it only because they'd made the decision to move toward original shows and big-budget movies). It was fun, a weekly party with Bill, a creepy puppet sidekick, and a Full Moon feature. One thing I was proud of was the final ten minutes of every show, which I carved out for Bill to interview a celebrity, usually a cult hero. Among my favorite interviews were Stan Lee, Roger Corman, and Alex Band.

Wait, what was that last one?

Yes, my son had suddenly become a full-fledged rock star! In 2001, the band he'd been playing with for five years dropped their first album. They'd named themselves the Calling, and the album, *Camino Palmero,* was a big hit in 2001. Alex wrote the songs, was the lead singer and lead guitarist, and the single "Wherever You Will Go" . . . well, you've heard that one for sure. It parked in the number one spot in the Adult Top 40 chart for nearly six months! That's second only to "Smooth" by Santana, whom, by the way, Alex promptly went on tour with.

Was I proud? Indescribably. Literally indescribably. Parenthood is so weird, like its own kind of messed-up time machine. Seeing Alex perform for thousands of screaming fans is overlaid in my brain with the memory of him as that shirtless seven-year-old, dancing and lip-syncing Madonna on a table in Italy. In some ways, for me, those two guys seem to exist simultaneously, both full of the same swagger, just slightly different sizes.

Yeah. I was proud. The Bands played on.

Well, not all of us.

Tragically, another reason I was back in America was my dad. He suddenly wasn't doing well. Health problems seemed to pop up all at once, including cancer, and I do think that for him the treatment might have been worse than the disease. I mean, he always had endless energy, endless drive to take care of things and get things done. Like me, he didn't want to be *taken care of*—that seemed backward! So being so weakened by those treatments, suddenly being diminished to the point where he couldn't feel useful and engaged . . . I think that broke him. His life was long (but not long enough) and full of joys and amazing stories and incredible adventures, but in June of 2002 Albert Band, son of the renowned artist Max Band, father of Charlie and Richard, died in Los Angeles at the age of seventy-eight.

One advantage of my selective memory is that I approach my life like a film editor: I generally only keep in the good stuff. So my dad's final years weren't something I had to "get over" in order to remember him at his best. I *always* remember him at his best. And that helps. The thing to get over, though—the thing I'll never get over, and that's okay, is *missing him*. He was my pal, my accomplice, and my *dad*. Whenever I had bright spots in dark times, and now when I'm having mostly good times, whenever anything awesome happens or I make something cool, that thought is always there with me:

My dad would've loved this.

He would've loved the Houdini mansion.

My dad was actually still alive when I found it. I was driving over Laurel Canyon sometime early in the twenty-first century when it attracted my attention—this weird property right off the side of the road, this mysterious place full of gypsies and vagabonds. In fact, I had a memory of it that's connected to my parents. CUT TO—

It was 1959, and we must've been in Los Angeles on some kind of vacation or business trip, because we were living in Italy by then. But I remember driving on Laurel Canyon Boulevard with my family. If you've spent any time in Los Angeles, you *know* that scene. The Valley is connected to Hollywood by very few roads through those hills, and absolutely everybody has to drive through those hills at some point. Hills filled with actors and rock stars and—on more than one occasion—members of the Band family. They're magical.

On this day, though . . . the mansion that Houdini had lived in had mysteriously burned to the ground, allegedly taking some of the secrets he had stored with it. People had gathered, gawking, exploring the weird property, grabbing half-burned film canisters from the smoldering ruins. My family drove by it, slowly, stuck in the inevitable Laurel Canyon traffic. I looked at that weird scene.

"Stop the car!" I yelled.

They didn't. We had somewhere to be.

Flash forward. It was the year 2000 and suddenly I didn't have that many places to be. But I was driving over the canyon, probably coming back from visiting the Valley-based wing of my family. The property again caught my eye and suddenly my childhood curiosity came flooding back. And there was something new there: a sign reading FOR SALE.

It was forty years later, and I finally stopped that car.

To say that the property was weird is a massive understatement. It was *bizarre*. Houdini actually never owned it—it was a loaner— but it was clearly his place. There were gardens and hidden paths and caves and secret tunnels everywhere. Real, natural caves, but excavated ones as well, connecting the property in weird ways. It had also become a homeless enclave, but not a typical one. If you were living on that remote, heavily wooded property at the top of the Hollywood Hills, that wasn't an underpass you'd stumbled across. You were there because you *meant* to be there.

I felt like I was meant to be there, too. The plan formed in my head all at once: I could buy the property, restore the serviceable but decrepit guesthouse, and live there while I rebuilt the mansion.

Did I have the wherewithal to do all that? Of course not. But I set about making it happen.

The owner was a strange dude, but he could tell my love for the place was real. Somehow I scraped together the cash and bought the property, with my only precondition being that he would politely but firmly ask the vagabond population—with whom he had a decent relationship—to move on. He agreed.

That first day I had it all to myself, walking around the grounds, it was everything I'd hoped—a magical place, full of apricot trees and lemon trees that produced these giant, bizarrely shaped mutant lemons. Secret gardens, terraces, waterfalls. In no time I'd put up a wall and planted trees to shield the place from the gawkers on Laurel Canyon, restored the guesthouse, moved in. A tiny house next door was for sale, and I bought it and moved the Full Moon offices in there so I could stay closer to my new love. I was down to a mere six or seven employees at that point, so I figured the arrangement could work.

Sounds a little obsessive, doesn't it? It was *love*. Although I had almost nothing left to sell and no realistic hopes of getting my mansion built soon, I pressed ahead and hired an architect to design my future palace. Insane.

But as immoderate and ill-timed as my passion for Houdini's mansion was, it was also rewarding. Of all the weird, wonderful places I've lived—Camino Palmero, the castle, Liberace's mansion—the Houdini property is the only one I truly *miss*. My boys loved it, too. Harlan and Zalman would spend their days prowling the property, hunting with BB guns or rampaging on the ATV that their rock star big brother Alex had brought home from his tour. We had a blast there, and that strange, magical, surreal place got woven into their childhoods—their own private Wonderland, nestled, impossibly enough, in the heart of Los Angeles.

Nowadays the "Houdini estate" is owned by a company that rents it out for weddings and other affairs. I've seen pictures, and it looks okay. I'm sure the place is happy enough with her new owners. But it can't be the same—they'll never love her the way I loved her. They'll never have what *we* had.

You might be tempted to point out that my affair with Houdini's place happened at a time in my life when, for the first time, I didn't have a stable romantic relationship with a woman. To that I say, "Well . . . *shut up*." It was what it was.

Besides, that was about to change.

I realize that all this might make me sound like an eccentric, down-on-his-luck recluse, holed up in his weird house on a hill. In reality, even during the bad times, I never lost touch with my family, never stopped trying to support everyone, and never stopped making movies. And I even managed to have a little fun.

For instance, in the summer of 2002 I got a call from Jim Gianopulos, who was busily making Fox Films relevant again. Jim and I had never lost touch. In fact, throughout the nineties, when he was leading international distribution for Fox, I'd often get calls from him that went like this:

"Hey, man, I'm in Germany, and I'm trying to get this deal secured, and things are all over the place, and I just need to get everybody on board. I feel like we need a change of venue . . ."

"You want to borrow the castle."

"I want to borrow the castle. Can I borrow the castle?"

"You can borrow the castle, Jim. I'll call Enzo and let him know you're coming."

Yes, we both said the phrase "borrow the castle" a lot. Wouldn't you?

Anyway, in 2002, shortly after my dad passed away, Jim had a great idea for a little pick-me-up. He called and asked if I'd be his guest at the Venice Film Festival, where his new movie was premiering: *Road to Perdition,* starring Tom Hanks and Paul Newman and Jude Law and a relative newcomer named Daniel Craig.

Over the years, I've probably turned down hundreds of invitations to glittery events like this. The whole red-carpet scene just isn't for me. But this one was different—I needed a break and Jim was a true friend. I brought Debi with me (as I said, we've always stayed close), and for once the experience was as enjoyable as it looked from the outside. Venice is a fantastic setting, obviously, and the whole vibe around the *Perdition* gang was positive and fun. We had a few meals with them, and what Debi and I remember most is how genial and funny Tom Hanks was, one of the rare stars who doesn't have to build a public persona—he is 100 percent *that guy*.

And I remember that Daniel Craig, possibly because he was a relative unknown on a screen full of household names, was endearingly insecure about his performance. He repeatedly asked Debi and me if we thought he was good, if he'd played it right, if we enjoyed it. It was pretty much the polar opposite of what you'd expect from a man who was about to become the next James Bond.

Back home, I kept plugging along. Though I had to scale things back, I was still making between four and ten movies a year, always keeping a hot set somewhere. The kids would visit those sets, too. Even Zalman, who was now in grade school. In fact, he dropped by a lot. His friends in school were all begging to be his guests, because where Zalman's dad worked there were blood and guts and monsters (and even more shockingly, there were boobies. Real, live boobies!).

As always, I kept things on my sets light and fun. Except for a one-day shoot that wasn't fun at all, which turned out to be one of the luckiest things that ever happened to me.

My friend and frequent collaborator Billy Butler brought me the script for *The Gingerdead Man,* the tale of a deranged murderer who gets executed and is brought back to life when his witchy mother mails enchanted dough to a bakery where—

—oh, you get it. A psychotic cookie comes to life and rampages. Okay?

To make things more interesting, just as we went into production, my casting people let me know that Gary Busey was available. And attainable: because of the weird story we'd written, I'd only need him for a one-day shoot as the murderer, and then when he's reincarnated as the cookie I'd only need his voice! Perfect!

For my leading lady, the daughter of the owner of the failing bakery where our evil Buseycookie comes to life, I found a young actress who had a great look and absolutely nailed the Texas accent I needed. Her name was Robin Sydney, and she had just moved to L.A. from Colorado with her mom, and she was . . . something.

I remember one moment during that first day on set, when I

made eye contact with Robin from across the room and felt that unmistakable *thing*. That charge. Something I'd only felt once or twice before in my life.

But I put that thought right out of my head immediately and got back to work. Robin was so young—*way* too young. And I . . . well, I wasn't all that young anymore. I'd turned fifty while trying my hand as a restaurateur in Italy. Besides, I had more than enough problems, one of them pretty immediate:

Gary Busey was a *nightmare*.

I guess that's not surprising. I knew his reputation, and I knew he had suffered a head injury in 1988, which had made him a bit more addled and volatile. But we only needed him to keep it together for one day. *One day!* How much nonsense could he get up to?

A fair amount, it turned out.

He was temperamental. He was weird. And he was an impossible lech. Almost immediately a couple of the women from wardrobe and makeup approached me and let me know that he was saying lewd things and being "accidentally" handsy. I advised them to steer clear and let me know if it got too uncomfortable. They said they could handle it. Honestly, I thought, I just need him for one scene. Like five shots . . .

Then he disappeared.

We'd gotten set up in a cool old diner in the Valley that we'd rented, a place where a million movies have been shot. We set up our "base camp" and craft services in the parking lot, and the only other thing there was the large trailer we'd rented for Gary, which was one of his demands to do the shoot. If he wasn't in the trailer, there was pretty much nowhere else he could be.

He wasn't in the trailer.

At least, he wasn't answering. Nobody wanted to invade his space, so they fetched me. Charlie, a.k.a. "the Maniac Whisperer." I knocked. Nothing. The clock was ticking. I went in.

Another of Gary's demands was a big basket of candy. Like, *really* big. And his people had been very specific about what kinds of candy. I don't remember exactly what it was, but it was the cheap stuff—pretty much a big basket of Halloween candy.

Anyway, Gary wasn't in the trailer. But the candy basket had been *decimated.* Wrappers everywhere, like a Candyland crime scene. Somewhere out in the naked city, Gary Busey was roaming, high on what must have been a full pound of refined sugar and corn syrup.

I stood there in the parking lot with my crew, flabbergasted. Things got quiet. Quiet enough that I started to hear something. A muttering. It seemed to come from behind the trailer, but the trailer was up against the wall. There was no "behind the trailer."

Except that there was. A tiny alcove, it turned out. I squeezed in, the voice getting louder as I went . . .

"Bush. The bush is gone. There's no more bush . . ."

I got back there. There was Gary, his already wild eyes amped up on a sugar high, and he'd somehow talked two women from my crew back there and he was lecturing them about the tragic loss of women's pubic hair in our society: "Everybody had bush back then. Bush is natural! But now, no bush. Nobody has . . . Do you have bush? Do either of you have—"

"Hey Gary?" I said. He whirled around. I looked at the women from my crew. They definitely had no interest in weighing in on the issue of bush. Before Gary could get my opinion on the issue, I hurriedly told him, "The shot's set up. We're ready for you." He seemed to focus a bit, and soon he was squeezing himself through the narrow space and back into the world, a complete maniac whose only job that day was to be a complete maniac.

He did a few takes and then took a break while we set up the next shot. It seemed like we might get through this.

Until Robin Sydney's mom, an incredibly sweet and competent woman, found me. "Mr. Band," she said. "My daughter is in Gary Busey's trailer. You've gotta get her out." Jesus, he really was like the Gingerdead Man—fueled by sugar, and you couldn't turn your back on him for a nanosecond.

I was on my feet instantly. Ran outside and into the parking lot, knocked once on the trailer door, and then pushed it open.

Gary had Robin in there, seated across from him as he held forth. Rambling, really, but fortunately no longer about bush. No, he was expressing his learned thoughts on the Craft of Acting. I suspect he was trying to impress her, but I could instantly see in Robin's eyes that she was humoring him but terrified. I quickly invented a reason why we needed Ms. Sydney on set.

Once we were out of there, I gathered the crew and pointed to the trailer door. "Pretend that's a crime scene," I said. "Nobody goes in or out."

We got through the day. The rest of the movie was a lot easier, because instead of Gary, we got to work with the cookie.

The Gingerdead Man did well, and I knew I had a potential franchise on my hands. I shot some other pretty good things too, including *Doll Graveyard,* one of two movies I made at my beloved Houdini estate. As I said, even in the lean times there was never a year where Full Moon didn't manage to release a movie or two. But it wasn't enough. The home video business was slipping away, morphing into something new. By that point I'd lost a lot of the revenue from my soft-core erotica. Hollywood Video had been taken over by a concerned Christian who eliminated all the non-wholesome offerings. They floundered not long after that, and they were bought out in 2005. Never bet against sex.

Blockbuster itself was starting to struggle. Netflix was on the rise, with their DVD-by-mail model, and suddenly owning hundreds of brick-and-mortar stores seemed like a foolish, expensive dinosaur of an idea. But how was an independent like me going to get shelf space in a world without *shelves*? How was I going to make money?

I thought I had an answer: an elaborate, must-see road show. And merch. Piles and piles of merch.

For the couple of years we did it, the Full Moon traveling road show was a crazy, wild, messy, wonderful thing. We had a truck that pulled a fantastic, custom-painted trailer full of products and props. We had a genuine guillotine onstage, where we'd perform nightly bloody "beheadings." We'd have celebrity guests— Bill Shatner did a bunch of the early ones. But mostly it was me, on the stage, P. T. Barnum-ing for a couple of hours, working my spiel, telling stories, keeping things moving. It wasn't the first time—Paramount had sent me out to entertain vendors a decade before, and this was just a bigger, funnier version of that. It was the Video Zone, but live.

And weirder. The audience got everything they'd gotten from my Full Moon movies: blood, behind-the-scenes stuff. Heroes, monsters, and even boobies. But those last three items were supplied by the audience.

I'll explain. Toward the end of every show, I'd demonstrate how easy it was to put together a horror movie. All you needed was a monster, a stalwart but kinda dumb hero, and a beautiful babe. The hero might get killed, the monster almost definitely would get defeated, and the babe, I said, almost invariably would lose her shirt at least once or twice.

And then I asked for volunteers to come onstage and let me talk through an improvised "movie shoot," people willing to be my Hero and my Monster and my Babe. That was the key—to tell them exactly what I was asking for so nobody felt uncomfortable or pressured. And you know what? I always got plenty of volunteers. These were fun, often drunk kids, whooping it up. It was spring break for horror nerds. There was always a clown who wanted to be the hideous monster, a jock who wanted to play the hero, and a boisterous babe who wanted to ham it up and, yes—when the plot called for it—spend a few moments topless to the deafening cheers and shrieks of the assembled audience.

And then, when it was all over, I would go to the lobby of the theater we'd four-walled and plant myself behind a table. For two hours each night, I'd meet, greet, and sign merchandise for people.

It was grueling work, running the show and then glad-handing for another couple of hours. It was fun, though. Especially because my son Harlan was with me at every single one of those road shows. He was in his early twenties and was psyched to travel and pitch in. He made himself a sort of apprentice to one of the roadies. The shows became a great father-and-son activity, just with a little more blood, raunch, and mayhem than most fishing trips.

But the pace was relentless—we might do twenty cities in thirty nights. I'd spend my days promoting, reaching out to radio stations and fan bases in whatever city we were headed to next, and my nights doing the shows. Unlike my crew, I flew back to Los Angeles at least once a week to see my kids and take care of business stuff. And, over time, to catch just one more dinner with Robin Sydney.

I'll get back to that in a minute.

But I think this is important: even though the road show was sort of a glorious failure from a financial standpoint (after the first few, we were lucky to break even), there was something really valuable about those signing sessions. For the first time I was out there, all over the country, meeting my fans. People in their twenties, thirties, even forties who'd grown up with my movies. They'd tell me how they begged their parents to let them rent *Puppet Master.* Or how they wanted more *Trancers.* And always there'd be at least one guy, always thirtyish, who'd tell me about how he couldn't use a bathroom for weeks after he'd seen that damn *Ghoulies* ad.

It was hugely touching. And super informative—I was being educated by hundreds of real fans about what they liked and didn't like about my movies. It was the kind of knowledge I could take to the bank.

Except that, increasingly, I had nothing in the bank.

All right, let me tell you the wonderful thing before I get to the terrible things: I fell in love with Robin Sydney. And improbably enough, she fell in love with me.

It started as "business dinners." Robin and her mom were running a burgeoning young wholesale company that sold clever point-of-purchase "impulse" items to retailers. She knew a startling amount about her business and had made a ton of connections just at a time when I saw retail merchandise as the future of Full Moon. So there was a reason for us to have dinner. Once or twice. But as time went on, I quickly became aware that I just wanted to dine with her, talk to her, be around her incredibly joyful, positive energy. We got to know each other, and the dinners got longer and longer. But she always brought her marbleized notebook with her and laid it on the table as she sat down. Because this was business.

She did this even after her mom started teasing her that there was no way this was business anymore. Robin told me that with a shy smile. But I didn't pursue the subject.

With signals like that, a younger incarnation of myself would've made his move long before. But I was hesitant. For one, there was the age difference. And times had changed. But more than that, it was a difficult, uncertain time in my life. And I had this fantastic, incandescent new friend in my life, a beacon of positivity and light in my increasingly gray world. I didn't feel like I could handle losing that friendship if I misread her signals and made an unwanted move. Me, a guy who never hesitated even when I obviously should have . . . and now, suddenly, I was flat-footed.

But one night, in our favorite Italian restaurant, I tentatively went for it. Tentatively. Giving her every possible offramp. I asked her if I could *ask her* to sit next to me after dinner. She said I could. And then, after dinner, I asked, and she sat next to me. We talked, and then I went ahead and gave her the lightest, most respectful kiss. But a real one. And then asked her if she'd liked that. She smiled and said, "Yeah. I did."

That was fifteen years ago. That restaurant is long gone. But we're still together.

Okay, kids, buckle up. We're heading for some turbulence. I'm going to do this as fast as I can, rip that Band-Aid right off . . .

The crazy, glorious road show ground to a halt. Comic-Con and Monsterpalooza and megafan events like that were suddenly thriving, so did I really need to invent the wheel yet again? I figured out that peddling my wares at conventions was a lot more profitable and wayyyy less effort. Besides, the debts were piling up. I had to sell the Houdini estate, obviously—owning that never made any real sense. But it hurt to see her go.

And still there were debts. It got so bad that I started throwing out letters and bills unopened, especially if the envelope looked dire and kinda like "legal" stuff. That was a mistake, obviously, but I knew I couldn't afford the legal help I'd need to sort it all out. See, I'd never shielded myself; all my businesses were in my name, all my debts belonged to me alone. It's like I never learned the lesson that had been handed to me, gift-wrapped, by the DMV, when I bought all those cars for *Crash!* I never learned to be crafty like Dino De Laurentiis, able to sell you a movie studio that he didn't technically own.

Bad things started to happen. I was at a convention in Texas, signing autographs and earning a few grand, when a sheepish fan who'd waited his turn walked up to my table and said, quietly, "I feel so bad, Mr. Band. I love your movies."

My first thought was, Poor kid, he must be from one of those strict evangelical families. I smiled gently and said, "Well, look, I admit that they can be kind of a guilty pleasure, but—"

"No, it's not—I feel bad because . . . you're being served!" he blurted, and he dropped some papers on my table and literally ran off out of the hall.

I tucked the envelope away as quickly as I could, hoping not too many fans saw that. It was mortifying. Awful.

That happened to me more than once. More than twice, in fact. I began to feel hunted.

If there were any bright spots . . . well, I still managed to make a movie or two, somehow. And Robin and I had moved in together. I actually moved in with her, in an apartment right near her mom's. Just like moving to Rome when I was a child, it was meant to be a temporary arrangement.

And just like Rome, but way less glamorously, it lasted ten years.

Any film buff knows there's a moment when our hero hits rock bottom, where everything seems hopeless and there's seemingly no shot at redemption. The end of Act Two. Like so many people before me, my rock bottom happened in Florida.

It was 2008, and I was working a convention. It had been a horrible year, but I was happy enough to be settling in for a weekend of signings and meeting fans and earning a few thousand bucks. It was Friday afternoon, and things were just getting started. The fans were just coming in, and various security people were getting themselves settled, so it didn't alarm me when two officers from the sheriff's department came up to my table. In fact, a lot of my fans are cops. When they meet me, they all generally say the same thing: "No shit! You made *Puppet Master*?" I greeted them warmly.

They were less warm. But they looked apologetic.

"Mr. Band, we are going to have to handcuff you and walk you out of here. Would you like to make this easier by stepping back behind the booth before we do it?"

It took me a good long time to process this. Would . . . I . . . like to step behind the booth . . . so these men . . . could handcuff and arrest me? Which they were going to do anyway?

Oookay. Now I understood the question.

I said that yes, I would prefer to do it that way. I got up and walked behind the booth. I'd be lying if I said I didn't contemplate making a break for the door. Maybe I could push over a display, cause a distraction . . .

They cuffed me. And walked me out. And read me my rights.

And took me to jail. When they nudged me into that holding cell and slid the door closed and it shut with that ridiculously loud metallic CLANG, I thought, Wow. The movies really don't quite capture what this is like.

It really, really sucks.

What I learned was this: There'd been a film lab that I used, in Pittsburgh, that I owed some money to. They'd gone out of business, but whoever held the debt was not playing around. Because we'd conducted our business across state lines, I guess, they were able to obtain a warrant and grab me in Florida. The cops told me that on Monday I'd appear before a judge and then be taken, in chains, into a van with other prisoners and transported to Pittsburgh.

Holy. Shit.

And wait—*Monday*?

Yeah. It was Friday evening. It'd be two days before the court would open. I'd be spending my weekend in jail.

My first thought was . . . Wow. There goes my convention money.

I called Robin. What else could I do? Even if I was endangering our newish relationship by being the fucked-up broke boyfriend calling from prison, I had to be honest. To my surprise, all she radiated was concern and a zealous determination to help me. Her mom, too. They vowed to make calls, wire me some money, fight this. I called Debi next, and she was instantly taking my side, promising to call her ex-boyfriend who was a lawyer with some connections.

I was kind of surprised that nobody yelled at me or just wrote me off at that moment. Maybe I was even a little shocked by the warmth, and I'm not sure I trusted it or knew what was next.

What I do know is that five minutes later I was back in that holding cell. For the weekend.

It wasn't a nice place. It was dark and dank and humid in that uniquely Floridian way. My cellmates were rough, and some of them were downright scary. Most of them were younger than me. And bigger.

I couldn't tell you much about that weekend. Mostly I stayed quiet, kept to myself, and mentally went to a place that I hadn't been since those terrible, gory weeks in those third-world hospitals. I went into survival mode. I let time pass. That's the key: Time is going to pass. Let it. I endured.

At one point, I remember, a policeman on guard duty motioned me over and talked to me through the bars. He wanted to know why I was there, probably because I was well dressed and middle-aged. And white. Florida, man. Anyway, I told him about the convention, about and how I was Pittsburgh-bound, the whole thing. He took a step back.

"No shit! You made *Puppet Master*!"

I admitted that I had. He was impressed. Then:

"What the fuck are you doing here?"

Well, officer, if you're reading this, now you know.

Monday morning they took me, cuffed, to the courthouse. A sack with my personal effects was with me, ready to be loaded into my next transport. It was a pretty grim scene.

But there at the courthouse, waiting for me, was a lawyer. Debi had come through. Robin and her mom had, too, with some money. After a quick hearing during which it was established that Mr. Band was a Respectable Citizen and Noted Filmmaker with no prior record who promised to make his way to Pittsburgh within the next thirty days . . . I was set free.

Ladies and gentlemen, if there is a drug better than "not being chained up and taken to Pittsburgh," I have never found it.

That night I was back in Los Angeles, hugging Robin, thanking her mom, calling Debi and the kids. One thing I knew, right away, was that I was never going to throw out those dire-looking envelopes ever again. I'd open 'em, face 'em, and pay off every penny I owed, even if it took years.

It did, in fact, take years.

But look, even though I still had some rough years ahead of me, if this is a story where our hero improbably finds his redemption and *wins* . . . the victory wasn't years later with a movie-related windfall. It happened right then and there. Robin and her mom, my mom, Debi, and all my kids . . . despite my self-appointed role of paterfamilias, the star of my own comic book in which I forked over reams of cash to my needy, insatiable clan . . . nobody shut me out now that I couldn't be the Provider. When push came to shove, it wasn't *about* that to them, and it probably never had been. The compulsion to constantly provide for and thrill everyone and never, ever be the needy one—that compulsion was mine and mine alone. I was valued for something different, something much more important.

Hell, I knew all that already. But it's one thing to know it, and another to experience it, especially when you're used to being the guy that everybody else is depending on. I don't want to idealize it, or gloss over some of the truly hard times to come. But that was my George Bailey moment. I was the richest man in town.

The Joy of Fake Sex

Once I discovered that erotic movies were my only remaining reliable cash cow, you'd think I'd just drop the other stuff and enjoy making 'em for the rest of my days.

You'd be wrong.

There are two reasons for this. First, horror and sci-fi, often with a comedy twist . . . that's just where my imagination lives. I could never stop making those. But second, there's a dirty little secret about dirty movies: they're not that fun to make.

Oh, they're fun. Moviemaking is always fun. But despite what most people think, there's nothing particularly sexy about shooting sexy movies. Often a new friend will smile and elbow me when the subject of my erotic movies comes up, nudging and winking about what a thrill it must be to work with all those beautiful, undressed people, getting them oiled up, going in for close-ups . . . and I have to let them down.

I guess the first time you make one you may get some cheap thrills. Like when I did *Cinderella* back in the seventies. Since these are my confessions, I'll confess that I may have experienced a boner or two. But that ended quickly. I soon became so jaded that to me, on set, there's little difference between banging two puppets together and banging two humans together.

When you think about it, getting excited on an erotic set ultimately is as unlikely as getting scared on a horror set. Yes, you have these two gorgeous, undressed human bodies (or sometimes three or four!). But you also have lighting people and makeup artists and PAs and cameramen. Just like with a puppet fight, the cameras are usually really close to the actors, too. Each shot has to be planned meticulously, rehearsed, set up, and then filmed. You want to make sure the camera is seeing exactly the right thing. And just like when you're shooting a puppet, there are certain things that it's really important that the camera *doesn't* see. Remember, this isn't hard-core! Not only do you want to leave a little to the imagination, you also need to hide the fact that, for instance, the dude that you're shooting has his most treasured possessions tucked away. And somewhat uncomfortably at that.

All that said, it *is* fun. There are laughs and banter and running gags and problem-solving, and everyone almost forgets that some of the people involved happen to be naked. Also, my erotic movies usually have some kind of sci-fi or comedy twist, so there's actual acting to be done and lines to play around with. In my genre of erotic movies it's not enough to send a pizza delivery guy into a scene and have a bored suburban MILF rip his clothes off. No, I've got to wrangle costumes and effects to create Sherwood Forest, spaceships, and Mexican villages. And tell an actual story. And *then* the clothes get ripped off.

13

Buried Treasures

(2009–Right Now)

I said I wasn't going to gloss over the bad times, but you know me by now: I'm not going to dwell on them, either. I kept finding ways to make movies, kept my brand and my business afloat. But I was a little wiser with money, and kept everything within my available resources.

I kept trying to innovate, too. Netflix had changed the industry by starting to stream its movie library, and I thought, Well, why can't a small independent with a lot of properties do the same thing? I built FullMoonStreaming.com, an Internet home where the true fans could see my movies. I was, I think, the first indie house to do that, and it was slow sledding at first. But I was convinced the future was there.

There were other tough breaks. In 2012 we lost my mom. She'd lived a full and long life, though, and she'd gotten to watch her kids and grandkids grow up and thrive. She even got to spend time with Robin. I remember the night after Mom met (and obviously liked) Robin and her mother. I was driving her home and she elbowed me and smiled wickedly and said, "You cradle-robber."

Sure, Mom. Cheapen it, why don't you?

I miss her.

When 2015 rolled around, I had to make a terrible choice. There was still one company that owned most of the rest of my debts. Coast Capital, they were called, and I think the debt was something like a million dollars. The Big Kahuna, debt-wise. They had a lien on basically the only two big possessions I had left in the world: My movies. And my castle.

Actually, it wasn't *that* tough a decision. I gave them the castle.

Now, the castle was great, obviously. But it had become more of a vanity. Still, let's be honest: an *awesome* vanity! I mean—I was a guy who owned a castle! That's a big, gaudy, amazing thing to be able to say.

But the kids were grown, I no longer had business in Europe, and the July family vacations were a thing of the past. And unless you're using them to protect the town from invading hordes, castles are for the young. I had been a kid with a castle! Now I was just a guy with a castle. Who had kids. Who were adults.

But my movies . . . no way was I going to let those go. It had to be the castle.

[Side note: The year after I had to sell the castle, in October 2016 came a series of earthquakes in central Italy, the largest in nearly forty years, centered in the Umbria region. One of the casualties was the Castle Giove, which suffered some massive structural damage and, as I write this, is *still* being repaired to make it habitable again. I'd actually forgotten that little detail, but Debi enjoyed reminding me. She considers it another case of the Dion Curse!]

But yeah, it wasn't a hard choice. I was still making movies—*Puppet Master* sequels, other sequels, even crossovers: in 2013 I made *Gingerdead Man vs. Evil Bong,* funny, creepy stoner fare that I could make on a budget, make a few DVDs, and put up on my site for my streaming subscribers.

By 2015, I'd built up to fifteen hundred subscribers. It wasn't a ton, but it was growing, and it was proof that the audience was out there. I started licensing more cult films and forgotten exploitation treasures, movies that would entertain my fans but that nobody else knew were out there. I'd been doing this stuff for a long time. I knew where the bodies were buried.

Which leads me to 2016, when I got a call from a fan named Chris. He told me he was a true admirer, that he liked my movies, and that he particularly liked what I'd done with Full Moon's streaming service.

Oh, I should also mention that Chris worked for a company called Amazon.

"We're starting up something new," he said. "Premium channels that subscribers can order à la carte, just add 'em to their Amazon Prime subscriptions." That sounded smart.

"That sounds smart," I said.

"What would you say to making a Full Moon channel be part of our first slate?"

I said yes.

We launched toward the end of a month, so the first report we got from Amazon, when it came to my office, only included the first six days' worth of subscriptions. There were seven hundred of them.

By year's end we had twelve thousand subscribers. The next year we launched in the UK and Germany. (Fortunately, I still had German dubs of a lot of the early stuff! But it was still a ton of work.) By that year's end we had twenty thousand subscribers. Nowadays that number is more like fifty thousand. With another seven thousand or so subscribing to what used to be the Full Moon website but is now a shiny, cool app that runs on everything.

All that doesn't make me a billionaire, but it's pretty cool. And because it's done on a subscription model, it's given me something I've never, ever had before—a steady, reliable stream of income. Which beats the hell out of my previous business model, which was essentially "Make something, put it out, get a check, celebrate, and then hope to god it's enough until you make the next one."

This is better.

But those are just numbers. In the real world, what this means is that I have all these weird, insane little movies that I've made over decades, and now, suddenly, there's an easy and cool way to connect them to the fans, and *the fans are out there*. Some of these movies had been covered up by the weird history of the industry, but people still want to see them, and they want to see those franchises continued in new, twisted ways. Maybe I haven't made a lot of great business decisions, but holding on to the things I made was one of the good ones. There was still value there to be unearthed.

Speaking of which . . .

During the hard years, I still always took time to have lunch with Chris Endicott, Dave Allen's old assistant. Chris had moved on to digital effects, which was a smart move, and he was doing well, working on tons of Marvel movies and other blockbusters.

[Sidebar! Since you're probably curious: Yes, I go see Marvel movies. I mean, come on: *Marvel*! But some of today's blockbusters leave me cold. By the time you get into that second hour, it's not so much about those amazing characters getting into weird, wonderful, unbelievably twisted situations. Instead, some of the movies follow a giant, world-destroying, cataclysmic explosion . . . with another giant world-destroying cataclysmic explosion. A mighty, skull-shattering knockout punch turns out to be the first of a *dozen* knockout punches. I've loved comic books for a long time, but if the second half of every single book had been a long, protracted battle sequence, I would've lost interest. Not a criticism—that's just my taste.

Okay, I'm going to get off of Stan's Soapbox here. That belongs to Stan alone, forever.

Anyway, Chris has worked on some of the Marvel movies I really dig, too. Like *Deadpool,* which I think had just come out when we had this lunch . . . so, back to our story.]

As I said, Chris and I got together like once a year. And every year the conversation went to the same place: Dave Allen's unfinished masterpiece, *The Primevals,* which was moldering in the vault. All the human photography was done, and it looked great. At least two-thirds of the stop-motion wizardry had been completed, maybe more, and it was awesome. But now what? It would take millions to finish it, even if we could find someone who had the time and talent to do it. Neither of us had millions to throw around (and if you remember, I had spent a few million on it already!). Plus, a stop-motion movie from the nineties wasn't going to earn back that money in the twenty-first century. There was no way forward.

But by 2016 I could finally breathe a little, uncoil from my defensive crouch, and start making assertive moves again. I thought I saw a way to do this. Dave's movie actually had sort of a natural ending twenty minutes before the ending he'd shot. We could trim it . . .

"No," Chris said. He wanted to preserve Dave's vision. But I kept working on him, over a year or two, because we both knew that time was just ticking on and on and on as Dave's film just sat there, hidden from the world. And so we came up with a plan.

A two-disc Blu-ray set. The first disc would have the shortened movie, a stop-motion masterpiece from beginning to end. The second would be Dave's entire movie, but the last few scenes would intercut the already-shot live-action stuff with Dave Allen's meticulous drawings and storyboards, complete with sound effects and my brother Richard's score, giving fans a real taste of what Dave had envisioned for them.

And the fans were still there. I set up a campaign on a crowdfunding site to get some of the money we'd need to put this thing out. Fans immediately kicked in—talk of this movie had been churning in their community for decades. We pulled the film from the vault and got to work. Editing, digitizing . . .

In 2022, fully twenty-three years after the great Dave Allen had passed away, we'll be releasing *The Primevals,* a big, crazy, weird love letter to classic stop-motion adventure, in the true tradition of Ray Harryhausen. Chris and I were finally able to raise a glass to our fallen comrade.

Here's to you, Dave.

The fans who've waited so long will gobble it up. There's a lot of pent-up excitement in finally seeing something so huge and mysterious that had been hidden away for so long.

Speaking of which . . .

In 2017, I called Enzo, the former caretaker of Castello di Giove. We kept in touch after the sale of the castle, and I still paid him to look after the other property, the one with the swimming pool and the turrets, that pleasant patch of land in that beautiful valley. It was really the only property I hadn't sold, and to tell you the truth, I'm not even sure why I *didn't* sell it. Maybe because there was a mystery there. Enzo and I were always curious about it, and I had always told him that when I had the money, when I managed to dig myself out of *my* hole, we were going to dig those turrets up and figure out what they sat upon—what was beneath that hill. So this was a good phone call to make.

"*Pronto.*"

"*Ciao, Enzo!*"

"*Charlie! Ciao.*"

"What do you say, Enzo? Are you ready to start digging?"

"Right away," he said. I could hear him smiling.

The ecstatic calls from Italy started coming in immediately. My email inbox began to fill with photos. Underneath the hill . . . well, it was big.

As near as we can figure, this is the history of the place: Back in medieval times, it had started as a fortress on the high banks above a river. At some point it was expanded and converted into a mill by building *down,* all the way down to the river. A giant waterwheel was constructed to turn the enormous millstone, and the place flourished. And then, sometime in the nineteenth century, the river was diverted, the mill was abandoned, and the whole structure eventually got buried and became part of the landscape, except for those two protruding turrets. So my art director Giovanni had been right, and he'd also been right; it was a fortress *and* a mill!

It was all still there underneath the hill. And it's *amazing.*

Enzo uncovered the gears, the giant wheel. The shaft that extended all the way down to a river that isn't there anymore. It's huge. And weird. And beautiful.

One part had been inhabited, and so it was easy to convert it into a really nice one-bedroom apartment. Between that and the now-restored (and absolutely fantastic) swimming pool, it's an ideal retreat for Robin and me. Or for the kids, when we can't be there. But we're going to convert the rest of the ancient stone behemoth, and soon it'll house the whole family when we need to. I'm excited to spend time there with the . . . um . . . *younger ones*. Okay . . .

In my mind I'm still young(ish). So I don't like to use the word "grandkids." But there's no denying that that's what they are. There, I said it. They are my grandkids. And they're awesome.

Anyway, it's not the castle. No, in fact it's way better. It's got greenery and olive trees and places to walk and frolic and live *well,* like they still know how to do in Italy. Why be a feudal lord, brooding in your high, cold castle, when you can be the head of the lively *famiglia,* strolling through his olive trees on a sunny afternoon, his loved ones screaming and splashing in the distance, his glass full of good wine and sunlight?

Don't worry, Full Moon fans. I'll be in Los Angeles most of the time, not far from where my dad and granddad arrived in 1941, and I'll be filling up the Internet with new, demented, hideous visions to keep us all entertained. I can't *not* invent things. Even as I tried to write this book, purportedly "locked down" during the coronavirus pandemic, my days have been jam-packed with planning, production, postproduction, licensing. In fact, I had to delay writing this last chapter (sorry, Adam!) in order to lock, promote, and release *Barbie and Kendra Storm Area 51,* which features Ms. Robin Sydney and hilarious overdubs of a truly bizarre sci-fi film made forty years ago. Something called *The Day That Time Ended*. By Charles Band. With a couple of tasty stop-motion shots by Dave Allen.

I've got a lot of irons in the fire, which is how I like it. In fact, as I write this, I've got a slate of twelve feature films that I'm planning for next year. Yes, you heard me. Twelve. It's the most ambitious production plan I've had since the nineties—culled from the two hundred or so items I've dropped in my Idea Box during this pandemic. It's a slate of projects that involve old pals, like Ted Nicolaou, and beloved, hideous monsters, like the Lovecraftian "Resonator" from Stuart Gordon's *From Beyond*. The coolest thing is that with streaming, I finally have a direct line to my fans—a subscription, delivered right to their homes, just like a Marvel comic!—and I intend to make the most of it.

But once or twice a year—I'm thinking at least in July—I will be in Italy, totally unplugged. Well, mostly unplugged. Unplugged for some of the time, for sure. I'll be hanging out, Italian style, the way I learned to as a kid, making and enjoying long, loud, laugh-filled dinners, four or five well-planned courses, not too much food, but served in just the right sequence, courses that take up the entire evening, with my weird, amazing patchwork family, on my strange and wonderful new estate. That's where I'll be.

Although, come to think of it, I may have to shoot a movie or two there. I mean, that stone mill is *ancient*. And cavernous. And god knows what could be lurking in those trees . . .

THE END?

AFTERWORD

At the end of 2020, not long after I completed this manuscript, my son Harlan passed away. It came at the end of a long, long struggle with addiction, and his death has devastated my family and me in a way that I previously could not have imagined. We've pulled together and propped each other up and moved forward—we always do—but we'll carry him with us as we go. Harlan was a deeply sensitive soul, and he had perhaps the biggest heart of all of us.

This book is dedicated to him.

ACKNOWLEDGMENTS

When you have a big family and make hundreds of movies, you meet people. I've been so lucky to have amassed such a great collection of friends and colleagues over the years, and I want to thank them here. Although some of them may not have appeared in this book (and some, sadly, have left us), they are very much a part of the story of my life!

I also want to thank the hundreds or perhaps thousands of people I've worked with and laughed with who are *not* on this list. I'm told that it's bad form to have your acknowledgments be longer than your actual book, but I'm deeply grateful to the giant cast of comrades, colleagues, and crazy people who've been part of this insane journey.

So, organized loosely, my deepest thanks to—

From Italy: Stefano and Thea Cacace, Jan Miracle, Tamara Alessi, David Gold, and Vincenzo D'Angelis.

From the movies: Frank Ray Perilli, Louis and Audrey Garfinkle, Dick and Sharon Erdman, Ron Carter, John Carpenter, Michael Pataki, Gary Allen and Barbara Toennies, Stan and Karen Winston, Lance Henriksen, Irwin Yablans, Andrew Davis, David Allen, Chris Endicott, John Carradine, Roddy McDowall, Phil and Sal Fondacaro, Ted and Becky Nicolaou, Bennah Burton-Burtt, Demi Moore, Mac Ahlberg, Tim Thomerson,

Helen Hunt, Megan Ward, Michael Wolf, Richard Moll, Jon Lovitz, John Buechler, Dallas Sonnier, Neal Stevens, Billy Butler, Mike Deak, Jeff Byron, Austin Furst, Nigel Greene, Linda Blair, Danny Bilson, Paul De Meo, Roberto Bessi, Rolando and Patrizia Cortegianni, Sherilyn Fenn, David Schmoeller, Peter Manoogian, David DeCoteau, Mickey Kaiserman, Sam and Luis Garcia, Stuart and Carolyn Gordon, Jeffrey Combs, Barbara Crampton, Brian Yuzna, Ken Dixon, Renny Harlin, Viggo Mortensen, Bill Maher, Shannon Tweed, Adrienne Barbeau, Courtney Joyner, Ry Mantione, Danny and Jojo Draven, Kenny Klimak, Jeff Jones, Gianluca Curti, Ed Seaman, Shane Bitterling, Jackie Lovell, Michael Citriniti, Anita Rosenberg, Adolfo Bartoli, Miles and Adriana Copeland, William Shatner, Debra Mayer, Jim Gianopulos, Richard Hamilton, Tommy Chong, Gary Busey, Jessica Morris, Amy Paffrath, Brockton McKinney, Cody Cameron, Tom Devlin, John Lechago, Libbie Chase, Arnie Mendoza, and Chad Nardiello.

My Full Moon family: Nakai Nelson, Robin O'Rourke, Chris Alexander, Bob Langer, Hugo Velazco, Brooks Davis, and Ryan Brookhart.

My family: Albert and Jackie Band, Robin Sydney, Debra Dion, Meda Christiani, Taryn Band Rodriguez, Alex Band, Harlan Band, Zalman Band, Robert Rodriguez, Haven Rodriguez, Mila Rodriguez, Shayna Band, Max Band, Richard and Marilyn Band, Joe and Jean Dion, and Marian Heymsfield.

At William Morrow I want to thank Mauro DiPreta and Nick Amphlett for their decision to preempt my story and their hard work to help me make a book from the three-ring circus that is the life of an exploitation filmmaker. I also want to thank Sharyn Rosenblum, Ryan Shepherd, Owen Corrigan, Shelby Peak, and Bonni Leon-Berman for all their hard work to help put this book into your hands, dear reader.

I also owe special thanks to Mauro and Nick's colleagues, the fantastic Judith Curr and Juan Milà at HarperCollins, who became aware that I was interested in publishing a memoir and alerted Mauro and Nick at William Morrow about that fact so they could snap up the book before my literary agent even had a chance to shop it around to any other publishers.

On that note, I want to thank Scott Mendel. I have never had a literary agent before, but I suspect that I am now deeply spoiled in that department!

And to my writing partner, Adam Felber, spending these Saturday sessions with you and careening down memory lane—during the pandemic—was a blast! I'm not sure if I would have been able to do this during (abby)normal times. Thanks for being so much fun to hang with on the phone, and for putting my bizzarro stories into such entertaining prose!

ABOUT THE AUTHORS

Charles Band is a renowned producer, director, mogul, and B-movie showman. He has directed or produced more than 360 films, including cult classics like *Ghoulies* and *Tourist Trap*, one of Stephen King's favorite horror movies. He lives in Los Angeles.

Adam Felber is an Emmy-nominated and WGA Award–winning writer and performer whose credits include *Real Time with Bill Maher* and the children's programs *Wishbone* and *Arthur*. He lives in Los Angeles.